PIL

Work and the Enterprise Culture

Work and the Enterprise Culture

Edited by

Malcolm Cross and Geoff Payne

Explorations in Sociology No. 38

 The Falmer Press

(A member of the Taylor & Francis Group)
London • New York • Philadelphia

In conjunction with the British Sociological Association

UK   The Falmer Press, 4 John Street, London WC1N 2ET
USA The Falmer Press, Taylor & Francis Inc., 1900 Frost Road, Suite 101, Bristol, PA 19007

First published 1991

British Library Cataloguing in Publication Data
Work and the enterprise culture.
   1. Great Britain. Entrepreneurship — Socioeconomic
aspects I. Cross, Malcolm II. Payne, Geoff
   338.040941

ISBN 1–85000–799–3
ISBN 1–85000–800–0 pbk

Library of Congress Cataloging-in-Publication Data is available on request.

Jacket design by Caroline Archer

Typeset in 10.5/12 Bembo by
Graphicraft Typesetters Ltd., Hong Kong

Printed in Great Britain by Burgess Science Press, Basingstoke on paper which has a specified pH value on final paper manufacture of not less than 7.5 and is therefore 'acid free'.

Contents

Contents

Chapter 1

Introduction:
Work and the Enterprise Culture

Malcolm Cross and Geoff Payne

The continuity of Conservative Governments under Margaret Thatcher during the 1980s has led to us seeing an apparent cohesiveness in the character of that decade. The rhetoric of public discourse has been focused on recovery from recession, 'getting the economy moving' and creating a new 'enterprise culture' to replace state controls and supposed inefficiency. Behind the facade of that coherence lies a period of economic and social change which has in reality been discontinuous, contradictory and disorganized. Tremendous changes have indeed taken place, but in complex societies political forces, demographic trends, cultural transitions, market pressures, technological innovation, and organizational restructuring do not all fit together neatly. One of the key tasks of the sociologist is to disentangle such components of large-scale, social processes, so that a clearer understanding of events can be constructed to replace conventional or ideological wisdoms.

This task is inevitably seen by those with a vested interest in the conventional wisdom as negative, or even subversive. At one level it is. If people buttress their own positions with selective accounts and simplistic appeals to vague symbols of legitimation — a problem that *all* politicians (not to mention others) have — then a social science perspective can only be perceived by them as threatening. At a different level, however, the social science project is marked by a concern for clarity, for better comprehension, for recognizing alternatives, and — by implication at least — for the construction of new and better policies. It follows that when the contributors to this volume raise questions about how the 'enterprise culture' actually has been manifested in the world of work, their prime concern is not to mount an ideological or narrow party political attack on enterprise, but rather to explore in specific contexts what has been happening in the 1980s.

The changes of the 1980s did not only alter the context of work, they also enhanced new forms of unevenness in both decline and renewal. The decade witnessed the increased significance of both space and time as boundaries of paid employment. The North–South divide is one example of the former; the crisis of the 'inner cities' is another. Similarly, work became increasingly concentrated within a shorter span of life. There was a redefinition of 'working age' as young people were excluded from work and as redundancies and early retirement sliced deeply into cohorts of the over 50s. In contrast to this early exclusion of young people from the labour market, the end of the decade saw a shortage of young people in the population with concomitant changes in employers' recruitment strategies as they sought to compete for them and for the older women re-entering the labour market after child-rearing.

As firms radically restructured to survive, they dramatically altered the labour process and the form in which work would be available. 'Flexible', part-time labour grew at the expense of more stable, full-time employment. With this change has come a renewed segmentation by gender as the new jobs are carefully tailored to low cost, malleable, and largely non-unionized female workers. Similarly, the relocation of plants outside high cost and increasingly inaccessible inner cities has had profound effects on the composition of those able to take advantage of the economic upturn. British people of Caribbean and Asian origin are still disproportionately concentrated in regions and areas of major decline, and therefore their lives have been made even more vulnerable by the coming of 'Enterprise Britain'.

On the other hand, the decade of the 1980s was also the one in which 'equal opportunity' and anti-discrimination legislation of the mid 1970s might have been expected to have an effect. The world of work does not exist in isolation from wider cultural and political processes. The exclusion of young people from the labour market during the earlier years of recession was matched by a rich variety of training and work experience schemes introduced by government legislation and promoted by unprecedented publicity. The question arises, as to how well these attempts at engineered social change have coped with the renewed segmentation by gender and race which have flowed from economic re-organization. At the same time, the ways in which sociologists study and think about these things have been changing, even more than in sociology in general. Sociologists of work have traditionally focused on class differences, for it is within that domain that relations of production are engendered. It became clearer, however, in the 1980s that class did not capture all that was important in the changing world of work. The salience of gender and race have in particular broadened our perspectives and added to our analytical repertoire. Age and the importance of locale are other examples of this growing sophistication. Ideas developed in other branches of sociology have cross-fertilized into what has hitherto been a narrower area: an analysis of graduate employment or the role of women in the miners' strike become newly relevant to what we mean by 'work'.

The sociology of work as a field of enquiry has also been responding to changes in its primary object of study, the social organization of the British economy and its associated processes. In the first half of the 1980s, as Britain's recession deepened, 'work' was redescribed by sociologists in analytically powerful ways. In the second half, as a re-organized economy began to recover, we have started to explore what we mean by 'enterprise' and whether or not the term 'enterprise culture' has a meaning which is precise enough for analytical purposes. How different is the new economy from the old? How well do the seeds of so called 'enterprise' grow in those areas hitherto laid waste by economic decline?

This collection is a book about both Britain's economy and how the sociology of work has been developing. Selected from among papers given at the annual conference of the British Sociological Association held at Polytechnic South-West, which took as its theme 'Sociology in Action', it represents a particular perspective of what the sociology of work should be like in the 1990s. At the centre of that project lies the idea that we need to engage with contemporary issues and events. The 'enterprise culture' is one such issue. Perhaps we run the risk of making too much of the term, or even of using it as a straw figure: we certainly use it as a convenient shorthand for a complex of notions. The authors of the chapters that follow are primarily concerned with exploring what real changes it signifies. Their enterprise lies in generating a better sociological explanation of work during a process of rapid social and economic change.

The Enterprise Culture

As Burrows and Curran point out 'enterprise' is a slippery concept that even its most frequent advocates find difficulty in defining. This itself suggests that it cannot readily be assumed to have very much explanatory power. Rather, 'the enterprise culture' is best regarded as a construct which has served to rationalize and thereby sustain political values of individualism, personal autonomy and supposed freedom from corporatist control (Bechhofer and Elliott, 1981). It is arguable that the true beneficiaries of economic changes in the 1980s have not been small businesses, but rather multi-national companies which have exploited deregulated markets, falling real wages, constrained unions and free currency movements to combine and extend their increasingly global concerns.

Burrows and Curran are sharply critical of theories of economic restructuring and of those that herald the significance of the petit bourgeoisie. In rejecting simplistic comparisons between the two, they are not suggesting that a stock of adequate theory lies elsewhere. Rather, a central conclusion they reach is that we have still no adequate guide to the rise and role of the small-scale entrepreneur.

3

Another crucial aspect of the enterprise culture is the changing culture of enterprise. We have, so it is claimed, moved from Fordism to Post-Fordism; from the perception that the culture of the firm is one characterized by an uneasy state of tension between parties with incompatible interests to one which identifies commitment and coalition as the pervading orthodoxy. But is this 'new culture' not the same as the 'paternalist capitalism' which pre-dated Fordism? Peter Ackers and John Black insist that a prior question is to explore what this earlier concept entailed and what led to its demise. Their conclusion is that in both an 'external' and 'internal' sense, paternalist capitalism was a reality. Some companies, usually with deep roots in nineteenth century technology and often cut off from other labour markets, were able to develop over long periods patterns of employee loyalty which ensured a stable workforce and quiescent industrial relations. Internally, paternalism could last longer, but in both senses it has rapidly given way to the pressures generated by capital concentration and changing competitive conditions. The same industries have not been immune from Post-Fordism, even though they may not have experienced much Fordism, and in this sense they could be said to be moving forward to the past. The reality of human resources management and associated practices is not, however, the same as old-style paternalism. One was born out of tradition and isolation, the other out of post-modernism and globalization. As they conclude, given the shifting pattern of management in the modernizing firm, any resemblance to old loyalties will be more apparent than real since it will be sustained by the cash nexus rather than by the warm glow of tradition.

If 'enterprise' is intended to be the solution to de-industrialization, then there can be no better test of its applicability than the South Wales coalfields. As Gareth Rees and Marilyn Thomas remind us, the gloomiest forecasts made by miners' leaders at the time of the strike of 1984–85 turned out to under-estimate substantially the actual numbers of pit closures and lost jobs. More important, these massive transformations have curtailed traditional avenues into employment for young people. 'Enterprise initiatives' in this context imply no less than an engineered change in the local class structure.

The empirical results of the study reported by Rees and Thomas clearly suggest that managed attempts at class reform run into major obstacles. Loans for enterprise sustain those who have already located markets and who have the educational and other resources to exploit them. Ex-miners will not tend to invest their redundancy payments in small businesses partly because of a reluctance to bear the risk involved and partly because of a rational evaluation of their chances of success. It is tempting to dismiss this failure as merely a reflection of a 'culture of dependency' on waged employment but the crucial point is the link between economic and cultural causes. It is one thing to be 'entrepreneurial' in the south-east of England where craftsmen are scarce and pockets full; it is quite another in South Wales where the market is weak and over-supplied.

The 'enterprise' remedy is prescribed for the ills of the 'inner city' as much as for the declining coalfields. But we know surprisingly little about what causes the symptoms of poverty and misery which are all too apparent in some parts of inner urban areas. Nationally, there is evidence of income polarization and Nick Buck identifies six hypotheses which could account for it. Using an innovative estimating technique derived from two major national surveys, he shows that economic changes associated with the demand for particular jobs (as estimated either by the incidence of unemployment or by differential changes in rates of pay) account for more of the changes in income distribution than other possible causes. Moreover, the analysis demonstrates a spatial effect in that polarization is greatest in Inner London, possibly as so-called 'global cities' come to develop a post-industrial occupational structure with an increasingly highly paid sector at one end, in which married women's incomes may be very important, and a growing poor, unstable sector at the other.

Age, Gender and Race in Production

Prior to 1980 it was rare to find studies of work and production that were embedded in anything but traditional class theory. Over the last decade, sociology itself has confronted the salience of other structured forms of inequality which cross-cut those of social class. The sociology of work is no exception and the six remaining chapters of this book focus on three of the most important, age group, gender and race.

During the 1980s, it became quite apparent that life-cycle effects were increasingly significant in predicting labour market experience, particularly so for the young (Wallace and Cross, 1990). The chapter by Ken Roberts and his co-workers reports on one part of a major ESRC initiative into the experiences of 16–19 year olds. The analysis uses longitudinal methods to unravel the pattern of 'trajectories' into the labour market. The major significance of educational qualifications in avoiding unemployment and the importance of area of residence in determining young peoples' prospects are clearly demonstrated. More important, it also confirms that the benefits of vocational training have yet to be reflected in enhanced career prospects. YTS entrants, for example, appeared to gain little in terms of employment chances over those following traditional paths into employment at age 16.

Enhanced labour demand, consequent upon the current demographic changes, could well undermine the supposedly permanent bridge created in the 1980s by the coming of YTS. Moreover, employment training for young people has been bedevilled by wide variations in quality which might well have been avoided if alternatives had been more seriously considered a decade ago. A move has now been made to dispense with a free-standing system in favour of funding employers to provide vocational training. The other possible avenue would have been to raise the leaving age to 18 and greatly increase funding to the school system. The immense amounts of public money funnelled through the Manpower Services Commission and its successor the Training Agency could hardly have been less well spent had this choice been made. Notwithstanding the ideological assault on education, young people who choose schooling over alternatives are making rational choices in terms of career development.

As Michael Maguire points out, the absence of a gendered perception in the sociology of work is surprising, given the nature of changes in the forms of employment consequent upon economic restructuring. So called 'flexibility' has been generated in part by the rise of part-time employment, and it is married women who are predominently employed part-time (Pollert, 1988). Maguire reports on research into the retailing sector in Northern Ireland. The Northern Ireland economy has experienced all the major changes associated with economic restructuring, except the upturn stemming from a growth in non-governmental services. Retailing has undergone the familiar capital concentration and globalization as individual shops give way to multi-national chains. From an industry dependent on full-time, male labour power, it has become one characterized by part-time, female workers. Wages rates are low, conditions for the most part unprotected by trade unions and women cluster at the bottom of the occupational hierarchy.

What is important is that demand-side issues for an inexpensive, mature and docile workforce have helped sustain ideological manifestations on gendered work. These in turn reproduce images of women that serve themselves to legitimize sexual divisions. Thus changes in the structure of work undermine the possibility of 'equal opportunity' by making women's work of lesser value. This could take place even where women had managed to penetrate 'management' posts, although in Northern Ireland they had not done so. The gendering process sustains profound structural inequalities without necessarily affecting access to all occupations. Policies to control discrimination can only operate outside gendered jobs, which is a severe constraint on their potency as strategies of social change.

The graduate labour market is precisely one where, potentially, equal opportunity policies could provide an opportunity for structural change. This is because economic restructuring processes are pressing in the opposite direction to those governing the utilization of unskilled labour power. Here, employers are anxious to adopt 'equal opportunity' approaches, with a view to giving themselves access to a wider pool of talent. As Tony Chapman argues, however, in his study of the graduate labour market, this does not mean that current anti-discrimination policies alone stand any chance of overcoming entrenched inequalities between men and women. In the first place, inequalities are sustained by socialized choices; second, they are underpinned by external constraints, and only third are they the result of direct or indirect discrimination in the workplace.

Mining communities again provide an important case study. Traditional community structures, which have adapted over centuries to the labour demands of coalmining, reveal an entrenched gender-based division of labour. Yet women clearly played a pivotal role in the 1984–5 strike, often seeming to provide the impetus to prolong the misery and discomfort which must have followed. In the research reported by Sandra Hebron and Maggie Wykes, however, the strike support groups were often led by women who had been active previously, and the researchers were unable to find major evidence of changing roles or consciousness after the dispute had ended. Change, particularly as measured by enhanced labour force participation, would have required a concomitant improvement in job availability. The evidence suggests transitory changes in the domestic division of labour which quickly reverted once shift work began again. The authors conclude, however, that women were more politicized and likely therefore to seek opportunities for less patriarchial relations if and when another chance occurred.

Plant based studies have made a major contribution to our understanding of patterns of access to occupational positions. Richard Jenkins (1986), for example, focused on the informal processes whereby discriminatory outcomes were sustained in a variety of industrial settings. Nick Jewson and David Mason report on research into the significance, if any, of *formal* recruitment and promotion procedures. They show that, where they exist, centralized and formalized recruitment procedures do have the effect of minimizing personal discretion which, providing a company has a commitment to equal opportunities, is likely to benefit ethnic minority applicants and employees. The problem, however, is that the drift of economic restructuring is in the opposite direction; towards decentralizing and delegating power and therefore shifting the locus of responsibility away from the personnel and human resource experts. Firms which are pressured to become flexible, pragmatic and performance (rather than procedure) oriented were not in a strong position to sustain what are essentially bureaucratic routines. Similarly, formalized procedures do not prevent 'acceptability' criteria predominating over job suitability. 'Acceptability' is determined more by an internal organizational culture which, when combined with a reliance upon internal labour markets, militates against change. Jewson and Mason suggest that there is no intrinsic reason why flexibility and informality should not be compatible with equal opportunity outcomes; it would simply require these to be included

7

as performance measures. In this sense, outcomes are more important than procedures.

Internal employment procedures are not, however, the only barriers to employment. A prior factor is whether individuals apply or are directed towards future employers. This is not a chance procedure but one which is socially organized. As John Wrench reports most young people leaving school at 16 pass through the Careers Service on their way to a job or further training. Historically, the service has existed to provide a counselling function to young people. As such it has lacked power to oppose the racism of employers and training organizations. However, under pressure to be part of a process whereby a poor vocational training record is reversed, the service has been steered towards fulfilling policy goals. These have been predominantly economic rather than social with the result that equal opportunity issues have become submerged. Again, we are reminded that equality of opportunity does not necessarily generate equality of outcomes. If this group of gatekeepers chooses to channel young people to schemes and jobs which they know will accept them, they mask the real barriers and help ensure the continuation of profound structural inequalities in the labour market.

The Sociology of Enterprise and the Enterprise of Sociology

Whatever else the 1980s may have done, they have set a new agenda for sociologists of work and labour markets. The essays in this book suggest that in tackling that agenda the key tasks will be, first, to generate an accurate picture of what has actually occurred. We still know far too little about what the implications of the changes have been. We need to balance the innovation of the enterprise culture, where indeed this can be shown to have occurred, against the continuity of decline and unemployment. It may be true that the changes of the 1980s are by no means usefully defined as the coming of the 'enterprise culture', but none can deny the importance of economic restructuring.

Second, in mapping the contours of these changes, there is an obvious need to develop a greater inter-disciplinarity. Research on the geography of production is one example, but there are many others. Finally, there is a need to return to the sociological well to rethink the nature of structured social inequality. As we have argued elsewhere (Cross, 1991a; 1991b; Payne, 1987; Payne and Abbott, 1991), it will no longer do to offer bolt-on additions of gender and race to what is otherwise a classical class analysis. Class is far from dead, but it lives in the workplace or in the labour market alongside equally powerful determinants of life chances.

Chapter 2

Not Such a Small Business: Reflections on the Rhetoric, the Reality and the Future of the Enterprise Culture

Roger Burrows and James Curran

The Discourse of the Enterprise Culture

The discourse of the enterprise culture has an elective affinity with what most social scientists would now accept has been a profound 'restructuring' of British society in the 1980s.[1] The economic and social symbols of earlier epochs of capitalist development have been transformed:

> deserted colliery wastelands [have] become lush green landscapes; once sprawling, elemental, fiery great steelworks [have] become spacious, tree-lined estates; noisy, bustling shipyards [have] become neat riverside nature parks and marinas; once labyrinthine railway networks [have] become 'eco-walkways' … the stricken, depressed looking 'unemployment queues of old' … [have been] … recast as individuals being trained for the better work 'opportunities' … [and] … rundown city centres … [have been] … transformed into designer precincts, with festivals and spectacles celebrating their symbolic rebirth (Ritchie, 1991, p. 21).

How best to interpret these changes has been a source of much controversy. A plethora of often contradictory attempts to make some sort of sociological sense out of the last decade or so have emerged.[2] Much of this literature has foregrounded small enterprises and self-employment to an extent hitherto unheard of (Curran, 1990; Rainnie, 1991). However, the more general categories of 'enterprise' and 'entrepreneurship' have hardly featured at all, much to the annoyance of the sociological New Right (Marsland, 1988, p. 219).

The reasons for this are clear. Whenever there are attempts to give the 'enterprise culture' any analytic solidity it melts.[3] Even its advocates appear confused over its meaning, as Pratt (1990) found when he was unable to elicit a definition from Conservative Central Office, the Department of Trade and Industry or the Department of Education and Science. However, this conceptual confusion does not mean that sociologists should repudiate the notion out of hand. We must take seriously the emergence of the rhetoric of 'business-like' discourse as a central cultural motif of the present period. Clearly, it is not just in the private sector that the rhetoric has taken grip. In spheres as far removed as education (Ritchie, 1990), policing (Hobbs, 1988; 1991), health and social services (Kelly, 1991) and other previously non-market based organizations, the discourse of business is becoming the legitimating, if not always the operational, basis for calculation.

However, whatever the constitution of the discourse, its popular and political appearance has been relatively recent. As Hobbs (1991) notes, throughout the 1970s the term 'entrepreneur' was generally regarded as a term of mild abuse. Entrepreneurship was not considered as mainstream activity but rather the province of unique, often obsessive individuals such as Freddie Laker and John Bloom. Clearly, since 1979 there have been dramatic changes as the Thatcherite project has attempted to articulate 'small business revivalism' as a panacea for the economic and social ills of the nation.

The past has been reformulated into an equation which allies an 'anti-enterprise culture' inspired by a social democratic collectivism with indulgency and degeneration and hence national demise. This prefaces more recent times which equate the enforced euthanasia of the manufacturing sector with stringency, cure and eventual rebirth. Predictably, the future within the Thatcherite scheme of things attempts to equate the new enterprise culture with industriousness, regeneration and true work, wealth, and happiness (Ritchie, 1991).

So far there have been few attempts to understand the affiliation between the reality of the restructuring process as it has, in actuality, implicated the prime moral subjects of the discourse — the petty bourgeoisie — and the wider rhetoric of the enterprise culture. The few attempts that have been made have been political, rather than analytic, in nature. On the one hand those on the political right have viewed the emergence of the discourse of enterprise as an exhilarating ideological force *antecedent* to the changes of the last decade or so.[4] On the other, many on the political left have viewed its emergence as little more than the latest in a long line of mystifications designed to bamboozle the masses into a state of acquiescence whilst new forms of capitalist exploitation can take shape. For them 'small business revivalism' and its analogues are little more than a convenient ideological smokescreen for increasingly global monopoly capitalist interests.[5]

Needless to say, the construction of such political and conceptual polarities has not been very productive analytically. The rightist interpretation of restructuring offers a crudely idealist 'agent-centred' model, whilst the leftist interpretation offers an overly materialist 'structure-centred' model. The objections to this dualism are now well documented (Bhaskar, 1979; Giddens, 1984); agent-centred models tend to negate social formations to problems of individual motivations whilst structure-centred models tend to negate human agency to problems of societal exigency.

Human agency is neither totally determining nor totally determined in relation to the enterprise culture. The old Marxian truism that people make their own history but not under circumstances of their own choosing, is worth remembering here. Clearly, an analysis of *both* agency and structure is required if one is to make any real sense out of the situation. We must reject both structural determinist and voluntaristic theories, and replace them with a model of social processes in which social structures are recognized as being *both* the medium and the outcome of human agency.

Consider, for example, spatial divisions of enterprise as represented by the spatial distribution of the *petty bourgeoisie* (Burrows, 1991b) or, obviously related to this, the geography of new firm formation (Mason, 1991). Explanations which attempt to account for such a gross structural patterning in terms of the 'enterprise mindedness' of local populations are unlikely to be of much use. However, it is also unlikely that we will be able to explain all of the variations by appeal to purely 'structural' factors: industrial structure; plant-size structure; occupational structure; and so on. As the results from a series of recent 'locality' studies have demonstrated (Cooke, 1989), although Britain may have been experiencing a process of socio-economic restructuring which has its origins in global economic shifts some forms of local — if not always purely individual — responses are possible which mediate such processes.

'Entrepreneurship' — a concept almost as difficult to get a handle on as the enterprise culture itself[6] — is thus a function of individual, situational and social variables. For example, after an extensive review of the geographic literature, Mason (1991) suggests that the most important factors influencing variations in new firm formation rates across localities are: an industrial structure that already has an inclination towards small independent economic units; employees working in problem-solving occupations who have close contact with customers; a concentration of technically-progressive small firms; a high awareness of past small business activities; banks and other financial institutions sympathetic to the needs of small businesses; the availability of help and advice; an affluent population and a social climate which favours individualism. The possibility of entrepreneurial praxis is thus historically conditioned and will always be inherently spatially uneven.

It is suggested then that although the enterprise culture is important as a *meaning system* from which some social actors can draw different rationalizing 'vocabularies of motive' (Mills, 1940) to make sense of their situations (Ritchie, 1991; Hobbs, 1991) it possesses only a small residual explanatory status in accounts of restructuring.[7] The enterprise culture is a discourse which provides a wide ranging semiotic rationale for the present restructuring. Such a period of rapid economic, social and political change has required an appropriate 'cultural' management. In this instance the state has encouraged the synchronisity which has emerged between these changes, the de-collectivization of social relations invoked (especially in relation to the strategies developed in response to the fiscal crisis of the state) and the discourse of individualism that increasingly legitimates so many contemporary social actions — articulated as the 'enterprise culture'.

Clearly, the notion of the 'restructuring' of Britain refers to a complex set of economic, social and political changes[8] which have had to be represented within some new set of cultural meanings (Harvey, 1989; Thrift, 1989) — dominant amongst which have been those supplied by the enterprise culture: individualism; independence; 'flexibility'; anti-collectivism; privatism; self-help and so on. The discourse of the enterprise culture thus presents itself as *the* justificatory language of social integration for a world characterized by an economic insecurity unknown in the more corporatist and collectivist world of the 1960s and much of the 1970s (Pollert, 1988). Further, it fulfils this function by way of a semiotic recourse to an imaginary world from which we have supposedly fallen from grace; that of a *laissez-faire* competitive capitalism populated by large numbers of small firms all equilibrating around some Pareto optimal set of conditions.

The discourse of the enterprise culture has been a contingent rather than a necessary feature of the present restructuring of Britain, and its survival as a discourse is by no means guaranteed. As a key element of social life within a period of rapid change it has had an obvious (even liberating!) appeal. However, its obligatory recourse to individualistic agent-centred solutions to the inherently structural emergent properties of social life are beginning to fetter its current hegemonic importance.

We confront a complex set of economic and social problems as we approach the millennium; problems which the discourse of the enterprise culture can only compound. It has now served its prime function as a justificatory discourse for the massive changes which have characterized the restructuring of Britain. The problems that we confront increasingly require the development of meaning systems and rationalizing rhetorics which justify actions in more than purely individualistic terms. The major crises of the age are now inherently collectivist in nature in that they derive from the emergent properties of aggregated individual actions: the crisis in transport; worries about the environment; the care of the elderly; adequate child-care provision in order to enable more women to enter an increasingly saturated labour market and so on.

However, as we discuss in the next section, none of what we have argued thus far is to deny that higher levels of self-employment and small business ownership than hitherto are going to remain important features of Britain in the 1990s; this now appears as an inherent and important feature of the economic structure now emerging in many advanced societies. However, it is to argue that the enterprise culture as a legitimating discourse for wider social actions will not for much longer be presented as a panacea for our social and economic ills.

Accounting for Petty Capitalism

As is now well documented, the 1980s saw something of a renaissance in petty capitalism in Britain (Department of Employment, 1989 p. 10; Hakim, 1988; Mayes and Moir, 1990) and to a lesser extent in other industrial societies, including the United States (Steinmetz and Wright, 1989). Self-employment grew from about 2 million in 1980 to over 3 million in 1988 and the number of businesses registered for VAT between 1979 and 1988 increased by over a quarter of a million.[9]

Accounting for petty capitalist activities in advanced capitalism has long posed problems for sociology. With some notable exceptions,[10] the discipline has tended to overly concentrate on large scale capital accumulation. However, as already indicated, the economic restructuring of the 1980s has had profound implications for petty capitalism as well as large. Much of the theorizing interpreting these changes has been quite explicit in offering a new significance to small scale economic activities. However, whether this new theorizing has been useful in accounting for the changing role of the small enterprise in advanced capitalism is far from clear. In the present context we will examine the two most influential contributions in this regard: *post*-Fordist theorizations and *neo*-Fordist theorizations.[11]

More radical interpretations — those often referred to under labels such as 'post-Fordism' (within Marxian models) or 'flexible specialization' (within more liberal models) — talk of a paradigm break with the economy of the past and the emergence of a radically new economic structure. As part of the latter, a new, more central role for petty capitalism is offered as well as suggestions on the new forms petty capitalism might take. Radical models of this kind are well illustrated by the work of Brusco and Sabel (1981), Goodman *et al.* (1988), Piore and Sabel (1984) and A. Scott (1988).

In accounts of supposedly Fordist economies, small firms were, when discussed at all, consigned to a peripheral role either supplying markets which dominant firms had not yet invaded or could not be bothered to enter because potential profits were too low. This was the orthodox interpretation of petty capitalism which prevailed generally for so long in economic sociology (Curran and Burrows, 1986; Steinmetz and Wright, 1989).

In post-Fordist interpretations, on the other hand, petty capitalism occupies a much more central role. The design, production and distribution of products become the subject of a new division of labour between firms and establishments (with an emphasis on small units) who form locally based networks. Within small firms themselves it is suggested that there might be a revival of craft traditions based on new technologies, with a widening of work roles to allow for flexible task performances by employees who would be working under owner-managers dedicated to quality and market responsiveness.

The break-up of Fordist mass markets as mass consumption ceases to be the engine of demand in advanced economies and the dawning of fragmented, rapidly changing markets, is expected to be matched by new small production units (small firms and small branches of larger firms) able to combine new technology and flexible human responses with the small batch production required to service new patterns of demand.

Although post-Fordist networks of enterprises and establishments are highly regional (Sabel, 1989), they are also held to be linked into the new international division of labour so that products might be distributed internationally. Again this is deemed possible through the harnessing of new technology, particularly information technology, which allows local economies to be in touch with, and to respond rapidly to, diverse markets throughout advanced industrial societies. This new order has frequently been typified under the label of the 'Benetton economy' (Murray, 1989).[12]

This new economic structure does not of course mean that large firms are no longer important but rather that their role in the economy is different and integrated with petty capitalism in new ways. The relative importance of small and large has changed in the new configurations of production and distribution characteristic of the post-Fordist economy with each having a key role to play in the functioning of the whole.

The post-Fordist model has come in for increasing criticism on several grounds. Some, such as Amin (1989), have suggested that it amounts virtually to argument by illustration. Too much, it is argued, has been made of specific examples of regional economies, particularly those of the 'Third Italy' (Weiss, 1988). These being impossibly over-generalized into a new economic paradigm for all advanced industrial societies. Whether Britain shows any evidence of the new economic regime is seen as even more doubtful. Storey and Johnson (1987 pp. 125–51) for example, contrast the 'Bologna model' of economic resurgence in Italy with what they term the 'Birmingham model' in Britain where sharp increases in the numbers of small enterprises in the 1980s is interpreted not as a symptom of regeneration but as recession-induced response to decline. In other words, it marks the continuation of 'Fordist crisis' (for want of a better term) rather than the beginning of a new economic regime.

Even the evidence from the Italian industrial district model itself has been increasingly questioned. Amin (1989) for example, examined the evidence for flexible specialization model in Italy and concluded:

> The empirical foundation for the theory of small firm flexible specialization ... appears to be thin. Evidence from the country which has inspired so much of the theory tends to demonstrate that very few, and only the oldest of the industrial districts come close to resembling the 'ideal type'. Furthermore, the organizational structure of these areas also appears to be changing, as new forces emerge to favour industrial concentration (Amin, 1989 p. 31)

Amin, along with others such as Murray (1987 p. 85) and Rainnie (1991), has also criticized the portrayal of the small firm in the flexible specialization model for its utopianism in suggesting an 'alienation-free' work environment for which the empirical evidence is distinctly slender.

Less radical neo-Fordist interpretations of restructuring proffer a rather different role for small scale economic activities in the 1980s and a rather more recognizable characterization of petty capitalism. For example, they suggest that large mass producers are simply adapting to changing circumstances. Flexible production based on programmable machines and computer based information systems, enable products to be differentiated to meet the needs of new or less stable fragmented markets without loss of the benefits of large scale operation or of large firm domination (Massey, 1984; Williams *et al.*, 1987).

It is also pointed out that while more fragmented patterns of demand may have been emerging, the persistence of mass production and consumption should not be understated. Replacement markets remain important especially when enhanced through redesigned and repackaged products (Solo, 1985; Williams *et al.*, 1987). Mass consumption markets are also constantly being widened as new Third World markets are added and soon, it may be expected, markets in Eastern Europe.

Under a neo-Fordism, the average size of plants falls. Large firms replace older technologies with programmable technologies which frequently operate profitably in small units serving local as well as international markets. The numbers of independently owned small firms may also rise because of an increasingly fashionable strategy for large firms to contract out (Rainnie, 1991). This achieves flexibility through cuts in stock levels and 'just in time' (JIT) tactics reduce labour control problems and the impact of demand fluctuations (Rainnie, 1990; Shutt and Whittington, 1987). In addition, the same fashion has resulted in so-called 'peripheral' activities — transport, printing, catering, security — also being increasingly outsourced. Again, some of the resulting opportunities have been realized by small firms, many of them newly created.[13]

Clearly, the small firm in a neo-Fordist economy is less central than in post-Fordist models. But equally clearly it is has greater importance than in previous economic regimes. The small firm serves and is dependent upon larger 'core' firms but becomes more crucial than in the past to the survival and successful functioning of large enterprises which dominate the economy nationally and, increasingly, internationally.

The type case of neo-Fordist small firm–large firm relations is exemplified in the clothing industry. Rainnie (1989) argues that while textiles and the retailing of clothing are dominated by large firms such as Marks and Spencer, the actual making of the clothes is by large numbers of small firms. The industry is extremely fashion sensitive and large high street retailers have only found it possible to cope with high levels of demand instability by contracting out production. Large numbers of mainly small producers allow for fast responses to fashion changes and minimize risks for larger retailers. But the strong bargaining power of high street retailers drives down the prices received by producers. The price of survival for individual small firms often results in 'sweat shop' conditions for employees and poor rewards for owners.

However, neo-Fordist models are in many ways no more satisfactory in their treatment of petty capitalism than the more radical restructuring theses discussed earlier. Some critics, such as Pollert (1988) have argued that increases in subcontracting and outsourcing in the 1980s were overstated.[14] Some of the examples cited to illustrate the neo-Fordist model (for instance, the clothing industry) are examples of long term small firm dependent relations rather than new ones.

Equally, neo-Fordist models do not deal properly with the role of petty capitalism in some of the 'leading edge' sectors of the economy. For example, the model stresses a new economic structure composed of 'core' and 'peripheral firms' with the latter, largely small firms, serving the needs of 'core' firms (NEDO, 1986). The implication here is that the larger 'core' firms remain the pace makers of the economy with small firms playing a supporting role. But in several high technology areas, it is small firms which have pioneered new products and markets (Rothwell, 1986) while the seemingly leading 'core' firms have often turned out to be economic 'dinosaurs' struggling to survive and sometimes failing spectacularly (Lloyd, 1986).

The argument challenging neo-Fordist emphases on the dependence of small firms on large may be put more generally. While there are economic sectors where relations such as those in the clothing industry obtain, in many others, small firms are demonstratively much more independent. In the hotel and restaurant industry, for example, there are large firms with hundreds of outlets but there are also hundreds of small, single output enterprises offering high quality or distinctive food and accommodation who survive and prosper (Gabriel, 1988). In printing, where there are large numbers of small firms who serve mainly other businesses, levels of independence are still relatively high.

Perhaps the most serious weakness of restructuring theories whether post-Fordist or neo-Fordist, is the over-emphasis on manufacturing. It is now commonplace to acknowledge the enormously increased importance of services and knowledged-based activities in Britain's economy but much of the restructuring debate still focuses on manufacturing in terms of the examples used in the arguments.[15] This weakness is doubly important when the role of petty capitalism in considered because the great bulk of petty capitalist economic activities is not in manufacturing (Burrows and Curran, 1989). One recent estimate, for example, suggests that nine out of ten of *all* small businesses are in services (Curran and Burrows, 1988 p. 53).

In short, restructuring theories, although giving petty capitalism a more prominent role in their analyses, remain manifestly inadequate. What is required is an approach which focuses on small scale economic activities as a starting point rather than treating them as derivative or residual to, larger firms. Of course, petty capitalism is articulated in many complex ways with larger firms and the state, but there can be no simple assumption that such links are all of a kind. To assume, for instance, such links can be subsumed under some global notion of 'dependence' (however elaborated) is implausible given the sheer variety of forms of petty capitalism and their presence in virtually every area of the economy.

The Future of Petty Capitalism[16]

For orthodox sociological theorizing, the recent renaissance of petty capitalism has been quite unexpected:[17] Marxist theorizing, for instance, represented this theoretical consensus very clearly. There was, it was argued, an inherent historical tendency for the long term expansion of capitalism to destroy earlier forms of production in which small scale economic activities were considered to be mainly embedded. But further, the concentration and centralization of capital lead to firms becoming larger both relatively and absolutely (Steinmetz and Wright, 1989 p. 981).

Above we reviewed some of the accounts which sought to explain increases in self-employment and small business ownership in the 1980s. In considering the longer term, we need to make explicit the central debate which underpinned the distinction between post-Fordism and neo-Fordism — the question of whether the 1980s represented a temporary reversal of the long term trend postulated in conventional sociological views of petty capitalism or whether they represented something more permanent. In short, was the revival of petty capitalism in the 1980s temporary — simply an historically familiar countercyclical response to severe recession accentuated by shifts in the make-up of the economic structure?

In the 1930s, for example, the last comparable period of severe recession of the kind occurring in the early 1980s, Foreman-Peck (1985 p. 406) reports that:

> Between 1926 and 1937 private company numbers rose by almost two-thirds, while there were fewer public companies at the end of the period than at the beginning ... the average size of the private company fell, whereas that of the public company rose, as if a dual economy was emerging.

As we know, in the 1950s, the first peace-time decade after the 1930s which was also a period of high economic activity, the small enterprise went into what many regarded as near terminal decline (Bolton Report, 1971; Chapter 5 *passim*). It might be therefore, that higher levels of economic activity and a slowing of the process of restructuring will see the reassertion of the long term trend in the decline of the small business sector in the 1990s.

Steinmetz and Wright (1989) have recently tested the thesis that recent rises in small scale economic activities in the USA were a counter-cyclical response. Given their general sympathy to a neo-Marxist perspective, their conclusion that there is no strong evidence for a countercyclical response interpretation is unexpected. They argue that:

> The traditional effect of unemployment on self-employment has been declining in the postwar period and in any case does not account for the increase in self-employment since the mid-1970s (Steinmetz and Wright, 1989 p. 1007).

Instead, they suggest that the shift to a services based economy has been accompanied by a proportionate increase in petty capitalism in the services sector and this offers a rather better explanation for the increase in small scale economic activities. But, further, they also report an increase in self-employment in longer established sectors especially construction and manufacturing.

The above findings are consistent with what has been observed in the UK in the 1980s. But, as Steinmetz and Wright argue for the USA, the increase in services self-employment and small businesses has only been proportionate to the expansion of the sector (Steinmetz and Wright, 1989 p. 1006) — paralleling a similar finding for the UK (Graham *et. al.*, 1989

p. 49). The discovery of an increase in small scale activities in traditional sectors of the economy — manufacturing and construction especially — is interpreted by Steinmetz and Wright as reflecting employer strategies to bypass unions and push down wages. For the UK, while the latter explanation has some force — not least because of government initiated increases in employer power in the 1980s[18] — other factors such as more subcontracting and new technology allowing smaller units to operate profitably, might also have played a significant part.

If the UK economy is similar to that of the USA — and it might well be since both are examples of older industrial economies which have resembled each other more than they do industrial societies such as Germany or Japan — the inference that could be drawn from the above is that history may not repeat itself, at least in the short term. The much greater importance of services as compared to the mid-century economy and lower concentration in services favours the continuation of the revival of petty capitalism. Of course, concentration in services could increase — a point to which we return below — but the basic character of services activities may restrict the extent to which this can occur. Services have a large personal relations element and successfully maintaining such relations is inherently more difficult as size increases offsetting the other scale advantages. In short, the countercyclical interpretation of the recent revival of petty capitalism does not appear well supported on present evidence and interpretations.

Questions involving the future of the structure of economic relations are never easy to answer and the social sciences — especially sociology — have such a poor track record that many would not even bother to try to answer them. On the other hand, attempting to answer them has at least the merit of suggesting key issues for the agenda for future research.

Assessing the prospects for petty capitalism in Britain over the next decade or so might start at several points. Here we take two: (i) cultural and political influences on self-employment and small firm ownership, and (ii) economic influences which make up the structure of opportunities faced by the self-employed and those who run small businesses.

Political and Cultural Influences

Earlier we discussed the importance of the enterprise culture in the 1980s and its relation to small scale economic activities, arguing that ideologically and culturally, notions of the enterprise culture prominent in dominant political discourses were only tangentially related to such activities. The bundle of assumptions, beliefs and values which made up dominant notions of enterprise and the enterprise culture, were, it was argued, essentially vehicles for interpreting radical economic change generally more than 'belief packages' guiding those involved in petty capitalism itself. Despite the important symbolic importance of petty capitalism stereotypes, 'believer driven' versions of the enterprise culture were empirically scarce among those involved in small scale economic activities.

It was also predicted that the 1990s will produce a swing away from individualistic interpretations of social experience which politically dominant versions of the enterprise culture have embodied. Already, it is commonplace to suggest that the 1990s will see a return to more collectivist concerns where market based solutions with any wide appeal seem hard to find. For petty capitalism itself then, any decline in the enterprise culture in dominant political discourse, might be expected to have little effect. As has often been demonstrated (Curran, 1986, 1987; Curran and Burrows, 1987b; Hakim, 1988; Ritchie, 1991) those directly involved in small scale economic activities do not utilize such cultural sets to interpret their experiences or guide their behaviour to any marked extent. Of course, discourses promoted vigorously by powerful élites have their cultural echoes even as they decline. One result of such an 'echo effect' is that self-employment is probably considered by a wider range of people than in the pre-1980s — a factor favouring the continuation of petty capitalism, other things being equal.

At a utilitarian level, government in the 1980s devoted a good deal of resources and legislative effort to promoting more small scale economic activities. A House of Commons Library background paper (Edmonds, 1986) estimated that between 1980 and 1985 government spent at least £1b supporting small firms with expenditure accelerating rapidly after 1983. In addition, from 1979 onwards, governments introduced well over 200 legislative initiatives designed to make starting, running and expanding a small firm easier. These ranged from changes in small companies corporation tax and simplifying VAT for smaller firms, to reducing the requirements of compliance with regulations and laws, to loans for start-up and expansion and cheap or free training (Department of Employment, 1989).

However, assessing the impact of these measures has not been easy. The sheer number of initiatives and the tendency to repackage and rename them after comparatively short periods makes following through their effects very difficult. More difficult still, are the problems of *additionality* and *displacement*, that is, estimating the extent to which such initiatives stimulated net increases in activity as opposed to activities which would have occurred anyway and the extent to which supporting some firms led to the decline or death of others not being helped (Ridyard *et al.*, 1989; Storey, 1983; Storey and Johnson, 1987).

Despite the above problems, however, there is some consensus on the effects of government promotion of small scale economic activities. Firstly, although Conservative administrations in the 1980s made much of the principle that problems cannot be solved by 'throwing money at them', some commentators such as Storey (1983; Storey *et. al.*, 1987) have argued that this was what happened in the small business sector. First, awareness of the aids available was slow to grow among those targeted and, hence, take-up of many of the measures was not anything like as high as government had hoped. Second, relative to the size of the petty capitalism sector government policies could not have had more than a marginal impact even had take up been greater among small firms.

Many of the legislative initiatives aimed at small firms required no action from small business owners themselves and therefore were less affected by awareness. Changes in employment legislation, for example, such as lengthening of the period in which employees could not complain about unfair dismissal or reductions in requirements to provide statistical information to government departments, apply to all small firms. However, even some of these measures probably had less impact than expected. For example, Curran and Stanworth (1986) argued that relaxations in employment law requirements would not have any great impact because many small firms did not observe the previous laws anyway and the most important determinants of levels and conditions of employment in the smaller firm were economic rather than legal. Similarly, small firms have long had a poor record in completing statistical returns for the Census of Production and so on. Allowing them not to reply was simply a recognition of what had always happened anyway. Research also indicates that small business owners often see the benefits of aid or legislative changes intended to help them as cancelled out by other more general policies such as high interest rates to curb inflation (Curran, 1987).

There are also indications that government is now trying to rationalize aid policies to small firms. For instance the current heavily publicized *Enterprise Initiative* represents a repackaging of a whole range of previous programmes and is aimed at a wider range of businesses. Whereas, previous aids concentrated on start-ups, the intention is now to target established firms. In other words, resources are being spread more thinly. In addition, many of the legislative initiatives introduced in the 1980s were one off changes which could not be repeated in the 1990s.

The implication of the above is that any fall in government aid to the petty capitalist sector in the 1990s will have only a marginal impact. Nor would this change substantially if Labour were to be elected in the 1990s. A Labour administration would be unlikely to devote the same levels of resources and legislative energy to promoting petty capitalism as the Conservatives did in the 1980s, but it would by no means be hostile (Labour Party, 1987). It might even be more favourable to some kinds of small business activities such as those in depressed regions and inner cities sponsored by local authorities.

Political culture is not the only cultural influence on petty capitalism. In the 1980s wider cultural changes occurred in Britain which also have considerable potential for affecting small scale economic activities. One set of much discussed changes are those associated with the various versions of *postmodernism* (Connor, 1989; Harvey, 1989; Lash and Urry, 1987). Post-modernism is a somewhat loose collection of ill-defined notions but the fragmenting of ideas and lifestyles and the elaboration of symbol over substance in everyday consumption are common to several versions of the thesis. Consumption, it is argued, becomes centred on symbolic meanings attached to objects and services much more than in previous eras. For instance, in fashion it is suggested that clothes are increasingly selected to make a statement about the wearer which is no longer simple, or even an assertion of wealth or class position.

Other aspects of postmodernism are argued to include the breaking down of the unity of previously dominant cultural forms such as classicism or modernism or the linear narrative form in books and especially in the cinema and video. In their place emerges a non-time specific, 'pick and mix' aesthetic which combines elements of previous cultures in new ways. The clearest example of the latter is in architecture where 1980s styles supplanted the modernist, 'box-like' buildings of the 1960s and 1970s with buildings which were increasingly pastiches of architectural styles drawn from previous periods.

At the level of the individual and group, postmodernist theses suggest a breaking down of the traditional class systems characteristic of earlier industrial society. Instead, people increasingly define themselves as members of fragmented, privatized groups which seek to establish their separate identities by distinctive symbols — language, dress, home decoration and so on — to mark them off from others. Also emphasized is the way consumption becomes short term, that is, there is an increased fluidity in consumption patterns because symbolic meanings change rapidly as individuals and groups discard and adopt new ones.

It is easy to criticize postmodernist theses for overstatement: the classes of earlier industrial society remain significant social forces, the narrative form in books, cinema and television remains popular and a good deal of domestic architecture is based on traditional designs popular for well over fifty years. But to the extent that such ideas capture some of the changes in culture and consumption patterns in the 1980s, they have some implications for the survival of petty capitalism.

The fragmentation of culture and consumption patterns has had a disorganizing effect on the economy adversely affecting larger, slower changing enterprises in their capacity to tap demand across the economy. The trend away from mass consumption towards niche or specialized, rapidly changing goods and services favours more responsive firms. New technology, as noted above, helps large firms to cope with these changes but smaller firms will also be in a strong position to reap the rewards of these changes.

Economic and Demographic Influences

Restructuring and its implications for petty capitalism have been briefly examined above. The conclusion drawn from the analysis is that, broadly, regardless of the model adopted, most were favourable to small scale economic activities. To the extent such tendencies continue in the 1990s then this favourable environment should continue also. However, it is already apparent that the 1990s will have their own special features which might affect petty capitalism adversely.

Recent economic forecasts (London Business School, 1989; NIESR, 1989; OECD, 1989) suggest that the early 1990s will see low levels of economic activity or even recession in the UK economy. On the whole, as in the early 1980s, low levels of economic activity do not necessarily hurt small business and may actually lead to increases due to counter-cyclical effects (Ganguly and Bannock, 1985 p. 168).

The extensive restructuring which marked the 1980s is unlikely to be so pronounced in the 1990s. For one thing, it is unreasonable to expect further sharp falls in manufacturing or the continuation of the massive 'shake out' of firms which were witnessed in the 1980s. For another, large firms in services will have much more experience and perhaps have developed techniques to allow greater penetration and control of markets. For instance, already in financial and business services, large firms are realizing economies of scope allowing them to link a variety of products to the same basic technology. This may well squeeze smaller firms out of the market as happened in property selling in the late 1980s. The historical parallel here could be with the 1950s and 1960s where a similar concentration occurred in manufacturing as the sector developed: services, in other words, might experience a similar increase in concentration accelerated by higher rates of economic growth in the late 1990s.

Before the later 1990s are reached, however, other factors may also have made life more difficult for small businesses. One such factor might be the single European market — as currently represented by the cryptic incantation of 1992! Views on its impact on small businesses vary ranging from those who optimistically emphasize the opportunities offered, to those fearful of its impact on ill-prepared and under-resourced smaller firms who will be unable to withstand increased competition. Surveys by the DTI report that many smaller firms doubt that it will affect them very much and only a minority claim to have taken any preparatory action (Department of Employment, 1989 p. 8).

Small firms' owners are notoriously short-term in their management planning but their views on the impact of the single European market are likely to be broadly correct. First, although the market offers access to 320m customers, less than 5 per cent of small firms already export (Storey and Johnson, 1987). Much more important, most small firms are in services ministering to local markets. The emergence of the single market will not automatically wipe out the extreme cultural variations throughout the Community which both provide a large proportion of the opportunities for smaller businesses and insulate them from competition from outsiders. The initial impact of market liberalization is much more likely to be on larger firms whose markets will be more attractive to encroachers. Indeed, the problems faced by larger firms in services defending themselves against open market competition may help small firms. The tendencies towards concentration mentioned earlier in this section may take longer to appear if larger firms have to devote more attention and resources to defending their existing markets and seeking others elsewhere in the Community. Thus, overall, in the early years of the single European market, small firms are unlikely to be greatly affected although, of course, the longer term — after 2000 — effects may be more direct.

Considerable publicity has been given to the demographic changes which will result in large transformations to the age structure of the work force in the 1990s (Atkinson, 1989; Goetschin, 1987). The impact of these changes on the small firm sector will be much greater than on the large enterprise sector for a number of reasons. Although the labour force as a whole will rise by 1m over the 1990s, most of the new members will be women and there will be a fall of 1.3m in the numbers in the labour force aged under 25 (Employment Gazette, 1989). The latter fall is particularly serious for smaller firms because they employ higher proportions of younger workers than larger firms (Storey and Johnson, 1987).

Indeed, the decrease in the under 25 age group does not tell the whole story here. Small firms also tend to employ larger numbers of school leavers and those with low or no qualifications than larger firms. The number of minimum age school leavers will also drop, and in the 1980s has been dropping faster than the demographic changes themselves would indicate because more are staying on at school. It is government policy also to push up the proportion of young people in higher education from the current 15 per cent to 23 per cent by 2000 (*The Guardian*, 28.9.1989). Again, smaller firms employ fewer graduates than larger firms. Some smaller firms who employ large numbers of young part-timers may benefit, however, from the switch to an educational loan scheme but, overall, these changes can only be coped with if small firms change their recruiting policies radically.

Changing recruiting policies would involve small employers overcoming the marked 'ageism' of their current employment strategies — more pronounced than the 'ageism' of larger employers even. The other alternative is to employ more of the women predicted to enter the labour market in the 1990s. But here small firms will be competing with larger firms for these forms of labour and may well lose the competition especially for women workers. Encouraging women to join the labour market depends, in part, on the provision of career break schemes, crèche facilities, flexible hours, job sharing and the like. Larger firms have more resources than smaller firms to provide many of these benefits.[19] Equally, for all employees, as labour markets get tighter, larger firms also have more resources to offer training, promotion opportunities and a wide range of other benefits to retain the workers they need.

Finally, a further factor which will drive up labour costs in the 1990s is skills shortages. Traditionally, smaller firms employ less well qualified workers than larger firms (Storey and Johnson, 1987) and offer much fewer opportunities for training. However, they do need some skilled workers and their traditional strategy is to recruit those trained by larger firms. But the sharp decline in training in the early 1980s and the failure to develop training to match the expansion of new sectors of the economy, means fewer trained workers and small firm employers in the 1990s will find competition for such workers an increasingly severe problem.

Demographic factors are also likely to have an effect on the supply of people to fill ranks of the petty capitalists in the 1990s. Research indicates that the 'age launch window' for entry into self-employment is between 25 and 44 when the combination of ambition, experience, energy and access to capital are at their most propitious (Burrows, 1991b; Curran and Burrows, 1988 p. 35). This age group will, in fact, not decline in the 1990s overall (Employment Gazette, 1989 p. 191). But this is also likely to be an age group very attractive to larger firms given the decline in the numbers of young people entering the labour market. As research has shown, entry into self-employment is often associated with unemployment or the threat of redundancy (Bevan *et al.*, 1989; Meager, 1989). If larger firms make greater efforts to retain workers in these age groups through appropriate rewards and opportunities, then this could undermine the willingness to risk entering into business for themselves. Given that the self-employed are very much a flow (with large numbers entering and leaving each year) rather than a static population, even if these influences operate only at the margin, the impact on the numbers entering self-employment could show up quickly.

Overall, therefore, economic and demographic factors are likely to have more impact than cultural or political influences on the future of petty capitalism in the 1990s. The factors mentioned are more specific than the overall trends considered in restructuring theories but likely to have at least as much impact. But it should also be emphasized that although it seems the 1990s will not be as favourable for petty capitalism as the 1980s, any decline will be at the margin. As previous periods have shown, even under much less favourable conditions such as those of the mid-years of the century, petty capitalism remained important in the economy — even if this was largely unrecognized by economists and sociologists.

Concluding Comments

Assessing the significance of petty capitalism in advanced industrial societies seems to cause all kinds of problems for social scientists. The immense economic restructuring which virtually all agree has been taking place over the last decade or so — even if they cannot agree on how to interpret it — has raised the question of the significance of petty capitalism in new and interesting ways. The prominence of notions such as 'enterprise' and the 'enterprise culture' in dominant political discourses linked to non-sociological interpretations of much of the phenomena allegedly associated with restructuring, has been particularly problematic for sociologists. On the whole, both sets of issues seem to be dealt with in much the same way: by a reluctance to engage with them directly or by alluding to them only superficially.

In this chapter we have sought to confront both sets of issues in order to suggest how they are linked to each other and how some of the most discussed recent sociological thinking on restructuring can be judged in relation to the problem of situating petty capitalism in industrial society. Finally, we have also sought to ground the largely macro-theoretical discussion of cultural and economic changes through an assessment of the prospects for petty capitalism in the 1990s.

On the relations between the dominant discourse of the enterprise culture and the economic significance and lived experience of petty capitalism, we have argued that the links are largely bogus. Whatever the claims of the right that their promotion of the 'enterprise culture' stimulated a huge increase in individual economic action in the 1980s, the evidence does not support such a connection. On the other hand, those on the left — as well as some social scientists — too easily dismiss the reality of petty capitalism and the increasing numbers of those whose economic lives are encompassed within it. It is facile to see these phenomena as simply the outcome of the machinations of global monopoly capitalism or a similar notion.

The discourse of the enterprise culture in its political and popular versions has considerable significance but as a historically specific and contingent semiotic rationale for the social and economic changes associated with restructuring in general rather than for what has been happening to petty capitalism in the last decade or so. The argument offered earlier that this discourse will lose its force as a meanings system to interpret change in the 1990s therefore tells us little about whether the recent sharply increasing significance of petty capitalism in advanced industrial societies is likely to continue or is simply a temporary reversal of a long term historical trend.

In an admittedly somewhat schematic examination of some of the more fully theorized attempts to account for restructuring, it was noted that they also offer a more or less explicit account of the role of petty capitalism in contemporary industrial societies. But a closer examination and a confrontation with findings on petty capitalism and its links with other aspects of economic life, shows that their accounts are hugely wanting. In other words, here we have another example of the seductive attractions of global level theorizing hitting the buffers of recalcitrant data and analyses, stemming in this instance from examinations of the reality of petty capitalism in industrial society.

At the level of lived petty capitalist activities and their complex interpenetrations with the wider economy, the 1980s were clearly a favourable decade as measured by the revival in the numbers involved and the size of the petty capitalist sector. It was argued that the favourable concatenation of factors which aided this revival is unlikely to continue in the present decade. This should not, however, be seen as a licence to slide back into previous inadequate orthodoxies on the significance of the role of petty capitalism in advanced industrial economies. Historically, the petty capitalist sector has demonstrated an extraordinary ability to survive. Change, therefore, in the form of any downgrading of the importance of petty capitalism in the economy is likely to be at the margin only: economic sociology still needs an adequate account of what involves about a third of all those involved in private sector economic activities, what, in other words, is not such a small business.

Notes

1 An introduction to this literature is provided by Allen and Massey (1988), Anderson and Cochrane (1989), Cochrane and Anderson (1989), Hamnett *et al.* (1989), Massey and Allen (1988) and McDowell *et al.* (1989).
2 For example: liberal (Piore and Sabel, 1984) and Marxian (Lipietz, 1987) analyses of changes in the dominant mode of production; liberal (Saunders, 1986 pp. 289–351) and Marxian (Gamble, 1988) analyses of the incompatibility between market capitalism and more socialized systems of collective consumption giving rise to the hegemony of the New Right; liberal (Hall, 1985) and Marxian (Mandel, 1980) analyses of economic long waves (Marshall, 1987); eclectic models claiming to be able to identify shifts from 'organized' towards more 'disorganized' forms of capitalism (Lash and Urry, 1987); 'culturalist' representations of recent times, conceptualised in terms of shifts from 'modernism' towards 'post-modernism' (Harvey, 1989); and so on.
3 See for example the various contributions collected together in Burrows (1990a) and Keat and Abercrombie (1990).
4 See for example Bright (1987), the Conservative Party (1987), HMSO (1985; 1986; 1988) and Young (1986).
5 However, this interpretation has not been adhered to by all on the left. Some have taken an extremely accepting line to recent developments (Hall and Jacques, 1989). For critiques, albeit from very different political perspectives, see Clarke (1990), Rainnie (1990) and Rustin (1989).

6　As Dale (1991) shows, there is no agreed sociological definition of entrepreneurship and as a consequence there is much semantic slippage between it,
petty bourgeoisie class status and self-employment. For a review of concep-
tualizations found in the economics literature see Hebert and Link (1989).

7　This confusion is related to the articulation of the discourse of the enterprise
culture with the wider discourse of Thatcherism. In much political rhetoric it
is assumed that Thatcherism has been, in some sense, an *independent* variable
which has had a causal impact upon a range of other *dependent* variables:
small businesses; self-employment; trade unions; manufacturing industry;
the public sector and so on. Indeed, the concept, based as it is upon such a
gross personification, encourages a fetishism for an analytic individualism of
the 'if only we could get rid of *her* things might get back to normal' kind.
Things are obviously much more complex, and this complexity can best be
understood by keeping the concepts of restructuring and Thatcherism distinct (Urry, 1989 p. 94). It is more useful to consider Thatcherism as the
political *expression* of deeper shifts in the national and the international
socio-economic system, than it is to view it as a political force with its own
specificity. Thatcherism, and hence the enterprise culture, has not been an
independent force invoking these changes, rather it has represented a contingent set of political and ideological practices which have mediated and given
expression to a socio-economic restructuring which would in all probability
have occurred, albeit at a different pace and mediated by a different set of
practices, even if Thatcher, and all that she stands for, had never existed
(Burrows, 1991c).

8　Martin (1988) provides the best schematic introduction to the theorization of
restructuring, however it is by no means the only one available. Harvey
(1989 pp. 173–88) provides a review of a number of other attempts (Halal,
1986; Lash and Urry, 1987; Swyngedouw, 1986). However, what all have in
common is an ambiguity concerning whether the different dimensions of
change that they note should be viewed as being *necessarily* related, or seen as
connected only in a *contingent* manner. It remains unclear if the notion of
restructuring (or its various analogues) should be treated as a conceptual flag
of convenience for a range of otherwise disparate changes, or whether it
should be regarded as a realist concept which has managed to capture an
ontologically real process of change involving a set of closely articulated
causal powers.

9　As has been discussed elsewhere (Burrows and Curran, 1989; Curran, 1986;
Dale, 1991) both of these measures have serious drawbacks as indicators of
the extent of small scale enterprise in the economy, they are nevertheless
suggestive of trends in petty capitalist economic activities.

10　See Curran (1986; 1990) and Curran and Burrows (1986; 1987a) for extensive
reviews of the literature which does exist.

11　This distinction is obviously a very crude one, but will be useful for our
purposes here. However, both approaches are unified by their concern to
theorize the crisis and (partial or absolute) breakdown of something called
'Fordism' — a concept which has itself recently been highly problematized
by Clarke (1991).

12　Other analogues to 'Not-Fordism' can also be found in the literature, such as

'Toyotism', 'Nextism', 'Proudhonism' and 'Japanizataion' — all referring to much the same set of ideas.

13 It is possible that some of these new firms are created by former employees of the larger firms offered the contracts for outsourced work.

14 Although Harvey (1989, pp. 189–197), one of the most influential writers on these debates, suggests otherwise.

15 Important exceptions to this observation include many of the contributions to Allen and Massey (1988) and Massey and Allen (1988).

16 An extensive elaboration of this section can be found in Curran and Blackburn (1990).

17 Economists and business researchers did not do much better in the past. For example, the Bolton Report (1971) was almost entirely wrong in its predictions of the future of the small enterprise.

18 See Goss (1991) for an analysis of this as it relates to the wider discourse of the enterprise culture.

19 There may possibly be some scope here for co-operation between coalitions of small firms on a district basis as suggested by the flexible specialization model, i.e. privatized collective consumption on an industrial districts basis — however, as things currently stand such a development seems highly unlikely except within the most utopian of scenarios. For recent research on employer responses to demographic change see Rainnie and Kraithman (1991).

Chapter 3

Paternalist Capitalism: An Organization Culture in Transition

Peter Ackers and John Black

Introduction

The Thatcher decade has spawned a cluster of apparently novel descriptions and prescriptions about the future direction of management's approach to labour in British industry. Concepts like Japanization, The Flexible Firm, Post-Fordism and Human Resources Management (HRM), share a common conviction that a management strategy based on the *control* of their workers, mediated through conflict and compromise with their trade union representatives, is giving way to a different relationship, of employee *commitment*, generated by direct management communications and employee involvement strategies.

Until the late 1970s, car firms, like Ford and Vauxhall, with their elaborate, work-studied division of labour, sophisticated payment systems, and complex procedures for negotiation and conflict management, were regarded as the model of the very modern British corporation. They met their workers' 'instrumental' work orientation (Goldthorpe and Lockwood, 1969), with a motivational 'cash nexus' and plenty of safety valves to handle the inevitable, periodic fall-out. Anyone who talked about employee 'loyalty' and 'all pulling together for the good of the firm' was regarded as a nostalgic crank who did not understand modern industry (Fox, 1966).

Today, even in these citadels of Fordism, such attitudes are passé. Instead, we hear of a host of employee involvement and communications initiatives, to win the 'hearts and minds' of workers, whose active participation at work is now deemed essential to effective manufacturing performance. These range from teamworking and quality circles, through team briefing and employee financial reports, to improved social welfare provisions, and profit participation and share ownership schemes. The overarching message, replacing the cynical, monetary realism of post-war pluralism, is that employees can be members of a team, all working together, towards an improved corporate performance: no need to fight over the cake, we can all make it bigger, together.

Several commentators have noted the similarity between the new thinking and an older body of management thought and practice, broadly described as 'Paternalism' (Kendall, 1984; Black and Ackers, 1988a). This applies as much to the general revival of a sense of management responsibility for motivating and nurturing their workers, as to a renewed interest in specific practices like social welfarism, industrial participation, and profit sharing. The objective of this article is not to draw some spurious identity between these recent developments, and the paternalist arrangements which predated modern pluralist, Taylorist industrial relations. Rather, it is to draw out the nature of old-style paternalism, what prompted and sustained it, and what led to its decline. We also consider the relevance of the old paternalism for the new HRM: which elements remain potentially viable in the contemporary world, and what constraints our modern, open society would set on any attempt to recreate the ideal of the committed, work team? There is clearly common ground in the idea of the firm as a social as well as an economic organization, in the emphasis on employee 'commitment' or 'loyalty', and in the underlying rationale that contented employees are more efficient workers.

We suggest an anatomy of paternalism, by comparing the characteristics of several industries and companies associated with it. Our starting point was our research into changes into Black Country industrial relations, conducted over the past decade. The three industries involved, locks, woven carpets and crystal glass, are all traditional to the area, and heavily concentrated in local occupational communities. Their employment relationships are widely regarded as 'paternalist', yet they also contain modern, dynamic elements projecting them into the future. To provide a broader base for generalization, we have set this primary material against the secondary literature on paternalism, in the chocolate, footwear, glass and other industries. We suggest that a paternalist model can be constructed from these experiences, representing a distinctive approach to managing labour. We look at the main elements of this and then at the trends in modern society which have unravelled it, and, finally, at its relevance for current HRM literature.

The almost total absence of doctrine and teaching in nineteenth-century labour management . . . should not deter us from understanding the central importance of paternalism in English industrial society. Indeed this absence was a reflection of the practical and piecemeal effectiveness of that paternalism (Joyce, 1980, p. 146).

Terms like Paternalism, Benevolent Paternalism, Paternalist Capitalism or, in the US, Welfare Capitalism (Zahavi, 1988) are frequently employed in academic studies of industrial relations; but usually as a loose, descriptive shorthand for some type of 'traditional authority' (Newby, 1977, p. 63) in the employment relationship, rather than as precise theoretical tools. They tend 'to be the subject of inference and assumption rather than definition' (Russell, 1987, p. 154). In these common sense usages paternalism often reflects workers' and management's own understanding of the type of company in which they work — and is indeed often used by them spontaneously. It usually refers to a general company 'atmosphere' rather than to any clearcut taxonomy of characteristics. At times, it just indicates any long-established 'family firm' with a correspondingly strong organization culture. Elsewhere it points, more narrowly, to a conscious welfarist strategy perhaps fired by some sense of religious mission or social obligation.

This style was spawned in the early small-scale stage of British capitalist development. However Joyce (1980, p. xx) suggests that the paternalism of the nineteenth century family firm, was longer lasting and, 'vastly more important than is generally recognized' as a mechanism of social and industrial control. He adds that, far from being a simply feudal hangover from early capitalism, a 'new' paternalism was consciously recreated by mid-nineteenth century Victorian employers, particularly in proto-modern industrial Lancashire. Finding their firms large, secure and profitable, and themselves with time to spare and imbued with a (predominantly Non-Conformist) religious sense of 'mission' and 'duty', they sought to construct a sense of personal and communal identity in the work towns which surrounded their factories. At this point of industrial maturity, 'as a fully developed factory industry consolidated its social effect', a strict economic *laissez-faire* attitude to wage-labour gave way to a more social-conscious employer paternalism (*ibid.*, p. 137). This was facilitated by the 'enormous influence' of the factory and work in these towns, which encouraged the mill owner to cultivate a 'moral legitimation of class domination' through the 'paternalist ethic' (*ibid.*, pp. xvi, xvii). Much more than ideology, this relationship was cemented by the dense social network of factory, family and community life, which successfully translated economic 'dependence' into social 'deference'. More widely, this period saw a growing working-class challenge to liberal capitalism, met by the widespread 'invention of tradition' as an instrument of social cohesion (Hobsbawn, 1988).

Joyce's perspective rescues paternalism from the clutches of a few remarkable exceptions, and restores it as part of the social fabric of industrial life, and 'everyday practice of the ordinary employer'. For 'most big employers' and many others,

> a piecemeal, almost instinctive paternalism ... grew out of the
> shared sense of community fostered by the industrial and urban
> conditions of the later nineteenth century (Joyce, 1980, p. 139).

Not only has this type of company survived into the late twentieth century, more widely than is generally recognized (in the USA, Endicott Johnson's paternalist 'Square Deal' was launched after the First World War (Zahavi, 1988); but, in addition, many firms which have outgrown their small scale, family origins, have nevertheless retained and developed elements of this cultural legacy. While powerful modernizing forces continue to undermine some central elements of paternalist capitalism, there are also new features in the modern industrial era which may encourage its partial survival and possible renaissance.

In this respect, it is worth reminding ourselves that, however benign, paternalism is still an aspect of capitalist control and power, as Wagner (1987, p. 48) recognizes:

> underneath the mateyness there was an element of obedience and deference on the part of the worker which was inherent in the relationship. How could it be otherwise when the employer was the all-powerful provider of the vital weekly wage?

Paternalism is 'essentially a form of authority' (Russell, 1987, p. 155), and a process of legitimation, which enables 'power relationships to become moral ones' (Newby, 1977, p. 64). As such it is riven by two 'inherently contradictory impulses' (Russell, 1987, p. 154): the need for 'hierarchical differentiation' from subordinate groups; and the attempt 'to foster a sense of identification and unity of purpose'. The main features of paternalism can usefully be placed into two groups: those associated with ownership and management; and those regarding the characteristics of the labour force.

An Anatomy of Paternalism: The Company

Large and Small Firm Paternalism

> Effective paternalism is ... related to size, for above a certain size, personal, traditional modes of control break down and a degree of bureaucratic control becomes inevitable (Newby, 1977, p. 73).

Paternalism is often associated with the small firm, where the size of the workforce enables top management to retain a personal contact with the shopfloor, and to do without specialist functions, like personnel. This was the case in the British footwear industry (Goodman, 1977, pp. 152–3), where the average firm was usually a single main factory, employing about two hundred shopfloor workers. These firms were 'usually owner-managed' and directors were 'directly involved in the day to day management'. There was a 'shallow' management hierarchy, and management's relations with their workers 'extended beyond work into the local community'. Linked to this was a lack of sophistication in management techniques and training, meaning that 'professional management was limited'. This corresponds with the conventional wisdom that Unitarism (Fox, 1966) — a closely connected concept — is no longer feasible as an approach to management control in large complex organizations, where the boss cannot be in touch with the shopfloor on a daily basis.

However, as Joyce suggests, later nineteenth century paternalism, which began in the small firms of early capitalism, found a new, more developed and deliberate form, in the larger, more modern companies. Indeed, this 'new' paternalism was a 'successful' response to this 'problem of size' (1980, p. 136). Our lock and carpet companies are medium sized firms, each employing about 2,000 workers on several sites, including some outside the 'industry town' and even overseas.

Those giants of paternalism: Clarkes, Rowntrees, Cadburys and Pilkington, are today huge multi-national concerns. The latter, which began as 'small family business' in 1826, was by 1983 the world's largest flat glass producer, with 38,000 employees, a turnover of £900 million, and 200 subsidiary and associate companies in twenty-nine countries (Norman, 1983, p. 20). Some forms of paternalism were clearly stimulated by this 'size problem'. The main welfarist thrust at Cadburys and Rowntrees came at the start of this century, when the latter — and smaller of the two — had expanded from 200 employees in 1883, to 894 in 1894, to 4,000 in 1906 (Wagner, 1987). In this respect, a distinction should be drawn between the 'primitive' instinctive paternalism of small firms and the more 'sophisticated' paternalism of medium and large companies. And since the small firm has remained part of the modern industrial scene, this distinction holds for contemporary as well as historical purposes.

This chapter is concerned with those relatively 'sophisticated' forms of paternalism, which cannot be reduced to a simplistic unitarism. In these firms paternalism has often accompanied modern scientific management techniques. Large Quaker employers pioneered 'professional management' (Child, 1964), and, at the start of this century, Cadbury combined 'a varied welfare programme' with 'systematic management procedures', including 'a modified form of scientific management' (Rowlinson, 1988, pp. 391; 386). Obviously the picture was more mixed at lesser firms, like our lock and carpet companies, who were still smallish firms at this stage, with stronger residual elements of 'primitive' paternalism. Or the crystal glass firm where, 'with the arrival of the stop watch paternalism was eroded' (Black and Neathey, 1989, p. 175). While the lock firm personnel manager described his firm as still low on 'clarity' and 'formality', and lacking 'well-defined management systems', his carpet counterpart recalled that, before the 1970s 'formalization' of industrial relations,

> We had no Procedure Agreements at all, we had no rules, we had no works and staff handbooks, it was not handled very formally.

Hereditary Family Ownership

> I'm conditioned in my thinking ... by the company and what I know about it, by my forefathers and by my successors. I want to preserve the company as it is ... a successful, private, family company that provides a living to a lot of people and a very good living for me personally ... we are only stewards ... for our time (Chairman, carpet company).

In ancient private limited companies, like this carpet firm, paternalism has been mediated through the persona of the hereditary family, in particular the company chairman — whose function the managing director compared to that of the royal family in British political life. Hereditary family ownership and control has been central to British paternalism. The British footwear firms (Goodman, 1977, p. 152) were often run by 'members of the family of the founder of the company, with ownership having passed from generation to generation'. A company, like the carpet firm, which has been run by the same family, producing the same basic product, in the same town, for two hundred years; and operating the same type of technology for well over a hundred, is likely to have evolved a strong and distinctive organizational culture (Ackers, 1988). While such firms remained private companies, great thought was given to the functional reproduction of the family dynasty.

In 1970, 142 years after its foundation, Pilkington (Lane and Roberts, 1971, p. 36) reached the fourth generation of family control — a 'tribute to the family's ability to produce large numbers of children'. But, a generation later, there were insufficient willing sons to command a Board majority — even employing both male and female lines of descent — and this was one reason for the decision to 'go public' in 1970. Anthony Pilkington is today 'the sixth and probably the last family chairman' (Caulkin, 1987, p. 43). Family members are still prominent in Cadburys, though it has long outgrown its family firm origins. When both Cadburys and Rowntrees became limited companies in 1899 and 1897 respectively:

> there were a sufficient number of young Cadbury and Rowntree men willing and able to provide continuity of management during the period of change. (Wagner, 1987, p. 67)

The large US Footwear firm, Endicott Johnson (Zahavi 1988), also remained a family firm long after it became a public corporation. Our lock firm became a limited company in 1916, 'went public' in 1936, but remained under effective family control until a 1965 takeover (with family brothers chairman and joint managing directors of the four man board). And even beyond then, it maintained the old company and brand names, product range, and management; including, until 1980, a 'family' managing director. Even after a further 1984 takeover, the personnel manager found it:

> A fairly paternalist organization, despite the changes in owner-
> ship, despite the changes in management ... there's a lot of
> non-change ... at grassroots level.

So if family ownership and control were crucial for the creation of a paternalist company culture, they seem less essential to its maintenance, albeit in a diluted form. In one footwear company (Goodman, 1977, p. 152), although

> ownership had passed out of the hands of the original family, the
> atmosphere of a family firm remained, given both the ideology
> and deliberate strategy of the management and the traditions and
> orientations held by the workers employed there.

In a similar local industry, crystal glass, 'with a variety of forms of ownership' from family firm to multinational; paternalist elements were found across the board (Black and Neathey, 1989, p. 172). One reason is that workers and plant management can carry on the paternalist mantle of longstanding personal contact, well after the family connection is broken. Thus the former lock convenor lamented the old personnel manager:

> That individual, as we've known him for a long time ... we could
> go and have a talk and understand each other, and we knew how
> far we could go ... he was a very good listener.

One attraction of paternalism in the private family ownership stage, is the 'preference of the long-term vision over the short-term presentation' (Caulkin, 1987, p. 441). This caused Pilkington to spend seven years of huge investment to bring their new float glass process to fruition. In the same vein, the privately-owned carpet firm continued to generate large capital investment funds throughout the profit-starved early 1980s. Management and shop stewards alike subscribed to this 'company objective':

> To remain a family company to prevent sudden unwelcome
> takeovers and to enable us to maximize investment and take a

long-term view free from public financial pressures, and to remain in a position where we can react effectively to severe fluctuations in trade.

Personal Relations

The special potency of the personal relations of master and men within 19th century paternalism can hardly be exaggerated (Joyce, 1980, p. 1351).

A core characteristic of paternalism is some tradition of personal relationships between directors and shopfloor. This 'family firm atmosphere', in the British footwear industry (Goodman, 1977, pp. 152–3) included 'close and direct relationships' between directors and workforce, whereby the former, 'would be seen daily on the shopfloor and usually knew almost all of their workers by name'. Virtually all allegedly paternalist companies mention this 'factory tour' in at least some stage of their development. Within the carpet firm, the chairman's Christmas factory tour symbolizes a tradition of 'first name' personal relationships between directors and the shopfloor, and especially the long-service, skilled male élite (at work and in the local town). When the present chairman joined the Board in the 1960s, older managers still referred to him as 'the young master'.

As late as 1969, Lord Pilkington (Lane and Roberts, 1971, p. 43) could argue that his firm's 'greatest asset' was a 'century of personal contact and established goodwill'. And, as Lane and Roberts point out, 'it is not the habit of traditional ideas to disappear suddenly', even when their material base has been severely eroded. However, if the efficacy of paternalism depends on 'face-to-face contact' (Newby, 1977, p. 66) this obviously poses problems even for medium-sized firms, like the carpet and lock companies.

Religious Mission

The roots of the new paternalism lay as much in religion as anything else (Joyce, 1980, p. 140).

Paternalist firms, like Pilkington (Lane and Roberts, 1971, pp. 139–40) still refer to their 'moral side', insisting 'that there is more to business than just making money'. Furthermore this moral philosophy traditionally married employee obligations 'to the firm and to hard work' with a sense of company 'responsibility for their welfare'. In this, and most other paternalist firms, a predominantly non-Conformist 'Protestant

Ethic' (Weber, 1971) was the formative influence. This 'tended to endow the pursuit of their business with high moral purpose' and 'created a sense of moral obligation to undertake public service in some form or other' (Lane and Roberts, 1971). In its various religious guises, this linked ideas of 'duty' and 'community' to 'the civilising mission of industry' (Joyce, 1980, p. 141).

This applied equally to the 'notion of kinship with the humble' which was 'closely linked to the brotherhood of the Congregationalists, the religion of so many employers' (Pilkington, Lever, Salt and the Crossley carpet family included) (Joyce, 1980, p. 142); and the Quakers' 'secular ethic' (Child, 1964, p. 294) with its four precepts: a dislike of exploitation; a view of business as serving the community as a whole; a principle of democratic leadership; and an abhorrence of conflict in industry.

Wagner (1987, p. 48) defines two traditional types of religious paternalist regimes in Britain: the 'more relaxedly expansive ... Tory Anglican' approach; and — far more common — the 'Liberal Non-Conformist', with its 'moral restrictiveness' and overbearing concern for the physical and spiritual well-being of its employees. In nineteenth century 'Carpet town', 'the division between the Church and non-Conformity was almost equal' (Smith, 1986, p. 175), though the latter were more active in public life. When, in 1839, an ancestor of the present company chairman became town mayor, he was a Congregationalist and a Whig-Liberal. Most nineteenth century paternalist families shared this inspiration when 'organized religion often provided a coherent world view which could oblige employers to expectations derived from religious ideology' (Newby, 1977, p. 65). This source of paternalism has all but vanished today, with the rapid secularization of twentieth century Britain, leaving only a moral residue.

Social Welfare and Public Service

> Works dinners and treats, trips to the countryside and the employer's residence, libraries, reading rooms, canteens, baths, lectures, gymnasia, burial societies and the like were to become the rule rather than the exception among the big employers (Joyce, 1980, p. 148).

Paternalist firms see themselves as social entities, with moral obligations to their employees and the local community (Ackers, 1988). One carpet 'company objective' is,

> To continue to assist the local community in whatever form it can as a major employer.

Since the last century the family have played a leading role in the social, cultural, industrial and political life of 'carpet town'. In the larger companies the personal, first-name paternalist relationship became hard to sustain at an early stage, even when family directors had a high profile. Within twenty years of his own life (Wagner, 1987, p. 65), Joseph Rowntree 'found himself unable to take the same paternal and personal interest in each individual employee as had been his wont'. Two factors seem to have compensated for this type of shortcoming — though a facade of shopfloor contact was rarely abandoned.

One was the institutionalization of the expression of care for your workforce through large-scale social welfare provision, at its most impressive in the style of Cadburys' Bournville, Lever's Port Sunlight, Saltaire or Rowntrees' New Earswick. Bournville illustrates the complex mixture of enlightened self-interest and disinterested social reform, which characterized such initiatives. Only half of the original Bournville tenants came from the firm; and the initiative had the wider objective of a mixed community and good working-class housing, in keeping with the contemporary Birmingham non-Conformist 'Civic Gospel' (Briggs, 1968). By contrast, Lever saw Port Sunlight more narrowly, as a form of 'profit sharing' (Wagner, 1987), to prevent his workforce spending their excess cash on 'booze' and dissipation.

Although George Cadbury was genuinely 'thinking more widely than merely providing for his own employees' (Wagner, 1987, p. 58) or his own interests, employers were well aware that their welfare policies paid 'material as well as moral dividends' (Child, 1964, p. 306), and were motivated 'in part from an interest in efficiency' (Rowlinson, 1988, p. 378). The idea that 'paternalism was a paying proposition' (Joyce, 1980, p. 146) rested on a virtuous circle (recently revived by the Labour Party) linking 'social justice' and 'economic efficiency': the belief that business efficiency and the employees' welfare are but different sides of the same problem (Lane and Roberts, 1971). By the mid nineteenth century, Pilkington had contributed towards sports facilities, a schoolmaster and a library; followed by a cycling club, works canteen, medical service and various sick, superannuation and OAP benefit schemes. However, in 1955, this welfare policy for employees still only cost about £75 per annum, per head, and was heavily skewed towards staff 'fringe benefits' (about £43s worth).

Joyce (1980, p. 180) points to the '*laissez faire* inflexion in English paternalism ... the mentality of the moral book-keeper'. Thus the Halifax Crossleys spent vast sums on the town, yet insisted that their workers paid, as far as possible, for their own canteen. Rowntrees (Wagner, 1987) docked a penny of every employee's wages — up to 2 per cent of earnings — towards the upkeep of a library for their use, in another example of compulsory, employer-administered 'deferred gratification'. As in the early days of the lock firm, employers with an 'improving tone'

(Russell, 1987, p. 157), often preferred to 'pump-prime' appropriate employee 'self-help' 'friendly society' schemes, rather than carry the full cost and responsibility themselves. Their 1949 Centenary Booklet lists a plethora of these: a Locks Welfare Society, a Sick and Dividend Club, a Savings Club, a Sport club with football, tennis, bowling and cricket branches, an Entertainments section, Refreshments Room and Coal Club.

The well-publicized cases of 'wholesale social engineering' (Joyce, 1980, p. 144) were less important than this more modest and general paternalism 'expressed through the factory itself'. Even as large a firm as Pilkington 'have not been public benefactors' (Lane and Roberts, 1971, p. 38). Likewise, the carpet firm provided an OAP welfare service and extensive sports and social facilites, but had a blindspot for inadequate pensions and sickness schemes.

Another channel was public service, political or otherwise, in the local community: 'town councillor, alderman, mayor, borough magistrate, school and hospital governor, poor law guardian, church or chapel dignitary and so on' (Russell, 1987, p. 157). This was particularly appropriate in an industry or company community, where the 'overlap of economic, social and political leadership' (including religious) facilitated a 'multi-dimensional' diffusion of paternal authority. The nineteenth century 'Carpet town' employers 'met fairly regularly as a body' (Smith, 1986, p. 178) and shared 'a common economic philosophy', which transcended their religious and political differences. In larger towns many employers preferred, from an early date, to immerse themselves in their industrial empires or retreat to distant rural estates (Briggs, 1968). The growth of the Labour Movement also circumscribed these political roles — with the defeat of a 'Pilkington' councillor in 1890, and the election of St. Helen's first Labour MP in 1906 (Lane and Roberts, 1971).

An Anatomy of Paternalism: Labour Force

Family Employment

The firm is in fact, a family firm in more senses than one. It is a firm which for over a century and a quarter has been owned, directed, and managed by the Pilkington family, and it is a firm in which family feeling is also experienced by the employees themselves . . . there are many families who have worked for two, three, or even four generations. The fact that there are so many families engaged at all levels, gives the integrated structure which is of great value in preserving the family spirit throughout the Pilkington group (Managing Director in 1955 — Lane and Roberts 1971, p. 41).

If the paternalist owner is often a father figure, steeped in the emotional involvement of generations of family control, this seems to be mirrored by traditional male, often craft-based, authority on the shopfloor, and by subordinate family structures of similar length and complexity. Even where, 'the manual workforce consists of a majority of females' (Goodman, 1977, p. 154); the skilled male labour aristocracy of clickers (footwear), weavers (carpets), hand-polishers, locksmiths and toolmakers (locks), or makers (crystal glass) dominate the shopfloor and the trade union. For Cadburys, at the turn of the century, it was the 'skilled men's section' (Rowland, 1988, p. 386) who formed an isolated bastion of trade union organization and offered 'resistance' to the introduction of scientific management. Lock unionization spread to women pieceworkers last, from an established core in the toolroom and the skilled production areas. The weaving élite played a similar part in carpet unionization and, like their crystal glass craft counterparts, endeavoured to control entry to the trade, while offering resistance to the new methods (Black and Neathey 1989). Indeed, in these industries, management authority is negotiated mainly through close relations between the all-male management and these labour aristocrats, with the majority female workforce playing a more or less passive role.

The whole workforce is closely knit together by the practice of children following their parents and relations into the company and industry, and the consequent presence of large complex, extended family networks. One lock shop steward commented, 'it's one big family here', and a manager argued:

It helps the general unity of the place, if you've got sisters and brothers who are working here, fathers and sons.

In the carpet firm, the 'ruling family' network going back generations is also mirrored on the shopfloor, where the pattern has been:

in-plant socialisation facilitated by the presence of a large core of long-service workers and by recruitment through family connections (Martin and Fryer, 1973, p. 84).

The GMB Convenor described the traditional labour force as 'institutionalized' by the fact that 'the carpet industry was the only employer' in the town. Children were pre-socialized to follow their parents into the industry and the company. The Employee Relations Manager joined the firm as a shopfloor worker, because: 'I'd got seven or eight close family ... it was the natural thing to do'. This pattern was particularly pronounced among the male craft élite, the weavers, where sons followed fathers for successive generations — as one shop steward described it:

> I'm the third generation ... and I've got a son here ... carpets
> [are] in the family, so automatically I was destined for the carpet
> trade and I've worked my way through the [traditional weaving]
> division from a lower level, all the way through 'til I [have]
> reached the ultimate now as a broadloom weaver.

Even today, most workers have relatives in the company, and many have
large extended families. In crystal glass (Black and Neathey 1989, p. 173),

> Due to the long historical association between the industry and
> the locality it is common for several generations of the same
> family to have had a lifetime of employment.

Employee loyalty and labour stability, have been motives for paternalism
(Kendall, 1984), creating 'typically long-service and ageing' (Goodman,
1977, p. 154) workforces with very low labour turnover. In the British
footwear study 17 per cent of workers had more than twenty years of
company service, with over 44 per cent between five and twenty years.
Labour turnover at the carpet firm was 0.6 per cent in 1979, and had been
very low even during post-war full employment; despite the high concentration of other carpet companies locally (Ackers, 1988). Yet, their
'new town' spinning plant had experienced severe labour turnover problems, on its opening in the early 1970s, when 51 per cent of all recruits
left within one year of engagement. This problem was tackled by recruiting 'former miners who tend to conform to group behavioural patterns'
similar to those in 'carpet town'. Paternalist management also tends to be
long-service, even in medium-sized organizations like the carpet and lock
firms, with 'little experience of other industries' (Goodman, 1977,
p. 153). At the carpet firm, most had either joined from school as management trainees, like the personnel manager, or risen from the shopfloor
via the supervisory layer, like the employee relations manager. This
created a personal and cultural closeness between management and the
shopfloor, as with the weaving shop steward and the employee relations
manager, who had grown up together.

With craft groups like carpet weavers and crystal glass makers,
family employment was functional in two respects: it kept young men in
the company during a long and arduous apprenticeship period; and it
provided a means of kinship control over these younger members. Harry
L. Johnson, the US Footwear paternalist (Zahavi, 1988) openly advanced
such arguments, against the high costs of skilled labour turnover.

Paternalist companies have developed a number of strategies to support this long service/low turnover pattern including: elaborate 'gold
watch' presentations, perks for long-service employees, and internal recruitment and seniority systems. The carpet and lock firms encouraged
employee loyalty by a policy of avoiding redundancy, giving redundant

workers first choice for vacancies, advertising posts internally first, and recruiting most departmental managers from the shopfloor. A carpet 'company objective' is 'to train and develop employees and promote from within, whenever possible'. Their Personnel Manager commented,

> We advertise all jobs in town, and we take the view that if you can get a good quality person from a family contact (that is ideal). There was a time when no matter how bad you were, if your Dad worked here you got a job.

The Lock Assistant Managing Director said,

> More often than not its been a case of the Personnel Department putting the word round and all the sisters and cousins and uncles and aunts come along ... the Lock trade must be in peoples' blood.

The Production Manager confirmed this:

> Whole families of people work here ... on the shopfloor and we tend to recruit a lot through our current employees.

In carpets, the lynchpin of these arrangements for holding and domesticating labour, is a shopfloor seniority system. This applies to redundancy and 'job choice' pecking orders; providing a career ladder for manual workers to move up, when a more senior employee leaves or retires; and acting as a strong disincentive to movement between firms or even departments. The Personnel Manager described it, as follows:

> We have a last-in-first-out system for selection of redundancy throughout the company. On the question of seniority systems and automatic promotion ... people are promoted to more senior jobs, not on merit, but purely on their service ... it provides a career structure to people in fairly low levels of jobs. It has enabled us to keep labour where we might otherwise have lost it ... they know that if they stay two or three years, they can get a weaving position. That has really helped us in times when labour was difficult to get hold of, if you go back to 1970.

A weaving shop steward described seniority as, 'a system we've had for years and years and years', and the Personnel Manager underlined this: 'It goes right back to the early years'. It originated amongst the weavers as a craft control to complement their strict apprenticeship system, and it remains strongest here, though it has spread with weaver's organization to cover the whole weaving workforce (including the female preparatory and finishing departments) and pockets beyond. A preparatory shop steward described her twenty-two year service as follows:

> I've been on the bobbin and I've been on cheese-winding ... all the jobs we took from seniority — like when your turn comes.

Occupational Communities

> The later nineteenth century town [developed] in such a way that the evolution of the sense of neighbourhood community was permeated by the presence of the workplace (Joyce, 1980, p. xxi).

Paternalism is normally found in two settings. In highly concentrated 'industry towns' or areas, like our 'lock' and 'carpet' towns, crystal glass in Stourbridge, footwear in Norwich or Leicester and its surrounding villages. And/or in 'company towns' or villages, like St. Helens, Street or Bournville, dominated or even created by one huge employer.

In the footwear study (Goodman, 1977, p. 155), 70–80 per cent of employees lived in the small towns near their factory. The industry's geographical concentration, its importance for local employment, and the lack of alternative manufacturing employment, saw several small firms drawing their workers from the same labour market. These conditions created 'a footwear occupational community', where workers from the same factory live in the same places, among workers from other factories in the area — a situation 'redolent with both kinship and out of work community based relationships'.

More usually, local urban employment depended on 'a relatively small number of larger-than average' (Russell, 1987, p. 156) enterprises, forming a 'unified élite' (Newby, 1977, p. 68) bound by industrial and/or religious ties, like the nineteenth century 'cotton town' of Glossop. The five firms of the Stourbridge crystal glass industry employ about 1,500 people, 'most of whom live within a five-mile radius of their work' (Black and Neathey, 1989, p. 173); while 85 per cent 'live in four clusters of half a mile or less in radius' — a situation very similar to the 'lock' and 'carpet' towns. Nearly 70 per cent of the British lock industry's 8,500 (Walker and Owen, 1984) employees are concentrated around its 400 year old centre. The lock firm (the industry's largest) has its headquarters and three main production plants, within walking distance, in 'lock town' itself.

In St. Helens, 'Coal was King' (Lane and Roberts, 1971, pp. 28–31), and it was only in the 1960s that Pilkington became the largest employer; with 36 per cent of jobs in glassmaking by 1970. Pilkington's dominance then became the 'dominance of the labour market' — with the threat of closure and the absence of alternative employment for local glassworkers. In Martin and Fryer's (1973) town, almost a quarter of the working population were employed by one firm, until the redundancies of the 1970s. As they point out,

> A community's economic development largely determines its social structure; it's economic and social structure mould and focus the attitudes of its inhabitants; these attitudes, in their turn, help to maintain the pre-existing structure (p. 27).

It is this complicated web and 'circle of causality', embracing workplace, family and community influences, which cements paternalism. The Carpet company Chairman described a:

> Womb to tomb sort of employment, which is general around here ... there's sixty-four people who have been with us for more than forty years, 58 per cent more than ten years. These are very, very stable workplaces and the ideas that they have are not likely to change through outside influence.

Isolation from Metropolitan Industrial Centres

> Geographical position made the development of paternalist capitalism possible, by minimising the 'contaminating influences' of the outside world and by increasing local dependence upon the Mills (Martin and Fryer, 1973, p. 83).

Geographical isolation from major metropolitan industrial centres (Goodman, 1977) helped to form and maintain these dense, 'parochial' occupational communities: preventing labour market competition for the industry or employer and innoculating the labour force against more secular ideological influences. Stable nineteenth century paternalism has often survived longest in 'isolated and/or self-contained work and community situations' (Newby, 1977, p. 66); especially in small towns whose combination of 'isolation' and 'totality' and strong sense of 'localism rendered people most susceptible to ruling class social, economic and political hegemony (Russell, 1987).

Martin and Fryer's 'company town' is characterized by 'geographical isolation and demograhic stagnation'; and workers who are predominantly 'locals' (1973, p. 29). Their 'Northern floorcovering town', closely resembles our West Midlands 'carpet town': dominated by a single industry and a handful of large companies; and isolated until the national motorway network and other road improvements recently linked it to the major regional industrial centre. In such cases the survival of paternalism appears 'an anachronism in the modern world' (Newby, 1977, p. 59) found in 'peculiar situations which are historical residues of a previous era'.

However, not all 'survivals' can be explained in terms of 'the town that time forgot'. Though highly traditional, 'lock town' is situated in the heart of the West Midlands engineering conurbation. And larger-scale individual paternalists, who are themselves the local industry, like Cadbury in Birmingham or Pilkingtons in St. Helens, have faced competition from other strong local industries, such as engineering and coal mining. In this respect, we should perhaps distinguish between an 'internal' paternalism, which depends almost entirely on the firm's own economic and ideological resources; and an 'external' paternalism, supported by a wider local industrial infrastructure. The giants like Cadbury, Rowntree, Clarkes and Pilkington would fall into the former category, while the lock, carpet, and crystal glass cases would better fit the latter. Some, like our relatively large lock firm surrounded by a shoal of smaller firms, would have a foot in both camps.

Collaborative Industrial Trade Unionism

> The stability and harmony of labour relations in Lancashire contributed much to the success with which paternalism elicited an affirmative response (Joyce, 1980, p. xxi).

For those mid-nineteenth century employers still opposed to trade unionism, 'paternalistic innovations . . . were seen as a powerful antedote' (Joyce, 1980), and welfare programmes were run in tandem with 'ruthlessly supressive strategies to control industrial relations and neutralise the threat of labour organisations' (Russell, 1987, p. 164). Even the socially progressive Quakers initially had a 'mixed attitude' (Child, 1964, pp. 300–1), seeing unions as potentially divisive to the family bond between master and man; until their religious beliefs pushed them towards 'the principle of joint control'. By the start of this century Edward Cadbury 'had a positive attitude to trade unions' (Rowlinson, 1988, p. 384). Elsewhere the 'unitary concept of society' (Russell, 1987, p. 155) probably yielded on more pragmatic grounds. As the lock deputy convenor put it:

> they realize that they've got to live in harmony with the trade union, because . . . we're not going to go away.

And since trade union membership became the norm in twentieth century manufacturing industry, a virulent anti-union employer attitude has sat uneasily with a self-proclaimed caring and a considerate attitude towards

employees. In the rather different political culture of the USA, the footwear manufacturer Endicott Johnson's (Zahavi, 1988) welfare capitalism
was deliberately contructed, in part at least, to pre-empt and exclude
trade union organization.

Today most well-known British paternalist employers have long
encouraged collective bargaining and well-organized trade unions. All of
the British industries and companies discussed here have approaching 100
per cent trade union membership, with high union membership since at
least the Second World War. The Pilkington case is fairly typical. At first
it 'did not take kindly to trade unions' (Lane and Roberts, 1971, p. 38),
and it was not until 1917 that they received recognition; but from then
onwards the firm adopted a more positive attitude, culminating in a
Union Membership Agreement with the GMWU in 1964. The lock
family actively encouraged union membership in the 1930s, and by 1949
it was strongly entrenched in the company and industry. In 1974 this was
formalized in an industrial closed shop. Even small lock and footwear
companies are usually unionized and covered by an industry agreement.

It is the character of the trade unions in most paternalistic companies
which commonly distinguishes them from other well-organized sectors
of British industry. As Lane and Roberts (1971) put it: paternalist companies (or industries) produce paternalistic trade unions. At Pilkington
'the paternalist corporatist relationship' (Caulkin, 1987, p. 45) between
union and management became so close that 'a historically respectful
workforce' felt 'unable to express accumulating discontents', leading to
the dramatic unofficial strike and breakaway union of 1971. But this was
a rare exception to a tradition of industrial relations characterized by
smooth, intimate relations between trade unions and management and
very little industrial conflict. As the carpet firm's GMB Convenor
recalled:

> The incidence of serious industrial dispute in this industry is very,
> very low.

Despite a bitter 1978 strike the weaving shop steward insisted, 'You can't
say that our union is a militant union'. While a lock shop steward and
union executive member argued:

> I think the management and the union should work together ...
> I don't believe in strikes, I don't think it achieves anything.

The crystal glass industry had only experienced five strikes, all over the
issue of craft controls, since the craft society was formed in 1851 (Black
and Neathey, 1989).

Where paternalism is located in a wider industrial community of
several or numerous firms, a locally-based industrial union — the Power-

loom Weavers (Carpets), NUFLAT (Footwear), Lock and Metal Workers (Locks), or National Union of Flint Glassworkers (Crystal Glass) — and an authoritative industry agreement are often features. Significantly, these small, parochial organizations limit the customary importance of union organization as a conduit for 'outside influences' (Russell, 1987) corrosive of localism.

As a lock director put it:

> We've never had any problems as far as the union is concerned
> ... I think there was a half day's strike once, but it's a small
> union and its basically a Lock union and nothing else ... They
> know the business the same as me ... it's not a big political
> union.

Localism also creates familiarity between industrial relations actors; with the union and management figures in company negotiations at the lock and carpet firms, reappearing at industry level (Ackers, 1988). This can be coupled with weak workplace trade union organization — shop stewards were late to develop in locks and footwear. In Donovan terms, the 'formal' system of industrial relations has held sway much longer in these industries than in others, like engineering, supported by an 'acquiescent' workforce (Lane and Roberts, 1971, p. 34). Even where company or plant bargaining has become stronger, there is often one dominant trade union for the hourly-paid, which has cultivated a collaborative and harmonious relationship with management. High membership density can disguise 'relatively weak and non-militant' (Lane and Roberts, 1971, p. 44) trade unionism.

However, such generalizations are inevitably fraught. For industries like carpets and crystal glass, strong craft groups exert powerful job controls against management, and maintain long and deep traditions of union workplace organization. And wherever union organization exists:

> Paternalism has been modified by the reality of a contested terrain
> in the workplace ... industrial relations pluralism co-exists with
> the paternalist culture, creating a pluralist or bargained paternal-
> ism (Black and Ackers, 1988).

Factors Undermining Paternalism

> Whilst this tradition is by no means dead, the circumstances no
> longer exist which would enable it to thrive (Lane and Roberts,
> 1971, p. 139).

Many aspects of paternalism can be regarded as hangovers from pre-industrial or early industrial times, which have been gradually undermined by the onward march of twentieth century capitalism (Kendall, 1985). In this view: the replacement of 'personal relations' family capitalism by the vast impersonal modern corporation; the spread of systematic Fordist/Taylorist labour control regimes with their associated pluralist industrial relations systems; and the emergence of an increasingly secular, differentiated and mobile labour force, forsee the gradual withering away of archaic paternalist elements. Joyce (1980) makes the point cogently:

> The relationship between labour process and mentality is inexplicable without an understanding of urban change. The fiction of paternalist community was effective to the extent that it accorded with the facts of neighbourhood community ... the social effect of paternalism is comprehensible only when the nature of population movement, and the changing ecological patterns of the factory town, are related to the characteristics of the factory workforce (p. xxi).

The Decline of the Occupational Community and Extended Family Structures

> We live in that time where a generation that knew there was a job for it, is now father and mother of a generation that knows there is no job for them there (Carpet GMB Convenor).

The decline of occupational community and extended family structures since the Second World War (Goldthorpe and Lockwood, 1969; Hoggart, 1977, Young and Wilmott, 1979) has followed greater personal mobility through car ownership, and changes in industrial structure — simultaneously reducing traditional industrial employment and providing new openings in the growing public, industrial and private service sectors. Paternalism has survived longest in those traditional enclaves of British society, least affected by these processes — the isolated industry towns of Martin and Fryer's study (1973) or our carpet firm.

More recently, the rapid decline of industries like carpets, footwear and locks, alongside improved communications links, has opened-up even these areas to change. The collapse of footwear employment and the growth of alternative opportunities in nearby cities (Goodman, 1977), undermined local occupational communities: encouraging an exodus of the existing workforce, and preventing young people from being recruited to the industry (and, as in carpets, the closure of local industry-linked training provision at local FE Colleges). The same trends saw the 'isolation' (Lane and Roberts, 1971) of the St. Helens decline, and with it the feeling of dependence on Pilkington for a livelihood. In short, when the 'economic base, industrially and occupationally' (Russell, 1987, p. 123) becomes 'less homogenous', the paternalist influence of 'a handful of employers' inevitably declines.

The decline of the British carpet industry (Ackers, 1988) over the past decade (from about 45,000 employees to 15,000), including the shedding of a quarter of the carpet firm's workforce (700), between 1979 and 1984, have made the company and industry just one employer among many, even in 'Carpet town'. Economic and social change have combined to make the firm, in the chairman's words, 'a lot less paternalist than it used to be'. Usage of the social club, which was 'the centre of people's social life', has declined with the advent of television and 'other centres of social life'. The weaving shop steward also noted changes in the composition of the workforce:

> It used to be a family concern ... you are finding individuals now on the shopfloor, not families.

Furthermore, industrial decline and technological change have begun to unravel paternalism's supporting structures, like the time-honoured weavers' seniority system. Today there

> are married men with families, of 33 years of age, and they've not got a loom ... because of the cut-back in the Department ... [and] a person can't get their lad on the company now.

Growing Out of Paternalism

> When a family business became a limited company, the change often marked the sundering of the bond between master and man, and the paternalism of the family firm was replaced by a kind of anonymous and rational organization (Wagner, 1987, p. 64).

Larger-scale paternalists were less dependant on a wider industrial and occupational community in terms of their management 'style'. However, they were affected by the problems of size, which poses problems for all developing paternalist firms; whether passing from small to medium scale, or from large to gigantic. Some like Cadburys and Rowntrees maintained a paternalist tradition for longer, 'because of the strong involvement of so many members of the second generation of the family' (Wagner, 1987, p. 65). But even the cohesive Quaker employers, faced with the growing 'bureaucratization' of industry and the 'growth in scale, mergers, introduction of outside specialist managers, and a lack of Quaker family members to carry on as Directors' (Child, 1964, p. 309), ceased to meet formally in 1948 — seven years after the last family chairman had retired at Rowntrees, and just two before the last family member left the board (Wagner, 1987). On a local scale, the same social processes dissolved the tight local political and religious élites.

Firms like Pilkington experienced a 'vast increase in the scale of operations' (Lane and Roberts, 1971, p. 45), from the 'St. Helens-based British firm of the 1960s' (Caulkin, 1987, p. 127), through 'the Anglocentric international one of the immediate past', to the ultimate point of growth: the 'fully-fledged global corporation'. As it expanded, the organizational structure underwent 'profound changes', including its approach to industrial relations (Lane and Roberts, 1971). As the firm became larger, more complex and impersonal, management recognized that employees had 'little interest in other, very different Pilkington operations' (Norman, 1983), outside their own plant. The company's first, highly traumatic strike came 'on the threshold of going public'. As Joyce (1980, p. 136) argues, 'It was the personal embodiment in the family or the family head that gave paternalism its cutting edge', and the arrival of the public limited company at the turn of the century 'was of crucial importance in the decline of factory paternalism'. By 1978 the firm could plan a new British plant 'away from the influence of the older St. Helens-based sites with its own separate agreement and a nine-point 'organization philosophy' in which traditional paternalism played no obvious part (Norman, 1983, p. 21).

There are obvious parallels with the carpet firm's 'new town' spinning plant: free from what the managing director described as, the 'archaic attitudes and practices' of 'Carpet town'; yet equally lacking the benefits of carpet culture. Thus the GMB Convenor argued:

> People who have not worked in the industry before ... can't achieve the results as people who for generations have been in the industry ... in productivity it can't be done.

The privately-owned carpet firm has also nurtured a growing bureaucracy, with overseas subsidiaries in Australia and USA, a large remote sales division, and an emerging graduate management stratum; all eroding the personalized family basis of paternalism. The personel manager stressed continuity:

> We are still a paternalistic company. The owners still do wander around ... a company that regards people as people and not as units of production.

But the weaving steward described the caring image as 'old bull', arguing: that the family are 'here to look after the family'; that his workforce were 'expendable'; and that he was 'looked upon now as a clock number'. While it had been an 'easy going sort of company' with 'personal relationships', where his father 'knew all the Directors by name and they knew him', you never saw the current chairman on the shopfloor. The latter conceded, 'I don't know as many people as I used to do'.

Similar complaints and observations were made at the lock firm. One shop steward commented:

Before it was more a family, you knew the top men more because they came on the shopfloor ... now you have to go through a procedure, well then you didn't.

Another added,

I don't think the personal touch is still there ... the people have changed.

And a Director agreed:

You haven't got the Managing Director going round the shopfloor, talking to Jack and asking how his hernia is ... there just isn't time to do those sort of things, even if we wanted to. So the family side is going out.

Takeover by a company with different traditions — such as BTR attempted at Pilkington — and Waterford, Nestlés and the Electronics firm succeeded at Wedgewood, Rowntrees and the lock firm respectively, is another stage in the dissolution of paternalist loyalty and identity. This depends partly on the organizational culture of the new parent: the Cadbury's takeover of fellow Quakers Frys, or the first takeover of the lock firm by another local lock and safe firm may have less dramatic implications.

Clearly this 'growing out of paternalism' is not simply caused by the 'depersonalising effect of the growth in size' (Newby, 1977, p. 72) (though gigantic multinationals do face particular problems), comcomitant 'functional specialization and bureaucratization', and the replacement of 'personal, informal "gaffer-to-man" modes of control' by 'impersonal, formal modes of control'. For some forms of paternalism have been precisely a response to this problem of size, and some paternalist regimes, notably in the chocolate industry, reached their zenith after going public. More likely, any major change of size or personnel endangers a traditional organizational culture, with its maintenance, in some recognizable form, depending on management will and skill as much as objective external variables.

Kendall (1984, p. 75) argues that large-scale paternalism in European companies, like Cadburys, 'is increasingly a thing of the past'. In 'a relatively backward economy' skilled labour is in short supply and training costs high, encouraging large corporations to attempt to 'domesticate' their labour force 'by a whole series of paternalistic welfare benefits'. Once they have invested in training an élite of the available population, they are 'reluctant to let it go elsewhere'. But 'as the economy increases in sophistication, the costs of domestication rise while the benefits diminish'. Seen in this light, paternalism dies because it no longer fulfils an important economic function.

The Trauma of Change: The Economic Fist Within the Social Glove

> It was in the most stable economic environments that paternalism thrived best (Joyce, 1980, p. xxi).

While paternalism may fade away gradually and imperceptibly, sudden economic and industrial traumas, like redundancies and strikes, can precipitate its decline. For the carpet company, both a bitter strike in 1978 and the restructuring of the 1980s were factors. Profits dived to 2 per cent in 1980 (Ackers, 1988) and employment fell by a quarter. Accelerated organization change — redundancies, new working practices and new technology — was a successful response to competitive pressures, as the firm moved into a new luxury product market niche.

Although the lock firm suffered some redundancies in the early 1980s, its traditional domestic product market has remained stable (buoyed by rising crime and security-consciousness) and its technology stagnant. In the absence of external pressures for change, inertia is a powerful force. As the assistant managing director put it:

> Organizations of this kind, this sort of size, have considerable inertia anyway. They don't change course very well.

Pilkington's 1970 unofficial strike coincided significantly with plans to 'go public' — a highly symbolic phase of growth — and was regarded as the death-knell of the traditional paternalist approach. The 1980s recession saw further restructuring, as at most other manufacturing firms. It was a period of 'the most difficult and far-reaching change' (Caulkin, 1987, p. 47) in the firm's history, 'embracing personnel, products and geographical spread'; including, the loss of half the St. Helens workforce (now down to 6,500), and £100 million in redundancy costs. Predictably, paternalism plays a less prominent part in company thinking today. At

Casterton Mills it was 'wholesale redundancies with product market collapse' (Martin and Fryer, 1973, p. 162) which finally broke paternalism.

As Russell (1987) stresses, in practice paternalism never ruled out 'the intermittent resort to draconian strategies'. However, since the 'privileges' accorded to workers in good times become regarded as 'rights' (Newby, 1977), the sudden display of 'the ruthless face of paternalist authority' (Russell, 1987, p. 164) is a risky business: tearing the social fabric, like a civil war or a family row, and exposing the contradiction between the social obligation of the paternalist to care and protect their workers, and economic pressures to treat them as 'impersonal commodities subject to the vagaries of the labour market' (Newby, 1977, p. 71). The ability of the employer to ride this contradiction, will depend, not only on their skill, but on the 'room to manoeuvre' provided by their own product market. In short, sudden changes in a firm's external economic environment (which demand redundancies; the introduction of labour-displacing, deskilling new technology; and general, rapid organization change, to maintain economic competitiveness) can quickly unravel a paternalist relationship carefully nurtured over centuries. As the employer deploys naked power to achieve their urgent objectives, 'the spurious symbiosis of unequals' (Russell, 1987, p. 162) underlying the paternalist relationship is questioned, and the search for a 'new style of authority' (Newby, 1977, p. 71) begins.

Human Resources Management: A Renaissance of Paternalism?

> The Japanese model is less the 'wave of the future' than a relic from the past (Kendall 1984, p. 75).

The 1980s have seen a challenge to the Donovan model of a 'modern' management labour control strategy. This assumed a Fordist/Taylorist system of production organization, supporting a pluralist, union-centred industrial relations set-up. Management communicated with their workers almost exclusively through the union representative channel; and sought to involve the workforce in the problems of the enterprise by incorporating shop stewards into forms of participation. The new prototype, is a Japanized, Post-Fordist, flexible firm pattern of production organization, married to 'direct communications' with the shopfloor, through techniques like quality circles, team briefing and employee financial involvement. Within this broader Human Resources Management framework, short-term conflict-management and relations with the union, should take second place behind the longer-term task of nurturing employee commitment *en route* to the optimum utilization of human capital (Atkinson, 1984; Black and Ackers, 1988; Guest, 1985; Murray, 1988).

In this context, the future may look more like the past than the present. We can expect the 'primitive', 'external' forms of paternalism to further decline, with the loss of the family touch and the supporting local community and industrial infrastructure — except as a shallow, small-firm unitarism. But, what of the legacy of 'internal', sophisticated paternalism? Contrary to Kendall's (1984) modernization thesis, there are signs of British industry, with and without a paternalist past, following 'the Japanese transformation from nineteenth century individual paternalism to twentieth century corporate paternalism and most recently welfare corporatism' (Joyce, 1980, p. 135). The current fashion of appealing to individual employee 'commitment', 'loyalty' and 'involvement', as against the drudging compulsion of impersonal Taylorism recalls the suspicions harboured by paternalists like Cadbury (Rowlinson, 1988) and Johnson (Zahavi, 1988) against over-reliance on mechanical, dehumanized forms of control.

The absence of labour market dualism on the Japanese scale in post-war Western economies, and the presence of universal, state-provided welfare provisions in education, housing and health, all under-mined the rationale for company-based welfare capitalism. But they left space for paternalist practices within the workplace, aimed at securing increased loyalty and employee commitment. Equally, Fordist/Taylorist production methods feeding a fairly homogenous mass market, full employment and strong trade union organization throughout large-scale manufacturing industry, underpinned pluralist regimes. However, the changes in the external environment and internal atmosphere of British industry, wrought by Thatcherism, world recession and the competitive crisis of British industry, have challenged these assumptions (Black and Ackers, 1989).

The lock company, which was in the final stages of jettisoning its paternalist past in favour of 'modern' pluralism, found itself taken-over in 1984 by a unitarist electronics multinational eager to secure employee commitment through company magazines, social outings and team briefing (Ackers, 1988). Under the pressure of economic recession and a highly competitive product market, the carpet firm has developed a HRM-style combination of new working practices, direct communications (quality circles, employee financial reports plus cascade briefing, profit participation etc.) and a more integrated manpower strategy — running parallel with established union-centred channels. The communications initiatives may be understood as an attempt to forge a new corporate relationship with the shopfloor, in place of the traditional paternalist ideological cement, during a period of rapid organizational change including redundancies, new technology, new working practices and relocation of the firm's manufacturing centre. They also reflect the demise of 'primitive', 'external' paternalism, with the growing remoteness of the family owners, and the collapse of the surrounding carpet industry, eroding the distinctive 'Carpet town' culture.

Nor are modern HRM notions of human capital far distant from earlier non-altruist rationales for paternalism. And whereas paternalist practices could benefit employers simply by reducing labour turnover, domesticating the labour market, and enhancing employee commitment; the USA experience, past and present, shows that it could also be employed, in an appropriate political and economic context, to undermine effective trade union organization. This has been the case at large non-union US firms, like Hewlett Packard and IBM (Barbash, 1987; Bassett, 1986; Grenier, 1988; Wentz, 1987); and direct communications with individual shopfloor workers, on the Michael Edwardes model, may be a strategy for by-passing and weakening collective workplace union organization.

For employers, traditional paternalism involved considerable personal and financial investment in their company and the surrounding community, spread over several generations. When, like the South Wales coalowners (Hywel and Smith, 1980), some found themselves facing antagonistic occupational communities, they could choose the opposite course of preferring to recruit labour from further afield, which diluted the identification between workplace and community. Serious HRM requires long-term conviction, and similar resource and personal commitments, to set against short-term profitability. It seems doubtful whether the depth of social relationships fostered over generations by the paternalist family firm, embedded in its local community, can be reproduced today. The impersonal, foot-loose multinational, with its mobile, diffuse, high turnover workforce, and even more transient management team, appears ill-equipped to fashion an emotional nexus with its workforce. As Kendall suggests, it may also be unwilling to carry the costs of the sort of 'retention management' required to buck the trend of current employee mobility. Where the HRM message is not connected to an attractive, immediate renumerative package, or to individual career progression, it may become no more than fashionable, but passing, management rhetoric.

Chapter 4

From Coalminers to Entrepreneurs? A Case Study in the Sociology of Re-industrialization

Gareth Rees and Marilyn Thomas

Introduction

The creation of an 'enterprise economy' has been a prime dimension of the economic transformation which has been sought by successive British administrations through the 1980s. Central to the Thatcherite prescription for economic renewal has been an emphasis upon the potential for innovation and growth held to be embodied in the activities of the self-employed and small-scale employers. As the 1986 White Paper, *Building Businesses . . . Not Barriers*, puts it:

> The prime aim of the Department of Employment is to encourage the development of an enterprise economy. The way to reduce unemployment is through more businesses, more self-employment and more wealth creation, all leading to more jobs (Department of Employment, 1986, p. i).

It is through the promotion of these forms of economic activity, then, that the dynamism of the (almost Schumpeterian) *entrepreneur* may be recaptured:

> The aim of our policy is thus to encourage the process of wealth creation by stimulating individual initiative and enterprise and by promoting an understanding of market opportunities combined with the ability to exploit them. (Department of Trade and Industry, 1988, p. iii)

Hence, central and local government, as well as regional agencies, have pursued a plethora of initiatives aimed at promoting economic regeneration through new business formation and small firm growth (Rees and Rees, 1989, pp. 2–4).[1]

Moreover, although the causal relationships are by no means established and despite the definitional problems involved, the official data undoubtedly do indicate substantial increases in self-employment and small business ownership during the decade (Casey and Creigh, 1988; Hakim, 1988). For example, the Labour Force Survey reveals that self-employment (including employers and self-account workers) rose by some 34 per cent (about 740,000) between 1981 and 1987 alone. What is involved here, therefore, is a major social development; whether conceived in terms of the rhetoric of political discourse, concrete state policies or the reality of economic restructuring.

Although these developments have aroused considerable analytical interest, the sociological contribution has been somewhat limited (for useful reviews, see Burrows and Curran, 1989; Curran and Burrows, 1986). Next to nothing, for example, is known about changes in attitudes and values with respect to 'enterprise' amongst the population *at large*. This is a point of no little significance, as it would require a *general* shift in attitudes for an 'enterprise culture' to become self-sustaining (Hakim, 1988, p. 429). Equally, although considerable scholarship has been devoted to the analysis of the *petit bourgeoisie* and the 'entrepreneurial middle class' (for example, Bechhofer and Elliott, 1985; Scase and Goffee, 1982), the effects of recent growth in self-employment and small business on the *recomposition* of class relations remain largely uncharted. Still less is the role of state policies in such changes properly understood.

In what follows, we attempt to explore some of these general issues by means of a case-study of the impacts of a single state initiative — British Coal Enterprise — on the social relations of a particular locality — the central South Wales coalfield. Whilst the usual methodological *caveats* clearly obtain, it should be emphasized that a focus upon one locality has important theoretical implications. It is well established that the form and pattern of growth of self-employment and small business are spread highly unevenly across the regional and local economies of Britain (for example, Whittington, 1984). In other words, the 'enterprise economy' (at least defined in these terms) is growing more strongly in some places than in others. In order to understand the processes of transformation involved here, it is necessary to explore how the pre-existing, historically shaped industrial and social structures characteristic of given localities articulate with contemporary 'enterprise' trends to yield determinate, but localized outcomes. Thus, past patterns of development in any local economy generate specific sets of opportunities for new enterprises, pools of relevant experience, attitudes toward self-employment and so forth. These, in turn, condition the contemporary pattern of growth in self-employment and small enterprises, resulting in locally specific trajectories of change and the emergence of new social and economic relations which are again characteristic of given localities.[2]

In this context, therefore, a study set in a coalfield locality is especially appropriate. First, there is a widely held analysis — not confined to sociologists themselves — which views the coal-mining community as the characteristic product of a history of highly distinctive relationships between the organization of industrial production and local social relations. Second, the dramatic restructuring of the industry during the 1980s has created severe employment problems in many coalfield areas, which would appear to have generated a fertile environment for the growth of an enterprise economy. Third, it remains to be seen how far the legacy of the social and economic relations of the coal-mining community impede the latter. Indeed, there is a sense in which the coalfields may legitimately be regarded as the ultimate testing-ground of the state's enterprise initiatives.

The Sociology of the Coal-mining Community

Despite the enduring influence of coal-mining upon the sociological analysis of working-class life in Britain, remarkably little is actually known about the reality of work in the industry or of social relations in mining localities. What is available, however, is a particular conventional account of the coal-mining community. This is portrayed as geographically isolated from other industrial activity, as a straightforward result of the geology and technology of mining. Equally, working conditions are highly distinctive: miners share common experiences of unpleasant and highly dangerous work. These working conditions also imply a high degree of homogeneity amongst miners, with a relative absence of occupational hierarchy. In the sphere of social reproduction, miners enjoy characteristically communal forms of leisure activity, in which workplace relationships are reinforced. Whilst within the family, gender roles are highly segregated, with women almost single-handedly responsible for domestic work, 'servicing' their men and enabling the latter's participation in mining work. In these ways, then, the characteristic features of both production and social reproduction combine to constitute the structural basis for highly solidary forms of social relations, which are expressed in the peculiarly militant and peculiarly 'macho' industrial and political cultures of the coalfields, in which the miners' union plays a central role (the classic empirical study is Dennis et al., 1956; for more analytical accounts, see Bulmer, 1975; Lockwood, 1966). And, of course, it is worth noting that this kind of conventional account provides a seemingly firm basis for the view that the coalfields are likely to be extremely hostile to government attempts to create an enterprise economy of the type sketched earlier.

However, there are a number of problems associated with this type of conceptualization of the social structure of coal-mining communities. First, it appears to fly in the face of the manifest diversity of social practices characteristic of different groups of miners and of social relations in different coalfield areas; a diversity which, of course, was cruelly exposed in the conflicts and divisions of the 1984–5 miners' strike (Rees, 1985). This, in turn, implies a need to trace through rather carefully the specificities of the social and economic structure in particular coal-mining localities and their determination in a unique set of historical conditions (cf. Massey, 1983).

Secondly, this is compounded by the fact that the empirical basis of this conventional account is extremely limited. More specifically, there have been surprisingly few systematic studies of the social organization of the coalfields as they are now, rather than as they were during the period immediately after nationalization in 1947, from which the majority of the classic coal-mining studies date (for example, Dennis *et al.*, 1956; Kerr and Siegel, 1954; Trist and Bamforth, 1951). Certainly, any contemporary analysis of a peripheral coalfield such as South Wales would have to take account of the effects not only of the substantial programme of mechanization and of colliery closure during the 1960s, but also the growth of employment outside of the coal industry, in manufacturing plants and, more significantly in numerical terms, in the services (for example, George and Mainwaring, 1988).

These latter changes, in turn, were associated with the very rapid rise in the employment of (particularly married) women from the South Wales coalfield; although the 1980s have witnessed a reversal of this trend (Winckler, 1987). Nevertheless, gender, as well as stage in the life cycle, have become increasingly central dimensions of working-class differentiation. Hence, whilst the social structure of coalfield areas such as South Wales remains overwhelmingly proletarian (witness, for example, the enduring allegiance to the Labour Party; the density of trade union membership; and so on), the industrial restructuring which has occurred over the past twenty-five years or so, has necessarily implied the internal recomposition and increasing diversity of the working class. And one important dimension of this has been the introduction of new types of employer, offering new kinds of jobs and implementing new patterns of labour relations and work organization (for example, Morgan and Sayer, 1988).

What these arguments suggest, then, is that there is a need to move beyond the sociological 'conventional wisdom' of the coal-mining community in order to understand the impacts of the state's current attempts to re-industrialize the coalfields through the promotion of an enterprise economy. More specifically, it is necessary to engage with the distinctive labour market conditions which have been generated by the closure and rationalization programme which followed the 1984–5 miners' strike.

Colliery Closures and the Reorganization of Coalfield Labour Markets

During the period since the miners' strike of 1984–5, the British coal industry has undergone a transformation greater than even the gloomiest predictions of Arthur Scargill, the President of the National Union of Mineworkers (NUM). And, of course, this transformation itself embodies a further dimension of the Thatcherite economic vision. Between 1982–3 and 1987–8, employment fell from some 208,000 to just over 104,000; almost 100 collieries were closed; and output of saleable coal from deep mines fell from 104 million to 82 million tonnes (Monopolies and Mergers Commission (MMC), 1989, p. 1). These changes were the predictable consequences of the strategy which has been pursued by British Coal (as the National Coal Board (NCB) was renamed in 1986), aimed at reducing substantially the costs of producing coal through the radical improvement of labour productivity.

The drive to achieve increases in labour productivity has been focused upon three inter-related elements: the introduction of new equipment in those coal-faces which remain in operation; the modification of working practices; and, of course, the closure of 'high-cost' collieries. It is important to understand, however, that the impact of these changes has not been felt uniformly throughout the coalfields of Britain. Not only have levels of capital investment varied considerably between the different areas, but also there has been no homogeneity in the acceptance of new working practices by miners. And, closely related, there have been sharp contrasts in the number of colliery closures. For example, in South Wales, one of the hardest hit areas, of the twenty-eight collieries operating on the eve of the miners' strike, seventeen had been closed (or amalgamated) by 1987–8. Employment fell during the same period by almost two-thirds, from over 20,000 to some 7,500 (although output declined only from 6.6 million tonnes to 5 million tonnes per annum) (Wass and Mainwaring, 1989).[3]

The effects of such intensive redundancy programmes on the local labour markets concerned have been extremely complex. Not only did they extend beyond the group of workers directly involved, but also they were not the same for all of the latter (for an extended discussion of these issues, see Rees, 1986; Wass and Mainwaring, 1989). Some miners, on the closure of their colliery, opted to take up the offer of transfer to another pit. Others, however, chose to leave the industry. Of these, many older miners in effect withdrew from the labour market altogether into early retirement. This reflects the relatively generous terms for miners over 50 years old of the Redundant Mineworkers' Payments Scheme (at least as it operated up until the autumn of 1986); as well as the results of many years of working in such an arduous and unhealthy industry. Equally, of course, these men knew that their chances of re-employment were extremely slight.

For those younger miners who took redundancy, however, their prospects of re-entry into employment were of crucial significance. Even lump-sum redundancy payments at the top end of the range possible for this group under the Redundant Mineworkers' Payments Scheme (which allowed £1,000 for each year of NCB service since the age of 16) were insufficient to provide an adequate household income in the long term. Indeed, in the aftermath of the miners' strike, many of these younger miners used their redundancy payments simply to clear the substantial debts incurred during the strike (Francis and Rees, 1989).

The direct impacts upon those miners who were employed in the collieries which were being closed were compounded by the job losses in the wider labour market. The removal of employment opportunities from a locality implied that the prospects for young people of obtaining a job there were reduced; young men who may have expected to be recruited into the local pit were likely to remain unemployed. This 'blocked recruitment' affected not only the places in which the closures actually occurred, but also those areas served by 'receiving collieries', to which men were transferred and in which, therefore, 'voluntary' redundancies were accelerated and recruitment stopped. To these may be added the multiplier effects of the initial round of job losses, both amongst firms which supplied the closed colliery and those enterprises which depended upon the expenditure of miners and their families. What is clear, then, is that the combination of these direct and indirect consequences of the reorganization of the coal industry in an area such as South Wales posed very acutely the question of how far the local labour market had the capacity to absorb extra workers.

Historically, of course, this capacity has been rather low; unemployment rates in the South Wales coalfield have remained above the average levels for Britain and even the South Wales region as a whole, for much of the post-war period. Even in the current context of declining unemployment overall (both officially-recorded and real), there has been little change in the differential between the local and national rates (for example, George and Mainwaring, 1988). Moreover, there is also evidence to suggest that even where alternative jobs have been available, redundant miners have not proven to be attractive to employers as prospective employees. Hence, a number of studies conducted following the colliery closures of the 1960s indicated that there were substantial problems in transferring the skills and work culture developed within mining to other forms of employment — factory work or whatever (for example, Town, 1975).

Although such direct analyses of ex-miners are not available, it seems likely that the changes in the nature and organization of the coalfield labour markets during the intervening period (which we sketched earlier) have exacerbated such problems. As numerous studies have shown, for most jobs, employers are less concerned with the technical competences which prospective employees have acquired through training or previous work experience, than with their social attributes — their age, gender, ethnic background and, perhaps most crucially, what are perceived to be their characteristic attitudes towards work and their employer (for example, Jenkins *et al.*, 1983; Rees *et al.*, 1989; Wood, 1985). Certainly, in the circumstances of the South Wales coalfield, where the new jobs which have been created have been disproportionately routinized, low-skill and poorly rewarded, it is these social attributes which have been the key criteria in recruiting workers.

For example, a recent study of the recruitment strategies of some 300 employers in the central South Wales coalfield revealed a marked preference for younger workers, not only because they were cheaper, but also because they were believed to be more responsive in learning what was expected of them by their employer. Equally, there was considerable evidence that recruitment to a wide range of jobs was shaped by employers' stereotypes of the attributes which men and women naturally bring to their work, as well as the beliefs which prospective employees have about what is an appropriate job for a man and what is appropriate for a woman (Rees *et al.*, 1989). More specifically, Morgan and Sayer (1988, p. 172), in their analysis of the development of electronics firms in South Wales, argue that there was a much more direct and specific exclusion of ex-miners (and ex-steelworkers), on the grounds of what were perceived to be both inappropriate technical competences and unacceptable behavioural attributes.

In fact, such evidence as is available suggests that the best employment opportunities which were opened up to such groups of redundant miners were through their social networks, and characteristically involved sub-contracting activities in their former workplaces. For instance, some ex-miners got jobs — albeit on a temporary and extraordinarily poorly paid basis — with the private salvage companies which were hired to break-up the collieries which had closed. Nevertheless, the extent of such employment appears to have been much less than that reported by Harris *et al.* (1987) in their study of the redundancy programme at the British Steel Corporation's Port Talbot plant, which reflected the very specific circumstances of a major construction programme in the plant (see also Fevre, 1989).

What these arguments suggest, therefore, is that the social opportunities which were available within this labour market were constrained both by the number and types of jobs, as well as the processes which determined access to them. It is not simply that there was insufficient employment overall, but also entry to the jobs which were on offer was rationed according to the criteria informing employers' recruitment strategies. And redundant miners would appear to have been especially disadvantaged in their quest for satisfactory re-employment.

It is in this context of widespread concern over the labour market problems confronting the coalfields that the full significance of the state's attempts to foster self-employment and the growth of small businesses becomes apparent. Its appeal here lies in the fact that, firstly, it offers the prospect of expanding the range of opportunities which are available in absolute terms. But, secondly, it also promises to do so in a way which does not disadvantage particular social groups in the manner that existing patterns of employment do: everyone can be an 'entrepreneur' now.

It remains, however, to investigate the extent to which this prospect has actually been achieved. In what follows, we outline some preliminary results from an empirical study of the operation of one state initiative, British Coal Enterprise, operating in the particular labour market conditions of the central South Wales coalfield.

The State and the 'Enterprise Economy':
The Case of British Coal Enterprise

Given the intensity of the labour market changes in the coalfields, it is not surprising that the need for special measures to generate new, alternative employment opportunities was recognized by the government relatively early on. Accordingly, in 1985, Peter Walker, then the Secretary of State for Energy, announced the establishment of British Coal Enterprise, a specialist agency and subsidiary of British Coal, whose aim was:

> ... to assist in the creation of long-term job opportunities in the coalfield areas of the UK and, hence, to assist in wealth creation for the country as a whole.
>
> The scale of the operation is intended to be such that all of the jobs lost in mining during the present restructuring will be replaced by alternative opportunities over a reasonable period of time. This may be judged to be five or six years. (British Coal Enterprise, 1985–6, p. 2)

British Coal Enterprise has four methods by which this aim may be achieved. First, it helps in the retraining of redundant miners through the Job and Career Change Scheme. Second, it supports the work of existing enterprise agencies, while thirdly, it assists with the provision of business premises and, in particular, it provides managed workshops as a safe environment for new businesses. And lastly — and most importantly — it provides loans to assist businesses which start up, expand or locate in the coalfields.

It is the last which we wish to take up, as it is this aspect of British Coal Enterprise's activities which bears most significantly on the wider development of an enterprise economy in Britain. What is involved here is the attempt to foster the growth of small business and self-employment, with a view to ameliorating the employment problems of the coalfields. Thus, three basic conditions must be fulfilled before consideration is given to a loan application: the project must create new jobs; it must be located in a coal-mining area; and it must be deemed viable on the basis of British Coal Enterprise's evaluation.[4]

However, it is important to understand that British Coal Enterprise's financial assistance is not restricted to redundant miners (despite the way in which the initiative has been portrayed popularly). Indeed, British Coal Enterprise has been quite explicit that it does not expect significant demand from older ex-miners either for the opportunity to start their own businesses or even for new employment (cf. our own earlier discussion). Rather:

> ... the critical demand arises amongst the younger generations, even those expecting to leave full-time education in the near future, who grew up in the coal mining communities believing that their future employment prospects lay either directly or indirectly in the local colliery, and who found that the changes in the coal mining industry now meant that the employment opportunities were reduced. (British Coal Enterprise, 1985–6, p. 4)

Hence, it is argued, the focus for British Coal Enterprise's assistance is provided by those individuals whose labour market opportunities have been adversely affected by the programme of colliery closures. Whilst those redundant miners who have remained economically active clearly constitute a major grouping of such individuals, others within the local population are targeted too.

It should be emphasized, therefore, that what is implied here is a social transformation of some magnitude. As a result of British Coal Enterprise's activities, what is envisaged is the effective reconstitution of the local class structure through the significant expansion of an entrepreneurial stratum of self-employed and small-scale capitalists — class places which have been markedly under-represented in the coalfield hitherto. Moreover, these places are to be filled predominantly by individuals whose principal socialization into the world of work has occurred in a milieu which, *prima facie* at least, is inimical to the development of those values and attitudes which have been widely identified as necessary to the growth of the enterprise economy.

In the next section, some of these issues are explored by reference to the results of semi-structured interviews with two distinct groups. First, we examine the characteristics of twenty-three small-scale entrepreneurs who were identified as those who had established and/or developed their business with the assistance of a British Coal Enterprise loan in the central South Wales coalfield up until 1986 (and could be traced). They are taken to represent those individuals who are responding positively to the state's attempts to foster an enterprise economy. Second, we explore the post-redundancy experiences of twenty-one ex-miners, who had been made redundant from Cwm Colliery (again in the central South Wales coalfield) in November 1986. Although most of these constituted a prime target group for the state's re-industrialization efforts, none of them had made use of the British Coal Enterprise scheme.[5]

Coalfield Re-industrialization: The Entrepreneurs

Writing generally of the *petit bourgeoisie*, Bechhofer and Elliott (1981) have argued that it fulfils essentially ideological functions in capitalist society, as the custodian of core capitalist values, in the light of which society is seen to be open and to reward those prepared to work hard, take risks and make sacrifices. The imagery of opportunity, competition and the free market thus conceals the reality of the dominance of large-scale capitalist enterprises. In contrast, as we have seen, the rationale underpinning the state's attempts to foster an enterprise economy is that the growth of entrepreneurship — defined in terms of self-employment and the small business — will significantly broaden the range of labour market opportunities. Accordingly, an essential starting point is to assess who is benefiting from the activities of British Coal Enterprise and how are they doing so.

Certainly, Storey and Johnson (1987), in a review of the international evidence on small firm formation, conclude that between 25 per cent and 50 per cent of all new businesses are established by workers who are unemployed, or likely to become unemployed, immediately prior to starting their business. Many of these businesses are in the services sector, where entry costs are low due to its labour-intensive nature (as, for example, in jobbing building, car repair, hairdressing, etc.). However, as the market for such services is overwhelmingly a local one and local demand is often fully satisfied, the effect is merely to displace existing businesses, without any expansion in the overall range of opportunities. Moreover, it would appear that this tendency is especially marked in relatively less prosperous areas, where the chances of genuinely innovative small firm formation are restricted (for a more detailed discussion, see Rees and Rees, 1989, pp. 15–17).

In fact, the businesses which were surveyed in the present study did not conform to this pattern. They were distributed across both manufacturing and services, in a diversity of industries, including electronics, engineering, agricultural supplies, packaging, photoprocessing and computers (see Table 4.1). Moreover, the owners for the most part had been in full-time employment prior to setting up, with only a handful faced

Table 4.1   The Entrepreneurs Identified as British Coal Enterprise Beneficiaries

Nature of Business	No. Employed			Non-BCE Public Assistance[b]	Number of Years Established
	F/T	P/T	T/S[a]		
1. Chemicals	50	—	—	RDG, SFA	20
2. Engineering	36	2	2	None	6
3. Cabinet manufacturer	30	—	—	WDA	4
4. Packaging manufacturer	26	6	5	RDG	2.5
5. Hand-tools manufacturer	25	—	—	WDA Investment	4
6. Engineering	24	—	1	RDG, WDA Investment	3
7. Agricultural merchants	6	—	2	None	1.5
8. Canopy manufacturer	6	—	1	None	3
9. Photoprocessing	5	1	1	RDG	1
10. Petfood wholesaler	5	1	—	None	4.5
11. Sheet-metal products	5	—	1	RDG, Mid Glam CC	1.5
12. Fire-place manufacturer	5	—	—	None	4
13. Scanning equipment	4	—	2	WDA R&D	1.5
14. Engineering	4	—	2	WDA R&D	1.5
15. Packaging services	3	10	1	None	2
16. Clothing	3	2	2	None	1.5
17. Car renovation	3	1	1	None	6
18. Restoration service	2	—	1	Mid Glam CC	1.5
19. Computer services	2	—	—	RDG, UDG	3
20. Industrial photographer	1	2	1	None	4
21. Signs/displays	1	—	1	None	2
22. Fishing-rod manufacturer	1	—	—	Mid Glam CC	1
23. Car repairs	1	—	—	None	10

Notes:
a. Figures include business owner(s). F/T — full-time; P/T — part-time; T/S – training scheme.
b. Mid Glam CC — Mid Glamorgan County Council grant; RDG — Regional Development Grant; SFA — Selective Financial Assistance; WDA — Welsh Development Agency Loan; WDA Investment — Welsh Development Agency Shareholder Investment; WDA R&D — Welsh Development Agency Research and Development Grant; UDG — Urban Development Grant.

with the prospect of redundancy. Should we conclude, therefore, that a consequence of British Coal Enterprise's intervention has been vastly to raise the quality of small firm formation, over and above what may be expected in a local economy of the kind found in the South Wales coalfield?

In part, of course, the atypical character of the businesses surveyed is explicable by reference to the method of their selection for the study. The fact that they were identified as having received support from the state necessarily implied that their business plans and chances of viability had been vetted extensively; the probability of their long-term success was therefore greater than the norm. Moreover, it is clear that this group of respondents brought with them significant resources — previous educational and work experience, as well as support from their families — unavailable to the majority of participants in the local labour market. In this respect, they appeared to exhibit many of the characteristics which previous research has found to be positively correlated with successful business formation and growth (for example, Storey, 1982).

Hence, educational qualifications were found to be relatively high amongst respondents, with a third having been educated to degree level or above. In some cases, their qualification was directly related to the field of business which the entrepreneur had entered. For example, an engineering graduate (who also had management experience) had set up an engineering company; a graduate chemist (who again had managerial experience) had gone into chemicals; and so on. For others, their educational attainment had gained them access to employment which, in turn, had enhanced their capacity to establish and run a small business. As one respondent, who had set up a packaging business, following a degree in public administration, put it:

> As part of my college course, I did a one year placement with BRS. I found that useful because I learned a great deal of respect for money in business — everything has to be accounted for, etc. ... So all that was good background work really for anything that you'd set up on your own.... [T]he one thing I got out of it was that I learnt how a business was run.

Moreover, the same respondent made clear the more widespread view that their educational backgrounds and past experience insulated these entrepreneurs from many of the risks attached to setting up in business on their own.

> If it all went to the wall, I could work for someone else. After two years of running my own company, making profits, with a degree, with a year's placement with BRS where I think I'd get a good reference, I don't think I'd struggle to get a fairly decent job.

The majority of respondents also had previous experience of management. This proved invaluable in providing financial skills, access to markets and business contacts, as well as in generating the confidence in their ability to establish a successful small business. Perhaps most significantly of all, it facilitated the negotiation of access to credit and other financial assistance. According to one of the partners in a firm of agricultural merchants:

> Both of us have had careers in corporate businesses. Both of us have been directors of large companies with turnovers in excess of £25 million per year ... Having had twenty years of fairly high-level management skills ... and having researched many industries from heavy engineering, through electronics, leisure, hotels and catering, we finally settled on agriculture, agricultural merchanting.

A chemistry graduate who had gained industrial and managerial experience prior to starting up his own chemicals business explained:

> I moved back to Wales from Corby and I joined AP as their engineering manager in Cardiff ... I got the job in Cardiff at an early age, with responsibility, and I gained excellent experience ... [T]hen an opportunity came along which allowed me to investigate the marketing of a product on a part-time basis. And I identified that here was a business which I would very much like to be involved in, so I did.

A family history of small business ownership was another characteristic of a number of respondents and this was an important factor in the decision and capacity to set up a business. For example, one business owner, a manufacturer and retailer of fishing rods, had not only been taught the technical skills of his trade by his father, who ran the same type of business on a part-time basis, but had also benefited from the business contacts which his father had made, from the good reputation of the family name and from the availability of credit which had been made possible as a result of his father's previous dealings. According to the respondent himself, these factors were crucial in enabling him to establish his business. Moreover, the fact that he knew 'an awful lot about the business' prior to setting up had clearly boosted his confidence in its likely success.

Family support also proved crucial to a number of respondents. In its direct form, this support consisted of inputs of finance from parents or spouse to help start up or develop the business, as well as of labour — most commonly, a wife performing book-keeping and clerical work. Indirect support was also important, as for example when the business owner was supported financially during the period before the business became profitable. Much more frequently, however, it was the domestic labour provided by the respondent's wife which was obviously crucial, as almost every respondent asserted that running a business demands vast amounts of time, including evenings and weekends (cf. Scase and Goffee, 1982).

What these findings suggest, then, is that the fostering of entrepreneurship through self-employment and small business development is restricted by the possession or otherwise of the requisite personal resources or cultural capital. It is most striking that ex-miners (of whatever age) were wholly absent from this group of relatively successful small businessmen. Neither were the latter drawn from that wider section of coalfield residents whose labour-market opportunities had been blighted by colliery closures. It remains to be seen, however, whether such individuals would feature more prominently amongst those ventures which had failed. Rather, it would appear that the effect of the public subsidies available through British Coal Enterprise is to facilitate entry to or expansion in the small business world of individuals whose qualifications, previous experience and family backgrounds equip them for such a career in any case. And, of course, many of these had no connection with the coalfield at all, either by origin or current residence.

Moreover, there was little evidence that the benefits of small firm growth were filtering out to the wider labour market as a result of significant employment creation within these firms (although, of course, they were for the most part at a very early stage of their development). The number of people employed in each business ranged up to fifty, but with only three firms employing thirty or more full-time employees and fifteen five or less. Average employment was eleven full-time workers, between one and two part-time workers and one YTS trainee. However, if the three largest employers are excluded, the full-time figure drops sharply to only seven. (See Table 4.1.)

Perhaps rather surprisingly, this sombre assessment was endorsed by the respondents themselves. In part, of course, their judgment of a small firms development strategy was coloured by their own experience of the problems and frustrations of obtaining finance, maintaining adequate cash-flow and so forth. Nevertheless, they were very firm in their assertion that self-employment and the small business sector were promoted in terms which were far too positive. And, certainly, they did not believe that simply anyone could embark upon an enterprise of this kind. More specifically, a number argued that redundant workers with lump-sum payments (such as ex-miners) should definitely not be encouraged to gamble their redundancy payments in starting up their own businesses.

Nevertheless, the question remains whether such redundant workers and others facing labour market disadvantages are in fact attempting to pursue this course of action. As Scase and Goffee (1982) have remarked of their sample of self-employed craftsmen: '... self-employment represented the *least disagreeable* way of "getting by" in a modern economy.' (p. 76; original emphasis) It is easy to see that the same may well be true for individuals confronted with the labour market exigencies of the South Wales coalfield.

Coalfield De-industrialization: The Redundant Miners

Of the sample of redundant miners, only two had become self-employed and a third was attempting to do so. (See Table 4.2.) One of these, who was 47 years old at the time of the interview, had been a mechanical engineer in the colliery for twenty-nine years. After being made redundant, he had applied unsuccessfully for a succession of jobs, before working briefly in a friend's small bus company. He had eventually started up in business, in partnership with his brother-in-law, as a subcontractor in the construction industry. His only access to state help had been through the Enterprise Allowance Scheme. He explained:

> We thought that with the development that's going on, in Cardiff and South Glamorgan in particular, there's an upsurge in the construction industry at the moment. We thought it would be worth having a go ... but the hardest thing has been finding enough work.

His hopes for the future of his business were extremely limited: '... just to be able to earn a comfortable living without being elaborate in any shape or form'. The other self-employed ex-miner was 36 years old and had been a face-worker for thirteen years. He was running a general store from a wooden shed which he had purchased for £4,000 from another redundant miner, who had tried to make a success of the business but had failed. He reported that:

> This shop was so run down, there was nothing in it when we bought it. You could have put all the stuff into two egg boxes. So it can only go up ... We've started on the bottom rung. Perhaps in time to come we'll buy a bigger shop, or build a bigger shop. But as we are, we're happy. We're doing all right. A wage — that's all we wanted. It's better than £31 dole.

The third member of this group was 37 years of age and had been employed as a face-worker for nineteen years. After redundancy, he had spent six months unemployed, followed by twelve months as a night-watchman on a building site. He was unemployed again at the time of the interview. He was trying to set up his own business to produce — ironically enough — commemorative plaques of collieries, an activity which he had recently taken up as a hobby. He said:

> You know, I'm 37 years of age, what am I going to do? If I don't do anything for myself, then no-one's going to do it for me.... To put it bluntly, if you sit on your arse for too long without

Table 4.2   *The Redundant Miners*

Age[a]		Mining Occupation	Years in Mining	Current Employment Status
1.	29	Face-worker	12	Factory worker
2.	30	Welder	15	General labourer
3.	33	Various	17	Farm worker
4.	33	Blacksmith	15	Factory worker
5.	36	Fitter	19	Factory fitter
6.	36	Face-worker	13	Self-employed
7.	37	Face-worker	19	Unemployed[b]
8.	39	Face-worker	13	Bakery assistant
9.	42	Fitter	24	Factory worker (temporary)
10.	44	Electrician	25	Clerk
11.	46	Banksman	23	Unemployed
12.	47	Face-worker	25	General labourer
13.	47	Fitter	29	Self-employed
14.	50	Fitter	32	Retired/sick
15.	51	Various	23	Unemployed
16.	52	Various	35	Retired/sick
17.	56	Various	29	Retired
18.	58	Various	35	Retired
19.	58	Labourer	42	Retired
20.	58	Various	30	Retired
21.	59	Various	25	Retired

Notes:
a. Age at time of intreview.
b. This respondent was attempting to become self-employed.

doing anything, you'll get into a rut, and once you're in that rut, it's very hard to get out of.

Clearly, then, these respondents had set up their businesses, or aspired to do so, as an alternative to unemployment or the type of employment available to them locally. Although the shop-keeper did claim that he had always wanted to work for himself, he admitted that he would not have left the coal industry voluntarily in order to do so. Moreover, it is at least likely that the kinds of activities which they had chosen to pursue would do little more than displace other, equivalent businesses, even if they were successful. In any case, these respondents had ignored the advice and financial assistance potentially available from British Coal Enterprise. In two cases, they said that they did not require capital or even business premises, as their enterprises were on such a small scale. The third did not appear to be aware of the availability of low-interest loans from British Coal Enterprise and had followed the advice of his accountant to borrow £4,000 from his bank.

The very limited nature of this move toward self-employment amongst these respondents does, of course, beg the question of why more individuals have not made use of state subsidies to enter the enterprise economy. One kind of explanation which is very widely held — not least amongst government ministers — is that areas such as South Wales are dominated by what may be termed a culture of employment, rather than a culture of enterprise and self-employment, as a consequence of the historical dominance of the local economy by large-scale and nationalized industries. Accordingly, individuals are imbued with expectations of being employed by someone else, rather than assuming responsibility for their own economic futures through individual enterprise. And, of course, this view is, to some extent, no more than a particular variant of the sociologist's conventional account of the coal-mining community which was discussed earlier

In actual fact, a majority of the respondents in this study *had* actively considered setting up on their own after redundancy, only to reject this as a viable course of action. Moreover, it is clear that cultural predispositions did play a part in this decision, although in ways rather more complex than is implied by any notion of a culture of employment. Hence, a number of respondents had been deterred not by any hostility to self-employment *per se*, but by a reluctance to undertake actions which are themselves necessary prerequisites to establishing a new enterprise.

For example, a 30-year-old former colliery welder had intended to set up a mobile welding repair service, in partnership with another redundant miner. He explained, however:

> The reason I didn't go into business was that the friend of mine — he was another welder with the Coal Board — he decided to spend all his redundancy money. He spent it wisely — he bought his house, built an extension and said that he didn't think that he could afford to go into it. You know, if you wanted to get on to the Enterprise Allowance Scheme, you had to have £1,000, and he didn't have that; then we'd have had to buy machinery, which was a couple of thousand pounds . . .

When asked why they had not borrowed the finance which they required, he replied:

> We didn't want to borrow money because I think that's a bad start to getting your business off the ground. If you can fund it up front, everything you've got coming in then, is basically yours. You've got no bills.

It is clear, then, that he did not recognize that borrowing money is a routine part of the creation and development of a business enterprise; let alone that such finance is available on favourable terms from British Coal Enterprise. He was unwilling to become indebted, in spite of the fact that this was essential to achieve his aim of self-employment. Equally, it is instructive that for this respondent it was *self-evident* that avoiding risk in investing capital was the most sensible course of action; 'bricks and mortar' were obviously a safer bet than a small business.

This emphasis upon the avoidance of risk was echoed by most of the other respondents. Even where the costs of entry to an enterprise were low, there was a marked reluctance to gamble their redundancy payments on the possibility of greater returns in the longer term. For instance, according to one former fitter in the colliery, who had been through a series of temporary, low-paid jobs since being made redundant:

> The risk was too great, and I think that my age [he was 42] is against me to start up [in business]. When I first started a job in Cardiff, I had to have transport so I bought the car. And I bought the house — so whatever happens, no-one can throw me out of my house.

With remarkable uniformity, respondents had opted for the perceived security of investment in their houses, even where they recognized the longer-term problems which this could entail when their lump-sum payments ran out. A 29-year-old ex-faceworker who had considered becoming self-employed as a roofer, expressed this very clearly:

> I welcomed having the redundancy money so that I could do what I wanted to do on the house, because I would never have been able to afford to do the things to the house if I hadn't had the redundancy; and we couldn't have afforded a holiday if we didn't have the redundancy money ... The redundancy doesn't last forever. It ran out more quickly than I expected.

For these respondents, therefore, it would appear that the potential future benefits of investment in their own small business were outweighed by the risks attached. Again, they had no hostility to self-employment in principle. Rather, they were not prepared to do what is a necessary prerequisite of achieving it — risk-taking. Hence, it may be argued that seeking out the immediate security of the familiar — clearly expressed in their decisions to put money into their houses — was part of their conventional 'cultural repertoire'.[6] On the other hand, however, their responses may be represented as a wholly rational response to their estimation of the chances of a small business succeeding in the structural conditions set by the local economy.

Certainly, a significant number of these ex-miners reported that they had not pursued plans to set up on their own because they believed that there was an insufficient market for their skills. Although a significant minority of the study group had been skilled workers in the colliery (fitters, electricians, blacksmiths and welders) and a number had taken re-training courses under the Job and Career Change Scheme (in, for example, plumbing and plastering), they argued that local demand for such skills was saturated and that, therefore, self-employment was not a viable option. For instance, one respondent, who had been a face-worker for twelve years, had considered becoming a self-employed roofer. He said:

> I was thinking of doing that, but it's a lot of overheads to start your own business, and you've got to have plenty of work on. And with the people that are around here doing roofing — there's loads.... There's so many people roofing in the valleys. There's roofers all over the place. Obviously, the ones that have been going for a while are going to get the business before the ones that are new.

Similarly, a former colliery electrician with twenty-five years service with the Coal Board, had been unable to get employment since his redundancy. Therefore, he had considered becoming self-employed:

> Financially, I could have started on my own, but in this area there were forty electricians finishing [from the NCB] ... So if forty of us had left at the same time and forty of us thought 'Right! I'm going to start up on my own', we might have jobs putting in an extra point or wiring up a garage, or something like that, but they wouldn't be actual 'bread and butter' jobs — you wouldn't get as far as the butter, because you just couldn't get enough of them.

In the light of the arguments presented earlier, it can only be concluded that these estimations of the prospects of such small businesses were pretty accurate. Local demand was so limited that the best that could be expected is a highly precarious existence in a highly competitive market. Moreover, it would appear that the resources which these individuals are able to command — not only in narrowly financial terms, but also their qualifications and past experience — are such as to mark them off rather sharply from the other group of respondents who had successfully set up on their own account. Certainly, there was absolutely no indication that these redundant miners had developed that capacity for innovation which is widely regarded as the key to the long-term success of a new business enterprise. In this context, therefore, the distinction between a response to changed labour market conditions based upon a traditional 'cultural repertoire' and one based upon the calculation of a rational economic strategy is much more blurred than may at first sight appear (cf. Crow, 1989).

Concluding Remarks

Clearly, these empirical findings have substantial implications for any evaluation of current state attempts to re-industrialize the coalfields, in the wake of the massive employment decline and colliery closures since the end of the 1984–5 miners' strike (especially in the peripheral areas such as South Wales). It has been shown that the major element of these state interventions has been focused upon a strategy — implemented through British Coal Enterprise — aimed at fostering the enterprise economy, expressed in the growth of self-employment and the small business sector.

The appeal of this strategy lies in its potential for extending the structure of opportunities in the labour markets of the coalfields, both absolutely and by broadening access to social groups which are disadvantaged in terms of entry to existing employment. For, although the coalfields do not conform to the sociological stereotype of single-industry, archetypally proletarian and patriarchal communities, labour market opportunities remain highly constrained. Not only are there now too few jobs to go round, but also unemployment is likely to rise relatively in the longer term, in part as a consequence of the restructuring of the coal industry. Moreover, entry to those jobs which are available is structured by the recruitment strategies of employers, which work systematically to favour some social groups and to exclude others.

However, it would appear that the impact of British Coal Enterprise on this structure of opportunities has in reality been rather slight. Hence, those individuals who have benefited from its activities have enjoyed the resources — qualifications, experience and family background — which are generally associated with successful small firm formation. To this extent, then, the state's interventions have not affected significantly what may be termed the normal process of small business growth.

Not surprisingly, therefore, other social groups — whether redundant miners, the unemployed or whoever — have not been drawn into this type of economic activity to any noticeable extent, in spite of the incentives available through government subsidies. Not only are they ill-equipped in terms of the requisite resources, but also they are culturally predisposed to avoid risk-taking and indebtedness, which are necessary prerequisites to small business development. Moreover, and perhaps most fundamentally, the same local economy which so cruelly restricts their access to satisfactory employment, also acts to block the potential for the development of self-employment and new small businesses. The reluctance of such groups to enter the enterprise economy reflects the interaction of an historically shaped 'cultural repertoire' with a strategy based upon the rational calculation of real local enterprise opportunities.

These conclusions further imply that the effects of state initiatives such as British Coal Enterprise on the reconstitution of the class structure of the coalfields are more complex than previously envisaged. To the extent that the growth of self-employment and small business is creating new entrepreneurial class places at all, they are being filled predominantly by individuals drawn directly from the service class. Moreover, many of these originate from outside the coalfield, their only connection being the location of their business. Certainly, there is no evidence (at least from this study) that local people, who would otherwise be members of an industrial working class, are being 'converted' into small-scale capitalists.

Even if a broadly based transformation of attitudes towards enterprise — the creation of an 'enterprise culture' — were to be achieved in the coalfield, it would be insufficient to generate an enterprise economy in the absence of significant changes in the resources available to coalfield residents and in the scope for the self-employed and small businesses to prosper within the local economy. However, these conditions are so far from being achieved by the state strategies which are currently being implemented, that it is difficult to escape the conclusion that, far from re-industrialization through the enterprise economy, the people of the coalfields should anticipate a future of continuing employment problems and further de-industrialization.

Notes

1 Clearly, this reduction of the notion of an 'enterprise economy' to the purported activities of the self-employed and small business owners presents only one, rather partial account of its potential (for an extended discussion, see Rees and Rees, 1989, *passim*).

2 These somewhat elliptical arguments draw upon the debates around the so-called 'restructuring approach' to the analysis of economic and social transformation; see, for example, Massey, 1984.

3 At the time of writing (early 1990), collieries in South Wales have been reduced to six, with further closures imminent; employment has fallen below 4,000.

4 Loans are normally payable up to a maximum of £5,000 per new job opportunity or 25 per cent of the total new funding required, whichever is the lower. Initially, British Coal was authorized to make £5 million available to British Coal Enterprise; this was subsequently doubled to £10 million, then to £20 million, to £40 million and eventually to £60 million (British Coal Enterprise, 1986–7; 1988–9).

5 The empirical research reported here was carried out by Marilyn Thomas. She is the holder of an ESRC CASS studentship and would accordingly like to acknowledge the financial support of the ESRC and Mid Glamorgan County Council.
    The list of self-employed and small business proprietors was drawn up only with the assistance of Mid Glamorgan County Coucil; whilst the redundant miners were identified with the assistance of the South Wales Area of the

National Union of Mineworkers. Again, this help is gratefully acknowledged.
6 The emphasis upon the security of home-ownership has particularly deep
roots in the coal-mining community, given a long history of evictions during
times of economic hardship. The 1984–5 miners' strike had provided the
most recent experience of such traumas, thus reinforcing the established
'cultural repertoire' (Francis and Rees, 1989).

Chapter 5

Social Polarization in the Inner City: An Analysis of the Impact of Labour Market and Household Change

Nick Buck

One of the key tasks of sociology is to understand the nature and significance of processes which determine the distribution of resources and life chances in society. Major changes in British society, politics and the British economy over at least the last decade have reshaped the distribution of resources. The changes have included a substantial upward shift in unemployment, occupational restructuring in the labour market, changes in the distribution of work within households, and changes in household composition itself, growing spatial divisions within and between regions and a government which has sought to reduce the role of the state in mitigating inequalities. This paper is therefore concerned with the impact on the distribution of resources of the changes which are associated elsewhere in this book with the growth of an 'Enterprise Culture'. A number of writers have in the past sought to account for the observed growth in inequality of incomes in terms of some of these factors. However there has been little attempt yet to measure the relative significance of some of the causal processes hypothesized. This paper begins to address this task, and presents evidence which allows a test of some of the hypotheses advanced.

The previous lack of analysis partly reflects the poverty of income related data sources in Britain, and there do indeed remain difficulties in measuring exactly to what extent inequality has increased. However sources of information do exist which could allow an analysis of the causes of distributional change, and this paper exploits a relatively little used source, the National Labour Force Survey, to estimate changing income distribution over the period from 1979 to 1985. In brief, the method relies on imputing incomes from the labour market and from welfare benefits, for 1979 and 1985, and simulating the effects on the overall income distribution of various changes in population characteristics and relative income levels which occurred over this period. The methods, as well as the reasons for preferring the LFS to some other sources which might seem more obvious are discussed below. This chapter reports work still in progress, and a number of developments of the methods adopted remain to be made.

This chapter arises out of research being carried out which compares processes of economic change and social polarization in London and New York (Fainstein, Gordon and Harloe 1990). It is in fact only one strand of this research which also concerns processes associated with race and immigration, housing allocation, changing labour markets and political change. As a result, one particular concern of this paper is with spatial variation in processes of social polarization, and in particular how far the distinctive nature of economic and social change in London has produced a distinctive pattern of social polarization. The significance of this question for our comparative study in the long term is to ask whether there are processes distinctive to large cities which are at least partly independent of their national context, and how important these are. For this reason the analysis of income change is carried out both for the UK as a whole, and also for Inner London, Greater London, and the Outer Metropolitan Area (i.e. the belt about twenty miles wide surrounding Greater London), and as a further comparison, the other conurbations of England — treated as a single group.

The chapter contains four sections. The first discusses evidence of increasing social polarization at a national level, seeking to clarify what we mean by social polarization. Six hypotheses are outlined to explain the changing distribution of household income. The second section discusses the methods used in the analysis and the nature of the data. The third section presents the main results for the nation as a whole, while the fourth section discusses the city-specific findings.

Social Polarization

The salience of social polarization and the discussion of social inequality as issues within sociology has varied over time and has returned to considerable significance over the last decade. In this discussion there have been three distinct, though related strands and it is useful to separate these. The first concerns the effectiveness, or otherwise, of the state in mitigating inequalities brought about by the market through tax and benefit policies. In past decades, the concern was whether the state could bring about a more equal society, but in recent years the main concerns have changed. As government policy has shifted away from using the state as a redistributive mechanism, and welfare policy has been restricted to a narrower role of providing a limited safety net, the analysis has shifted to the numbers in poverty, and to understanding increasing levels of inequality (O'Higgins, 1985; Townsend *et al.*, 1987; Walker and Walker, 1987). This has been reinforced by a concern with the social effects of rapidly rising unemployment in the early 1980s, itself in part a by-product of government policy to restructure the economic system. A more diffused set of changes, which may be labelled as moves towards an 'enterprise culture', including changes in the taxation system in particular, have tended to encourage a relatively rapid increase in earnings at the top end of the income distribution. This has worked with the grain of economic restructuring towards privatized industries and away from manufacturing.

The second strand of thinking has been much more concerned with the social effects of widening inequality, and particularly the effects of state and market processes combined with spatially specific social processes, in creating an underclass (Dahrendorf, 1987). The underclass was seen as being excluded from most of the material benefits of society, being denied many of the benefits of citizenship and, at least potentially, being at war with society. The so-called underclass a is phenomenon both of the inner city and of declining individual regions and it tends to take on different forms in different areas, in ways related to the economic changes those areas have experienced. In the inner cities the phenomenon is particularly related to the increasing instability of the economy, while in the declining individual regions economic problems are more related to long-term unemployment. In many ways the concept, particularly as applied to the inner city has similarities with many formulations of the 'dangerous classes' of Victorian cities (Stedman Jones, 1971). I would argue, following Stedman Jones on Victorian London, that the growth of the concept has as much to do with middle–class ideologies as with the economic and social processes of the inner city. The underclass is not a major theme of this paper, but it is worth pointing out that it does not readily correspond with the poorest in income terms, who are largely made up of single pensioners and lone mothers.

Related to concern with social polarization in the inner cities, most significant in the 1960s and early 1970s, was concern about an increasing segregation of classes, and the departure from the cities of middle and higher income groups. This followed from the socially selective nature of decentralization processes, at their height in the late 1960s and early 1970s, which were largely to new private owner occupied housing. The move to the New Towns, and other planned decentralization measures were quantitatively less significant, particularly in the South and Midlands and even then tended to be skewed to the skilled working class. Survey evidence for London suggests that there was a threshold income below which outward migration was very low, while the census suggested that less skilled manual workers had markedly lower chances of leaving London than other groups (Buck, *et al.*, 1986). This decentralization, combined with an economic restructuring of the cities which saw a rapid decline of manufacturing and related activity, and some growth in private sector services, and combined, too, with a more modest level of inflow of younger higher income households through gentrification has led over the last two decades to a restructuring of the population of the inner cities. A more bipolar form of social distribution is developing in some areas, with relatively fewer middle income groups. However, different forms may be emerging in different types of cities depending on the scope and scale of the different flows. This strand of concern with polarization and inequality leaves us with a focus on both the changing social composition of areas, and also on the industrial and occupational restructuring of opportunities in the labour market.

The third strand of concern with social polarization focuses on the interaction between labour market changes and changes in the household. Pahl (1988), for example, has argued that the growth of employment of married women, combined with benefit regulations which discourage the employment of the wives of unemployed men, have led to the polarization between work-rich and work-poor households. The distinction between individual incomes and household incomes which this raises is important since it is not immediately clear how changes in individual earnings and welfare benefits will translate into household level distributions. There are signs of polarization of individual labour market incomes, with the growth of more 'flexible' forms of employment such as part-time and temporary contract and casual work (Hakim, 1987), with relatively low hourly earnings, whilst incomes of full time, particularly non-manual private sector workers, rise more rapidly. However, Pahl argues that for the distribution of household incomes, these trends are mitigated by the fact that most of the worse paid 'secondary' workers are married to the better paid 'primary' workers. The major source of inequality, on this argument, is in the difference between households with no workers, and dependent on welfare benefits, and household containing at least one worker.

A related point of importance is simply that a major source of variation in household income is household composition. Poorer households tend to have fewer members, elderly households tend to be poorer, as do single parent families. These factors need to be taken into account in discussing income distributions (see O'Higgins, 1985, on the use of the equivalent income concept for taking into account household structure). Moreover changing household composition will tend on its own to lead to changing household income distribution. For example a growth in the proportion of elderly households will, other things being equal, increase the proportion of low income households and increase measures of income dispersion. Some means of controlling for this factor is necessary in explaining how income distributions are changing. Rather than using equivalent scales this analysis seeks to measure directly the impact of changing household composition on overall income distribution.

Social Polarization in the Inner City

Table 5.1 Changes in Income Distribution 1979–85, UK.

	Gross Normal Income			Share of Aggregate Income		
	1979	1985	% Change	1979	1985	Difference
Lowest 20% of households	33.09	50.46	+52.5	5.49	4.65	−0.84
Second quintile group	68.18	106.81	+56.7	11.32	9.85	−1.47
Third quintile group	110.13	182.70	+65.9	18.29	16.84	−1.45
Fourth quintile group	150.33	273.31	+81.8	24.96	25.20	+0.24
Highest quintile group	240.53	471.37	+96.0	39.94	43.46	+3.52
Average	120.45	216.93	+80.1			

Source: Family Expenditure Survey 1979, Table 46 and 1985, Table 22.

There is in fact clear evidence of an increasing degree of inequality, whether this is measured in terms of widening differentials between those at lower and higher incomes, or in terms of the share of total income received by the rich and the poor. The most commonly used source of evidence on income distribution in Britain is the Family Expenditure Survey which collects information on both income and expenditure from around 7,000 households. Data from this survey on changes between 1979 and 1985 are presented in Table 5.1. The incomes of higher income groups have been increasing significantly faster than those in lower income groups, and the share of aggregate income received by the richest 20 per cent of households increased from 40 per cent to 43.5 per cent. As an alternative measure the ratio of higher quartile earnings (i.e. the income level with 25 per cent of the sample above) to lower quartile earnings rose from 2.91 in 1979–80 to 3.30 in 1985–6. On this same measure inequality in London increased by an even greater degree, from 2.93 to 3.54. In this same period the real incomes of the lowest quartile may even have declined (Townsend et al., 1987).

Six Hypotheses on Causes of Changing Income Distribution

The above discussion has suggested a number of competing explanations of changes in income inequality. These are summarized briefly here, while the next section discusses how they are implemented in the methodology of this study. Conceptually they can be grouped into two types, first those which relate to levels of incomes received by particular types of household, and those which relate to the changing composition of households with different characteristics. The significance of spatial variation in the impacts of each of these factors is also briefly discussed.

a) The changing level of state social benefits compared with labour market incomes. In the period between the spring of 1979 and the spring of 1985 average earnings rose by over 90 per cent, while on average rates of

83

welfare benefits rose by around 80 per cent. This would tend to lower the proportion of aggregate earnings received by poorer households dependent on benefits. In principle the effect of this factor will be equivalent across the whole country, but its effect on aggregate regional income distributions will differ according to the proportions of benefit recipients in each region.

b) *Differential growth of labour market incomes in different occupation groups.* The growing demand for more qualified white collar workers has tended to lead to their earnings rising significantly faster than those of manual workers. Table 5.2 gives some examples of changing rates, derived from the New Earnings Survey. Higher growth rates are clearly concentrated in non-manual occupations with higher initial incomes. One would expect these changes to raise the proportion of income earned in the highest income group relative to middle income groups. The only factor mitigating this is that women's earnings have tended to rise marginally faster than men's. There has been some impact from government policy given the attempt to hold down public sector wages and salaries more than those in the private sector. Like factor A, inter-area differences will be largely compositional, though there have been some significant regional variations in the relative rates of income changes.

c) *Changing household composition.* As suggested above, changes in the distribution of household types (defined in terms of numbers of members, marital status and age, rather than labour market factors) will have an effect on the distribution of incomes. Changes over the period 1979–85 are shown in Table 5.3. The most significant changes have been a 3.6 percentage point decline in the share of households containing working age married couples, a small decline in the number of single person non-pensioner households, a small growth in single person pensioner households, a relatively large growth in single parent families, and a large growth in other household types.[1] These changes in aggregate would be expected to lower household incomes. There have been some significant regional variations in these trends, particularly in London, with a more rapid decline of married couple households, a stronger growth of single elderly in Inner London, and a more rapid growth of 'other' household types.

d) *Changing levels of unemployment.* The rise of national unemployment over this period from 1.2 million to 3.2 million, on official figures, has clearly depressed the incomes of a very large number of households. Its impact on the income distribution will depend on the propensity of people at different levels of the occupational hierarchy and the income distribution to become unemployed. Labour Force Survey evidence suggests that in fact manual workers are around three times more likely than

Table 5.2 *Change in Weekly Earnings by Occupation: Full-time Workers*

	Men		Women	
	1979 Weekly Earnings	% Increase 1979–1985	1979 Weekly Earnings	% Increase 1979–1985
Professional etc. supporting management & administration	129.0	+109.5	94.6	+105.9
Professional etc. in education, health and welfare	113.1	+97.3	80.1	+96.3
Professional etc. in science, engineering, technology, etc.	119.2	+92.5	75.1	+103.6
Managerial	114.4	+100.3	70.7	+108.6
Clerical	83.7	+90.4	60.0	+96.7
Sales	94.5	+83.9	47.3	+108.5
Security	104.5	+112.5	82.0	+122.9
Catering, cleaning, etc.	74.2	+78.7	51.2	+85.9
Making & repairing (metal & electrical)	100.7	+77.5	63.4	+75.7
Painting, routine assembly, etc.	91.4	+73.6	58.7	+83.3
Construction, mining, etc.	94.6	+69.7	—	—
Transport & storage	93.1	+74.8	59.4	+89.7

Source: Department of Employment, New Earnings Survey, 1979 and 1985.

Table 5.3   Distribution of Households by Type

	1979	1985
Household headed by a working age married couple	57.8%	54.2%
Single person, non-pensioner	10.6%	10.1%
Single person, pensioner	12.9%	13.2%
Two person pensioner household	10.4%	10.4%
Single parent family	3.8%	5.0%
Other	4.5%	7.1%

administrative, professional and technical (APT) workers to become unemployed. This would tend to lead to a much greater widening of the income distribution than if all groups faced an equal risk of unemployment. There have been marked regional variations in the impact of this factor.

e) Married women's participation. As suggested above it has been hypothesized that a growth in married women's work would tend to sharpen the degree of inequality between the lower portions of the income distribution and the middle and upper portions. However there are difficulties because of tendencies pulling in two opposite directions. On the one hand there has been an increasing tendency for wives of employed men to work (an increase from 57.6 per cent to 63.7 per cent), but wives of unemployed men have a much lower, and declining, probability of working (29.7 per cent in 1979, 26.1 per cent in 1985), and the proportion of households with unemployed husbands has increased sharply. The probability of the wives of unemployed men working is particularly low in the case of the long term unemployed. In aggregate there has been almost no change in the proportion of married women working. The simulations below however focus solely on the growing participation of wives of employed men, on the assumption that the opposite effect has been taken into account in the simulation of unemployment growth. Inter-regional differences in the pattern of change in participation have been relatively slight.

f) Occupational restructuring. The rapid decline of manufacturing employment and the growth of a number of service industries have sharply reduced the number of manual workers, and raised the number of administrative, professional and technical (APT) workers, and to a lesser extent those in other services such as sales, catering and security. Technical and other labour process changes within individual industries have reinforced these trends, particularly the growth of APT workers and have also led to declines in more routine non-manual workers, such as clerical workers. APT workers increased as a proportion of all workers by 8 percentage points, while manual workers declined by an equivalent amount, and service and clerical workers increased and declined by 1.5 per cent percentage points each respectively. The expected effect of these changes within the employed population would be to raise the proportions of higher income workers relative to lower income workers, though there would be some compensating effects in the growth of lower paid service workers. Both compositional effects and variations in local rates of change would be expected to lead to significant variations between areas.

It should be clear from the discussions of the six factors above that there are strong interactions between them. These interactions occur at both the causal level and at the level of the impact of the factors on income distribution. For example, the growing demand for skilled non-manual workers (F) will tend to contribute to their growing relative earnings (B). However the growth in relative earnings will itself increase the impact on income distribution of the growing proportion of APT workers. There will be similar strong interactions between household composition change, unemployment and married women's participation. In the main this paper seeks to examine the separate impact of the factors, but clearly there are difficulties in distinguishing them. The next section discusses this further in the context of the methods used.

Data and Methods

As suggested above, the Family Expenditure Survey is the richest source of data on household incomes, however in this analysis I have preferred to use the Labour Force Survey, which though it contains no direct income information, has very much fuller information on labour market participation. In addition to this advantage, the LFS has a much larger sample size than the FES, with about 85,000 households in 1979, and 64,000 in 1985. It contains information on occupation at a detailed level (i.e. the 547 OPCS Occupation Unit Groups) and hours of work for each individual (for both main jobs and second jobs if any). The analysis in this paper was based on imputing labour market earnings and welfare benefits for each household on the LFS data tape, making use of information about the household structure, labour market participation and job characteristics of each individual. This information was combined with New Earnings Survey occupational wage rate data[2] to estimate hourly and weekly earnings for each male and female worker separately, using their detailed occupation unit group. Adjustments were then made for inter-regional differences in occupational wage rates and differences in wages received by different age groups.[3] After labour market earnings were estimated for each individual, they were recombined into their households and state benefit entitlements were estimated for each household on the basis of composition, age and labour market status and earnings of members. This exercise was carried out for both the 1979 and 1985 surveys, and for each survey the appropriate incomes were calculated on the basis of both 1979 and 1985 wage and benefit rates. Thus two derived data files were created each containing imputed weekly household income on two bases.

In spite of the advantages of the LFS there are a number of gaps in the information compared with the FES, which need to be summarized briefly, since they account for some of the differences between the results obtained here and results from the FES. There are a number of sources where income could not be imputed reliably from the available information. The most significant of these were occupational and other earnings related pensions. According to the 1985 FES, only 46 per cent of one and two person pensioner households were mainly dependent on state benefits, and this had fallen from 52 per cent in 1979. The effect of this omission is that too many pensioners are concentrated in the bottom three deciles of the income distribution (and conversely the concentration of other households in these deciles is underestimated), and there is an underestimation of the level of income of these deciles. Second, there was no information on investment income. Overall this accounts for 3.3 per cent of household income, with the highest proportions of incomes in second quintile (e.g. pensioners living off income from savings) and in the highest. Thirdly, the calculation of benefits reflects entitlements rather than actual receipts, and thus will tend to over-estimate income from benefits with a low take-up rate, such as Family Income Supplement. On the other hand a number of benefits received by relatively few people, but at a high rate are excluded (e.g. Industrial injuries disablement benefits). In addition a number of other relatively minor sources of income such as student grants and alimony are excluded. Two other forms of FES practice could not be replicated. First, owner occupiers have the imputed rent from their house treated as a part of income (this represented around 5 per cent of aggregate income). Second, the FES treats those who have been unemployed for less than three months as if they are still receiving their former income — on the basis that their pattern of expenditure is liable to reflect their former standard of living rather than that of a temporary period of unemployment. Supplementary payments for housing (in 1979) and housing benefit are excluded from the analysis. The latter were not included in the FES, but the former were included.

Once estimated total household incomes had been obtained, the distribution of household incomes were analyzed. The basic method was to divide the distribution into deciles — ten groups with equal numbers of households, ranked by income. Mean values for the income of each of these groups, as well as their share of aggregate household income were calculated. The basic calculations for 1979 and 1985 for the UK are shown in the upper half of Table 5.4. It should be clear, looking at either the changes in decile incomes, or at the change in decile shares of aggregate income, that there has been a substantial increase in income inequality. It should also be clear that it is the fourth and fifth deciles which have experienced the sharpest relative decline in income. It is necessary to stress here that decile groups are statistical artefacts, and not social groups. It is not necessarily implied that, for instance, the fourth decile group contained the same specific types of households in 1979 and 1985 and that this particular type of household experienced a sharp relative drop in income. The effect shown in the table could have occurred through large numbers of households originally in higher deciles suffering falls in income — for example through unemployment — and swelling the number of low income households. Such change could even come about if the income of households of all types increased at the same rate, if the distribution of household types changed sufficiently.

As some check on the method, Table 5.4 may be compared with Table 5.1, based on the Family Expenditure Survey. The two tables represent entirely independent measures of change in income distribution over the same period. Two different comparisons are available on the rate of growth, and changes in share of total income. The former suggests that the method here produces rather low estimates of income and rather high estimates of income growth. The low estimates of income level follow from the income sources missing from this analysis. Part of the difference in the estimation of growth rates may follow from the different timing of the LFS at the NES and the effects of inflation. 1979 was a year of relatively high inflation and while NES measures are taken in the spring, the FES continues throughout the year. This could have made a difference of up to 5 per cent in the estimated rate of growth. The estimates of changing shares are much closer, with basically similar patterns of the sharpest losses of income occurring in the second and third quintile, and the largest gains in the highest quintile. The most serious difference of estimation relates to the lowest quintile. This is likely to result from the underestimate of pensioner earnings, referred to above, leading to an excessive concentration of households exclusively dependent on social benefits, and hence an insensitivity to changes in market incomes.[4] Nevertheless the comparison gives some confidence that the income estimation procedure used here is modelling changes in income distribution quite closely.

In considering the methods used to explore the six hypotheses advanced earlier to explain changing income distributions, it is important to stress that the analysis used here constitutes a simulation of the changes to overall income distribution that would be expected given other compositional or wage rate changes. It does not present direct longitudinal evidence as to what happened to a fixed group of households, and in this sense only provides an indirect means of explaining changes in income distributions. The method used was to reanalyze the 1979 data in order to predict the 1985 distribution on the basis of changing characteristics of the

Table 5.4 United Kingdom: Changing Income Distribution 1979–85

Decile Income Groups	Mean weekly income		% Change	% Share of Aggregate Income		Difference
	1979	1985		1979	1985	
1	18.60	33.78	+81.61	1.91	1.83	−0.08
2	22.79	39.12	+71.65	2.35	2.11	−0.24
3	32.65	56.83	+74.06	3.36	3.07	−0.29
4	57.79	80.83	+39.87	5.95	4.37	−1.58
5	83.77	140.14	+67.29	8.62	7.57	−1.05
6	101.73	187.33	+84.14	10.47	10.12	−0.35
7	119.98	230.03	+91.72	12.35	12.43	+0.07
8	140.25	276.11	+96.87	14.44	14.92	+0.48
9	166.15	336.99	+102.82	17.10	18.21	+1.11
10	227.81	469.63	+106.15	23.45	25.37	+1.92
Mean	97.15	185.08	+90.5			

Change in share of aggregate income predicted by:

	Benefit/wage growth differential	Occupational wage rate differential	Household composition	Unemployment	Married women's participation	Occupation shift
1	−0.08	+0.04	+0.03	+0.06	−0.02	−0.01
2	−0.11	+0.04	0.00	−0.12	−0.04	−0.02
3	−0.09	+0.03	0.00	+0.03	−0.04	−0.02
4	−0.03	−0.04	−0.20	−1.00	−0.05	−0.08
5	+0.01	−0.15	−0.10	−0.49	−0.01	−0.03
6	+0.01	−0.14	−0.06	−0.12	+0.06	−0.03
7	+0.02	−0.10	−0.03	+0.06	+0.09	+0.01
8	+0.05	−0.05	+0.01	+0.27	+0.05	+0.02
9	+0.07	+0.10	+0.07	+0.49	+0.01	+0.04
10	+0.12	+0.29	+0.27	+0.83	−0.05	+0.07
Sum of positive values:	0.28	0.50	0.38	1.74	0.21	0.16

population, and changing wage and benefits rates. The type of question asked was 'what would the income distribution in 1979 have been if households had been exposed to the risks of unemployment they experienced in 1985?'. In practice, a different method is used for the first two hypotheses, as compared with the last four. In the former case the 1985 money rates were substituted in the calculation of the 1979 distribution, or an adjusted version of these rates in the case of the analysis of the wage/benefit differential. In the four latter cases, concerned with changing household or labour market characteristics, weights were applied to the sample so that households with particular characteristics in 1979 should have the same probability of occurring as in 1985. This exercise was carried out separately for each region considered, using distinct regional weights — e.g. the analysis of the effect of occupational recomposition in Inner London was carried out on the basis of the changes in the occupation distribution of the Inner London population. All the data on changing population characteristics was derived from the Labour Force Survey itself, so that for example the analysis of the effect of unemployment changes was based on LFS estimates rather than claimant counts.

More explanation of the method is required in the case of unemployment. This was carried out on the basis of the employment status of the 'primary earner' in the household. This clearly requires further refinement since it leads to the assumption that there has been no change in the relationship between the 'primary earner's' unemployment and the earnings and probability of unemployment of other household members. As suggested above there has in fact been a small decline in the likelihood of the wives of unemployed men working, which is not taken into account here. It is also necessary in measuring the effects on income of unemployment to assess the changes affecting other household members e.g. working age children, and also interactions in other household types — i.e. those not containing couples. In reweighting the sample it was necessary to both increase the weights attached to unemployed households, and correspondingly reduce those attached to employed households. This was done so that lower weights attached to households with the primary earner in occupations with a higher probability of unemployment.

A number of the same considerations apply to the analysis of occupation recomposition as to that of unemployment. This also was carried out on the basis of changes in primary earners occupations. Ideally some account should be taken of changing occupational opportunities of other household members. The occupation recomposition calculation used changes at the level of four broad sections: administrative professional and technical workers; clerical workers; service workers and manual workers. A more disaggregated approach might produce stronger effects.

Once the samples were reweighted, new distributions were calculated, and the shares of income in each decile were calculated separately

Table 5.5 Greater London: Changing Income Distribution 1979–85

Decile Income Groups	Mean weekly income			% Share of Aggregate Income		
	1979	1985	% Change	1979	1985	Difference
1	18.26	33.92	+85.8	1.71	1.52	−0.19
2	22.46	37.83	+68.2	2.10	1.69	−0.41
3	33.85	56.65	+67.4	3.17	2.54	−0.63
4	63.83	96.68	+51.5	5.97	4.33	−1.64
5	88.70	172.49	+94.5	8.29	7.72	−0.57
6	108.72	227.52	+109.3	10.17	10.19	+0.02
7	131.33	278.66	+112.2	12.28	12.48	+0.20
8	156.93	338.40	+115.6	14.68	15.15	+0.47
9	187.06	419.70	+124.4	17.49	18.79	+1.30
10	258.15	571.58	+121.4	24.14	25.59	+1.45
Mean	106.93	223.34	+108.9			

Change in share of aggregate income predicted by:

Decile Income Groups	Benefit/wage growth differential	Occupational wage rate differential	Household composition	Unemployment	Married women's participation	Occupation shift
1	−0.07	−0.05	+0.04	+0.03	−0.03	−0.01
2	−0.09	−0.06	−0.04	−0.10	−0.03	−0.01
3	−0.07	−0.13	−0.08	−0.08	−0.05	−0.04
4	−0.02	−0.11	−0.26	−0.81	−0.06	−0.09
5	+0.01	−0.10	+0.05	−0.26	−0.04	0.00
6	+0.01	−0.07	+0.10	−0.09	+0.02	+0.03
7	+0.02	−0.03	+0.10	+0.03	+0.08	+0.01
8	+0.05	−0.02	+0.08	+0.23	+0.05	+0.02
9	+0.06	+0.17	+0.11	+0.47	−0.03	+0.04
10	+0.11	+0.40	−0.10	+0.59	+0.09	+0.06
Sum of positive values:	0.26	0.57	0.48	1.35	0.24	0.16

Table 5.6 Inner London: Changing Income Distribution 1979–85

Decile Income Groups	Mean weekly income		% Change	% Share of Aggregate Income		Difference
	1979	1985		1979	1985	
1	17.50	32.95	+88.3	1.79	1.63	−0.16
2	19.50	35.50	+82.1	2.00	1.76	−0.24
3	30.72	50.82	+65.4	3.15	2.53	−0.62
4	52.82	72.42	+37.1	5.41	3.60	−1.81
5	77.26	134.12	+73.6	7.91	6.67	−1.24
6	94.93	188.83	+98.9	9.72	9.39	−0.33
7	116.32	243.76	+109.6	11.92	12.12	+0.20
8	142.64	303.53	+112.8	14.61	15.10	+0.49
9	174.70	392.88	+124.9	17.90	19.54	+1.64
10	249.84	550.49	+120.3	25.59	27.63	+2.04
Mean	97.62	201.03	+105.9			

Change in share of aggregate income predicted by:

	Benefit/wage growth differential	Occupational wage rate differential	Household composition	Unemployment	Married women's participation	Occupation shift
1	−0.07	−0.05	+0.03	+0.02	−0.04	−0.01
2	−0.09	−0.05	−0.03	+0.12	−0.05	−0.01
3	−0.09	−0.11	−0.05	−0.22	−0.08	−0.03
4	−0.05	−0.13	−0.15	−1.01	−0.13	−0.08
5	+0.02	−0.08	+0.03	−0.38	−0.17	−0.06
6	+0.03	−0.01	+0.20	−0.11	−0.13	0.00
7	+0.02	−0.01	+0.21	0.00	−0.09	−0.02
8	+0.04	−0.11	+0.17	+0.26	−0.10	−0.07
9	+0.06	+0.08	+0.11	+0.58	−0.15	−0.01
10	+0.12	+0.48	−0.51	+0.74	+0.93	+0.29
Sum of positive values:	0.29	0.56	0.75	1.72	0.93	0.29

on the basis of each of the six hypotheses. The difference between this share and the original decile share is the prediction of the effect of the factor for each decile. These differences are presented for the five areas in the lower halves of Tables 5.4 to 5.8. The upper half of each table shows the estimates of 1979 and 1985 income distribution for each region. It should be noted for the lower half of each table, that because these are the predicted changes in the share of aggregate income, they sum to zero across all deciles. There may in consequence be apparently strange corresponding effects to the more predictable effects — for example although the differential decline of welfare benefits has little direct effect on those in the highest income deciles, their share of aggregate income rises as that of those in the lower deciles falls.

Considering the results for the United Kingdom, most are broadly in line with expectations. The most significant points relate to the relative scale of the effects and which parts of the distribution they most directly effect. The overall scale of the effects is measured by summing values across deciles, which gives an indication of the proportion of income shifted as a result of changes in the factor. The benefit/wage growth differential does appear to lead to declining shares of income at the lower end of the distribution, though the scale of the effect is not particularly large in relation to overall estimated changes. The effects of occupational wage rate differentials are rather stronger, and the positive effects are strongly concentrated in the top two deciles.[5] The household composition effects are perhaps the most difficult to interpret. The increase in poorer households (single pensioners and single parents) would explain the concentration of negative effects in the fourth decile, but it is more difficult to explain why positive effects are concentrated at the top of the income distribution. Part of the explanation could be a growth of multi-earner, non-family households, included in the residual category of households.

The unemployment effects are clearly the strongest of all, and account for much of the decline of the fourth and fifth deciles. Corresponding positive effects are progressively more concentrated in each decile from the seventh. This concentration of positive effects at the top of the income distribution reflects in part the higher risk of unemployment of manual workers compared to APT workers.

The married women's participation effect broadly has the expected pattern, but its effects are surprisingly small. This result provides little direct support for Pahl's contention that the increasing concentration of work in multi-earner households is significantly increasing the degree of polarization (Pahl, 1988). However, the increase in the number of work-poor households — encompassed by the unemployment effect — clearly has led to greater inequality. It is the increasing concentration in work-rich households which does not appear to be significant in its effects. Further analysis is necessary to investigate whether there has been any

Table 5.7 Outer Metropolitan Area: Changing Income Distribution 1979–85

Decile	Mean weekly income			% Share of Aggregate Income		
Income Groups	1979	1985	% Change	1979	1985	Difference
1	18.85	34.43	+82.6	1.81	1.57	−0.24
2	25.78	48.92	+89.8	2.47	2.23	−0.24
3	39.11	68.35	+74.8	3.75	3.11	−0.64
4	73.58	137.69	+87.1	7.05	6.27	−0.78
5	94.18	190.91	+102.7	9.03	8.69	−0.34
6	110.16	232.44	+111.0	10.56	10.58	+0.02
7	127.64	274.64	+115.2	12.23	12.50	+0.27
8	147.37	321.58	+118.2	14.13	14.64	+0.51
9	172.51	380.47	+120.6	16.54	17.32	+0.78
10	234.07	507.09	+116.6	22.44	23.09	+0.65
Mean	104.32	219.65	+110.6			

Change in share of aggregate income predicted by:

	Benefit/wage growth differential	Occupational wage rate differential	Household composition	Unemployment	Married women's participation	Occupation shift
1	−0.09	+0.01	−0.01	+0.04	−0.03	−0.02
2	−0.08	−0.01	+0.14	−0.06	−0.03	−0.03
3	−0.07	−0.02	+0.22	−0.34	−0.05	−0.06
4	+0.01	−0.09	+0.10	−0.60	−0.04	−0.03
5	0.00	−0.18	−0.02	−0.09	0.00	+0.01
6	+0.01	−0.13	−0.07	+0.03	+0.05	+0.03
7	+0.02	−0.04	−0.08	+0.12	+0.09	+0.05
8	+0.04	+0.06	−0.10	+0.25	+0.03	+0.01
9	+0.05	+0.21	−0.11	+0.35	−0.01	+0.01
10	+0.10	+0.17	−0.08	+0.28	−0.01	+0.02
Sum of positive values:	0.23	0.45	0.46	1.07	0.17	0.13

Table 5.8 Conurbations*: Changing Income Distribution 1979–85

Decile	Mean weekly income		% Change	% Share of Aggregate Income		Difference
Income Groups	1979	1985		1979	1985	
1	18.46	33.22	+79.96	1.96	1.97	+0.01
2	20.96	36.49	+74.09	2.23	2.16	−0.07
3	31.77	55.10	+73.43	3.37	3.27	−0.10
4	53.42	69.37	+29.86	5.67	4.12	−1.55
5	81.04	116.99	+44.36	8.61	6.94	−1.67
6	99.09	167.33	+68.87	10.52	9.93	−0.59
7	117.37	209.85	+78.79	12.46	12.45	−0.01
8	137.36	255.31	+85.87	14.59	15.15	+0.56
9	162.03	310.77	+91.80	17.21	18.44	+1.23
10	220.20	431.12	+95.79	23.38	25.58	+2.20
Mean	94.17	168.55	+78.98			

Change in share of aggregate income predicted by:

	Benefit/wage growth differential	Occupational wage rate differential	Household composition	Unemployment	Married women's participation	Occupation shift
1	−0.08	+0.08	+0.02	+0.07	−0.02	0.00
2	−0.09	+0.09	+0.04	0.00	−0.03	−0.01
3	−0.10	+0.10	+0.05	+0.02	−0.03	0.00
4	−0.04	+0.05	−0.01	−1.18	−0.03	−0.07
5	+0.02	−0.13	−0.07	−0.97	−0.02	−0.05
6	+0.01	−0.12	−0.05	−0.25	+0.05	+0.01
7	+0.03	−0.10	−0.05	+0.01	+0.08	+0.03
8	+0.05	−0.06	−0.01	+0.35	+0.04	+0.03
9	+0.08	+0.03	+0.04	+0.70	−0.01	+0.05
10	+0.12	+0.06	+0.04	+1.25	−0.03	0.00
Sum of positive values:	0.31	0.41	0.19	2.40	0.17	0.12

* i.e. West Midlands, Merseyside, Greater Manchester, South Yorkshire, West Yorkshire, Tyne and Wear.

further concentration of workers through changes in the unemployment probabilities of other household members.

The occupation shift effect is even less significant than the participation effect — though its shape is in line with expectations. This is surprising given the extent of occupational change. As with the previous factor there is some question of whether the effect is fully measured both because the analysis has not been able to explore the effects of occupation change on all household members, because there is an interaction with unemployment change and because a rather coarse classification of occupations was used for the simulations. However a further analysis of the income distributions of households with primary earners in different occupation groups suggests that differences in overall household income are not in fact particularly large — owing largely to the equalizing effects of the earnings of other household members.

The analysis at this stage has not yet been able to explore the interactions between effects. The addition of the predicted changes across the columns would suggest that these factors are predicting total estimated change relatively well, though the absolute value of the sums of the predictions tend to be rather lower than the estimated change (e.g. in decile 4: −1.40, compared to −1.58; in decile 9:, +0.78 compared to +1.11; in decile 10: +1.53 compared to +1.92). One explanation of these remaining differences are factors which are missing or have been imperfectly specified. The discussion of household composition and unemployment above suggested one direction for further development. The occupation change analysis was carried out using four very broad groupings — it is possible that a more disaggregated approach might achieve a stronger effect. An example of a factor missing entirely is that there is no account taken of changes in the number of hours worked.

One must use considerable caution in summing across the columns, since there are undoubtedly strong interactions between some effects, and there is no certainty as to whether two effects combined will have a weaker or a stronger effect than the two separately. An example of an interaction is that the occupation effect is rather stronger if measured in terms of 1985 wage rates rather than 1979 rates, since a greater differential in the wage rates of growing occupations and declining occupations existed at the latter date than at the former.

Regional Variations

The previous section has suggested that at the national level estimated income distribution changes may be rather powerfully predicted in terms of a number of hypothesized social, economic and policy changes. Further, it is the economic changes associated with the growth of unemployment and the very unequal rates at which earnings have risen in different occupations which have had the most powerful effects. This section explores how far these patterns have varied in different regions of the country.

If we first compare the estimated extent of change that has occurred, it would appear that there have been significant regional variations in the degree of income redistribution though in all cases the distributions have become more unequal. Measuring the sum of positive values, Inner London (with a 4.4 per cent shift) and the conurbations (with a 4 per cent shift) have experienced a greater degree of change than the UK as a whole (3.6 per cent) while change in Greater London as a whole has been marginally less (3.4 per cent) and in the Outer Metropolitan Area (OMA) change has been significantly less (2.2 per cent). Thus it appears that change has been greater in areas of higher unemployment and with more people initially in poverty. Inner London, though not the conurbations, was also an area with a higher than average degree of inequality at the beginning of the period. It should also be noted that there are differences in the estimated average level of income growth with significantly higher growth in all the parts of the London region, and significantly lower growth in the conurbations. These differences are confirmed from FES data on income change.

Considering the predictions of changing income shares, differences in the effects of the benefit/wage growth differences are relatively slight, and appear to be in line with differences expected on the basis of population composition. There is more variation in the impact of occupational wage rate differentials. In London, the effects appear to be somewhat stronger, and much more concentrated at the top of the income distribution, though in the Outer Metropolitan Area they are somewhat weaker than the national effects.[6] In the conurbations the wage rate differential does not seem to be having the same effects as elsewhere, with little relative gain at the higher end of the distributions. This effect is thus related strongly to the pattern of growth of higher wage service industries in this period.

The overall effects of the household composition factor are rather stronger than average in the parts of the London region, and rather weaker in the conurbations, however there are also significant differences in the pattern of effects. The weaker effects in the conurbation are similar in distribution to those in the UK. By contrast the effects in the OMA are almost reversed. This follows from differences in the pattern of household change, with a fall in proportions of elderly households in the Outer Metropolitan Area (OMA). In London itself the pattern follows that of the country as a whole, except for the decline in the highest decile. This is difficult to interpret without further analysis of some of the household types involved.

The pattern of unemployment effects is broadly similar in all areas, and the overall effects vary with the level and rate of change and unemployment. Hence in the OMA, the area with the lowest level of unemployment, the sum of positive values is 1.07, compared with 1.74 nationally, and in the conurbations 2.40. The one area where the unemployment effect is below expectations on this basis is Inner London, with significantly above average unemployment, but an overall level of effect around the national average.

In all but one of the regions considered, the married women's participation effect has similar effects to those in the country as a whole. The exception is Inner London, where the effect is much larger, and indeed second only to unemployment among the effects. Moreover all the positive effects are concentrated in the highest decile. This was not caused by a higher degree of movement towards dual earner households. The rate of growth of such households was marginally lower than nationally. One explanation may be that more married women in Inner London than elsewhere work full-time rather than part-time, and at least some of them in rather higher paid occupations than elsewhere, so that married women's earnings make up a higher proportion of household earnings with the effect that the growth of such households has much stronger and more concentrated effects.

To a lesser degree the same regional differences as applied to married women's participation apply to the occupation shift effect. It is approximately twice as significant in Inner London as elsewhere, and its positive effects are concentrated in the highest decile. In this case the degree of occupation change was greater than elsewhere, but a further factor is that the earnings differential between occupation groups is greater in London, and there is a stratum of very high earning households depending on high individual earnings, rather than a multiplicity of earners. London's increasing role as a global financial centre does in this respect appear to have an impact on income distribution.

This section has suggested that the regional pattern of income distribution change is in fact significantly related to the processes of economic restructuring which have occurred in the 1980s. The areas of economic decline and of higher levels and growth rates of unemployment have experienced a stronger polarization of income distribution. Inner London, and to some extent London more generally stand out as areas where rather different processes seem to be operating. Gordon and Sassen (1990) have suggested that in the global cities such as London and New York a distinctive polarization within the labour market is emerging, between very high wage jobs and very unstable low wage jobs. The impact of this pattern on inequality appears on this analysis to be particularly exacerbated by the distinctive household structures of Inner London.

Conclusion

The methods developed in this paper provide an opportunity to assess a number of causal models which seek to explain changes in income distribution and account for a growth of social polarization. The results point to the major importance of unemployment in increasing the degree of household income polarization. A second significant factor has been the increasing differentiation of occupational wages, whilst changing demographic patterns of household composition have also had effects. Perhaps the most surprising findings have been the relatively low significance of compositional changes within the employed population, either in terms of an increasing concentration of employment in multi-earner households, or in terms of the shift towards non-manual higher qualified occupations. These conclusions must remain somewhat tentative, for reasons explained above, particularly the risk that some of the change due to both effects has been absorbed within the unemployment factor. Further analysis is required to disentangle these effects.

The analysis has then pointed to the strong link between the processes of economic restructuring and widening inequality. The direct effects of rising unemployment have been the most significant, but they have been supplemented by changing patterns of labour demand, and to a lesser extent by occupational change effects. This must raise a question of the likely prognosis with declining unemployment levels. In fact evidence from the 1988 FES suggests that over the period 1985–8 when unemployment was falling, the income distribution was becoming still more unequal, with the share of income received by the top quintile rising from 43.5 per cent to 45.5 per cent, and all other groups losing relatively. This suggests firstly that the processes identified for the early 1980s are not the only mechanisms by which inequality may increase, and in the late 1980s a different combination of processes is clearly at work. It is not likely that the processes at work will have changed completely although it may be that in the late 1980s they were driven much more by occupational wage rate differentials, and possibly more strongly than before by participation effects, since part-time female employment was rising rather faster. Moreover, in this period, unemployment, though falling, tended to become more concentrated, and the proportion of the long-term unemployed tended to rise. This new combination of processes requires further work along the lines outlined in this chapter.

Notes

1 Some further exploratory work is needed on the nature of this last group, and whether its growth reflects any change in household definition.

2 This annual survey, with a very large sample, covers hourly and weekly

earnings of individuals, and the published data contain averages by age, region, occupation and industry.

3   No allowance has been made for any differences between the earnings of employees and the self employed. However FES data suggests at least that earnings of the latter are not higher than those of employees of broadly equivalent occupation.

4   According to the FES the proportion of income in the lowest quintile not derived from social security benefits fell from 21.8 per cent in 1979 to 18.6 per cent in 1985.

5   The paradoxical small positive effects at the lower end of the distribution follows from the fact that few households in these deciles receive labour market earnings, so they do not expeience the negative relative decline suffered by deciles towards the middle of the distribution. Similar arguments explain similar results for unemployment.

6   This may be explained by the fact that the regional wage rate differentials applied were based on place of residence, and many OMA residents work in London and receive the higher London wage rates.

Acknowledgment

This paper derives from a project on 'Economic Change, Urban Revival and Social Polarization: London compared to New York', supported by the Economic and Social Research Council, and the Research Fund of the University of Kent. I am grateful to Ian Gordon and Chris Pickvance for their comments on this paper. The Labour Force Survey data used in this paper was supplied by the Office of Population Censuses and Surveys through the ESRC data archive, neither of whom bear any responsibility for the analysis reported here, or the conclusions reached.

Chapter 6

Young People's Transitions into the Labour Market*

Ken Roberts, Glennys Parsell and Michelle Connolly

By the time longitudinal research produces results, the questions being asked can be very different from those that influenced the design of the enquiries. Youth unemployment was among Britain's leading domestic issues when the ESRC 16–19 Initiative was planned in the mid-1980s. Joblessness had spread dramatically during the recessions of the 1970s and early 1980s, and the effects among school-leavers were exacerbated by the prevailing demographic trend. The rising birth-rate from 1955 until 1965 sent increasing numbers of school-leavers onto the labour market throughout the 1970s and up to 1982, the year when Britain's economy began recovering from its deepest recession in post-war history, but it took several years before the upturn in output made any impression on the level of unemployment. Subsequently, throughout the course of the ESRC enquiries, as Britain's economic recovery continued, employment increased steadily and unemployment fell. There has been much debate over the extent to which the quantity of employment has really increased, and likewise as regards the decline in unemployment, but the trends are not in dispute. By 1988 public opinion was sensitive to the turn-around in the demographic tide with the size of school-leaving cohorts having begun a decline which must continue until the mid-1990s. There was concern over an impending shortage of new entrants, especially the better-qualified (National Economic Development Office, 1988). The education and health services, financial institutions and high technology manufacturers were wondering where they would all find enough recruits suitable for training. The ESRC enquiries were designed to distinguish the new routes into the labour market that had been created during the

* The research on which this chapter is based is supported by the Economic and Social Research Council. The views expressed are solely the authors' and are not necessarily shared by other researchers on the 16–19 Initiative.

spread of unemployment, and to investigate the effects of their loss of producer-roles on 16–19 year olds' economic and political socialization. When completed, the evidence will reveal how young people have fared during a period of rising demand for labour.

The core research in the 16–19 Initiative comprises longitudinal studies of representative samples of young people from four parts of Britain — Kirkcaldy, Liverpool, Sheffield and Swindon (see Bynner, 1987). These areas were deliberately chosen for their contrasting economic histories and recent labour market conditions. Two cohorts have been investigated. The younger subjects were in their final year of compulsory education when the research commenced in 1987, while the other cohort was then two years older. The samples have been surveyed by mailed questionnaire on three occasions in 1987, 1988 and 1989, but the findings presented below are from the first two surveys only. A total of 4,874 individuals (82 per cent of the achievable samples) replied in 1987, and of these 73 per cent, 3,468 young people, also responded in 1988. At this stage the samples were boosted with 779 individuals from the same cohorts and areas who were not in the original study, so the total response in 1988 was 4,247.

On a descriptive level, the evidence allows us to assess the extent and ways in which economic recovery and the new demographic trend were transforming the prospects of different groups, with different levels of educational attainment for example, in various parts of Britain. And the evidence can also be interrogated to answer questions raised during the course of the research in response to the new trends, including whether the education and training provisions introduced for 16–19 year olds in the early 1980s were becoming securely locked in place by the end of that decade. Unlike earlier special measures, the initiatives of the early 1980s were not intended as just another set of temporary palliatives. They were designed to last. The intention was ambitious: to transform youth unemployment from a problem into an opportunity to end Britain's allegedly abysmal record in the vocational education and training of young people, and to enable future beginning workers to keep abreast of an expected growth in the economy's skill requirements. If the initiatives were based on a sound diagnosis of school-leavers' transition problems, and if the chosen measures were appropriate, one would expect the new pathways not merely to survive, but to be strengthened by economic revival. However, we shall argue that the continued prominence of the new measures up to 1988 was due mainly to economic revival and the new demographic trend making little impact on young people's prospects in many parts of the country.

Another set of questions arises from criticisms of the conceptual foundations on which the ESRC Initiative was launched, partly on the basis of evidence that has become available more recently. The Initiative was designed with the declared aim of identifying young people's main 'trajectories' from education into the labour market (Bynner, 1987; Roberts, 1987). Subsequently, however, the application of this trajectory concept to 16–19 year olds' movements has become controversial. Furlong and Raffe's (1989) analysis of the Scottish Young People's Surveys which followed the 1984 cohort up to age 19 has cast doubt on the possibility of identifying a limited number of clearly-bounded routes. Similarly, the initial analysis of the 1984 England and Wales Cohort findings has distinguished dozens of routes through the YTS alone (Clough *et al.*, 1988). Young people from the 1984 fifth-form cohort entered this scheme with different qualifications and at different ages, sometimes directly from education but in other cases following spells in work or being unemployed. They remained on the scheme for varying lengths of time, then proceeded to many different destinations in further education, training, jobs and unemployment. Hence the argument is that there is simply too much flexibility in present-day 16–19 year olds' opportunities, and too much variety in their movements, to permit meaningful talk of trajectories with the implication that different groups are somehow propelled along prestructured routes to predetermined destinations.

If 16–19 year olds' opportunities and movements really have become characterized by variety and flexibility, this will amount to a substantial change from the earlier situation in Britain. Until the 1970s, when the majority of 15 and 16 year olds made 'traditional transitions' straight into jobs, the kinds of employment they entered were highly predictable from their places of residence, sex and educational attainments (Ashton and Field, 1976). And the kinds of initial employment that most school-leavers obtained were excellent predictors of the levels of the occupational structure at which they would settle. Our reading of the ESRC evidence indicates that little has changed in these respects : that 16 year olds' routes forward have been restructured rather than destructured, and that trajectory is a highly appropriate concept for analyzing their movements. Even if the new education and training provisions were not historically secure, they occupied clearly-bounded niches in the overall structure of our samples' opportunities.

Main Positions from Age 16–19

Each of the three annual questionnaire surveys asked respondents about their 'main positions' during successive three-month periods. This information does not amount to a comprehensive history of the samples' educational and labour market experiences because only 'main' positions in every quarter were recorded. However, the simplified biographies

Table 6.1   Main Positions at Three-Month Intervals

| Cohort I | | 1985 | | | 1986 | | | | | 1987 | | | 1988 |
	Q2	Q3	Q4	Q1	Q2	Q3	Q4	Q1	Q1	Q2	Q3	Q4	Q1
Full-time education	73	37	49	44	40	25	32	32	36	34	8	23	23
YTS	7	24	27	28	23	21	17	15	11	10	6	3	2
Full-time employment	6	13	13	17	21	30	33	35	35	39	51	53	54
Part-time employment	3	8	4	3	4	8	5	5	2	3	9	5	5
Unemployed	11	14	7	8	10	14	12	14	13	12	19	13	13
Other	—	2	1	1	1	2	1	1	2	2	6	3	3

| Cohort II | | 1987 | | | | 1988 |
	Q1	Q2	Q3	Q4	Q1
Full-time education	90	75	41	55	51
Y.T.S.	2	8	23	25	25
Full-time employment	1	4	13	12	15
Part-time employment	1	2	7	2	2
Unemployed	5	9	12	5	6
Other	1	1	5	1	1

throw the samples' main patterns of career development into all the sharper relief.

Table 6.1 presents the 'raw' results from each cohort up to spring 1988. The older respondents were asked about their situations between January and March 1987 in both the 1987 and 1988 surveys, and the differences between the percentages placing themselves in the various positions on these two occasions are due mainly to a bias in the non-response. We know that in successive surveys the members of both age-groups who continued in full-time education beyond age 16 have become more-and-more over-represented, while other groups, especially those proceeding through the YTS and experiencing unemployment, have become more-and-more under-represented. So the real proportions still in education in spring 1988 would have been significantly lower than in Table 6.1, and the real proportions in other positions, especially un-employment, would have been correspondingly higher. Eventually the Initiative's findings will be weighted to compensate for the bias in non–response. At present, when consulting the raw data to compare the positions of the two cohorts at similar stages in their careers, such as during their first autumn beyond compulsory education, it is necessary to bear in mind that at this point the younger sample had been biased by a double drop-out, whereas the older cohort answered the relevant questions in the first survey.

The main difference between the two cohorts' career development was that the younger respondents were the more likely to have remained in full-time education at age 16. The width of the difference in our raw data will be partly due to the double-drop from the younger sample, but we know that there was a nationwide trend in the late 1980s towards education retaining a higher proportion of 16 year olds. The stay-on rate in England and Wales rose steadily during the 1970s and reached 48 per cent in 1982 before falling back to 45 per cent in 1983 when the YTS became available. However, after 1985 the upward trend resumed, which is reflected in our evidence. It is noteworthy that despite the continuing economic growth, there was no rise between the cohorts in the proportion making direct transitions into employment. Nor did YTS recruitment expand despite the re-launch as a two-year scheme in 1986. The decline in unemployment among 16–17 year olds in our survey areas between 1985 and 1987 was due entirely to the higher proportion remaining in full-time education.

The proportions of both cohorts reporting full-time education as their main positions dipped in the third quarters, the summer vacation periods in each year. Many of the individuals who resumed full-time studies later would have always intended doing so. However, there is independent evidence of the threat of unemployment leading to higher stay-on rates in education (Raffe and Willms, 1989), and we will demonstrate later that some of the post-summer returns by our respondents were due to the individuals' inability to obtain suitable employment. If the summer periods are ignored, the proportion of the older cohort in full-time education can be seen to have declined to just under a half during their initial post-compulsory year, to around a third during the second year, then to just over a fifth. However, as explained shortly, there were considerable differences here by area, as well as according to the qualifications that individuals had already earned.

In both cohorts a minority of the respondents reported main positions outside education during what should have been their final compulsory year at school. There could have been a handful of over-age pupils in the relevant year groups, or some errors in sample selection, but these findings may be regarded as corroborating anecdotal evidence of persistent truancy among a minority of secondary school pupils, and of some under-age teenagers succeeding in obtaining jobs and YTS places.

The proportion of the older cohort on the YTS rose to a peak of 28 per cent during the winter after they completed their compulsory education then declined gradually. The YTS was normally a one-year scheme when this cohort entered. Some who were on the scheme during their second year beyond compulsory schooling were late-entrants, but others were taking advantage of the 'bolt-on' periods that were already available in some areas. How had some managed to survive on the scheme another year on? Some of the 2 per cent from the older cohort who reported that they were still on the YTS in spring 1988 may, in fact, have been on other schemes such as the Community Programme. Our 1989 survey distinguishes between different kinds of schemes. However, some of the older cohort who reported that they were still on YTS in 1988 will be further examples of education and training provisions never working quite as tidily as their regulations suggest.

The percentage of the older cohort in employment rose sharply during each summer period, and more slowly throughout the intervening months to reach 54 per cent at the time of the 1988 survey. Even at this stage in their lives, when those who had remained in education had already completed two years in sixth forms or at colleges, only just over half the cohort was in employment. The proportion in full-time jobs remained beneath the combined total of those unemployed and on the YTS throughout the first year following compulsory schooling, after which employment became the most common position of all who had left full-time education.

The proportion in part-time employment rose to 8 and 9 per cent during each summer vacation period, but otherwise fluctuated around 5 per cent. This low figure may be treated as confirmation that out-of-school teenagers have made only slight inroads into Britain's expanding part-time labour markets. As explained below, however, the proportions in part-time jobs varied between socio-demographic groups, and while part-time work accounted for less than 10 per cent of all 'main position' employment, it could be more meaningful to talk of around a quarter of all who would otherwise have been unemployed having taken part-time jobs.

The level of unemployment peaked during each summer period, but otherwise rose to 10 per cent during the older cohort's first year beyond compulsory education, then fluctuated between 12 and 14 per cent. Of course, there were variations within the sample, and we will demonstrate below how the apparent scale of unemployment can be varied considerably according to how the rate is calculated.

Unequal Opportunities

The best predictors of the positions our respondents would occupy after age 16 were their educational qualifications and where they lived. Sex also made a difference which will be understated in the evidence currently being presented since males and females differ not so much in their likelihood of remaining in some form of post-compulsory education, entering the YTS, or obtaining employment as in the kinds of courses they take, and the occupations for which they are trained and subsequently enter. However, it is well-known that girls are marginally the more likely to remain in full-time education after age 16, though this does not result in more females obtaining the qualifications required for higher education since their lead is primarily on vocational courses. The vocational qualifications that girls tend to aim for, especially in office work,

Table 6.2   Older Cohort

	Autumn 1985		Spring 1987		Spring 1988	
	Males	Females	Males	Females	Males	Females
Education	46	52	28	34	23	21
YTS	27	27	14	13	2	1
Full-time jobs	16	11	40	34	54	54
Part-time jobs	4	4	1	4	4	7
Unemployed	7	6	16	16	15	14
Other	1	—	1	1	3	4
	100	100	100	100	100	100

Spring 1988 Occupations

R/G Classes	Males	Females
1.	2	1
2.	12	12
3a.	26	55
3b.	30	9
4.	26	23
5.	4	2
	100	100
(N)	(570)	(600)

are better-recognized when employers recruit from external labour markets than most other 'non-academic' credentials (Raffe, 1990). Among our older cohort, there were more females in education, and more males in jobs throughout the two years immediately following compulsory schooling, after which these sex differences disappeared (see Table 6.2). So the principal difference between the sexes' main positions at age 18–19 was that a higher proportion of the females were then in part-time jobs. However, there were considerable differences between the kinds of occupations in spring 1988 that the males and females in employment had entered. More than twice as many females were in lower-level non-manual occupations, while three times as many males were practising or being trained for skilled manual jobs (see Table 6.2).

There were clear and persistent differences when respondents were divided according to their educational attainments (see Table 6.3). The better their qualifications at age 16, the greater the likelihood of individuals remaining in full-time education for one further year, then another, and then beyond. The overwhelming majority of the best-qualified quartile in our older cohort, 87 per cent, entered some form of full-time post-compulsory education. Only a small minority left at age 16. According to our evidence, Britain's pool of such well-qualified 16 year olds who are available for immediate employment has become very small. Correspondingly, only a small minority of the least-qualified quartile, just 17 per

Table 6.3   Older Cohort: Main positions by Educational Attainments at 16-plus

	Autumn 1985 Ed. Quals*				Spring 1987 Ed. Quals*				Spring 1988 Ed. Quals*			
	1	2	3	4	1	2	3	4	1	2	3	4
Education	17	32	57	87	4	12	30	70	3	4	15	49
YTS	40	42	26	6	18	20	14	3	4	2	1	1
Full-time jobs	20	17	13	6	36	44	45	23	48	69	67	41
Part-time jobs	3	1	1	—	5	4	2	1	9	5	5	3
Unemployed	19	7	2	1	37	19	9	2	34	16	9	4
Other	1	1	—	—	1	2	2	1	3	3	3	3

*Educational qualifications
  1 : bottom quartile
  4 : top quartile

Occupations: Spring 1988 Ed. Quals*

R/G Classes	1	2	3	4
1.	1	1	—	2
2.	5	6	17	18
3a.	26	37	38	57
3b.	22	25	20	8
4.	38	28	23	13
5.	8	3	2	1
n =	153	233	281	246

cent, remained in post-compulsory education for even one year. During the older cohort's second post-compulsory year, 70 per cent of the best-qualified quartile remained full-time students, whereas by this stage very few from the less-qualified half of the age-group were still in full-time education. Even another year further on, when the majority of those concerned had taken A-levels or Highers, 49 per cent of the best-qualified were continuing as full-time students.

Needless to say, the members of the best and least-qualified quartiles who stayed-on had tended to take different post-compulsory courses. The key distinction here is probably according to whether young people remain in the academic mainstreams taking the A-levels in England or the Highers in Scotland that will qualify them for higher education. Among all those in the older cohort who remained in full-time education for at least one post-compulsory year, almost exactly a half were still studying for, or had already obtained such mainstream academic qualifications another year on. Staying-on to obtain such qualifications was not only most common among the best-qualified. These 16 year olds rarely stayed-on to take any other courses, whereas when the less-qualified did remain in post-compulsory education it was usually to take courses outside the academic mainstreams (see Roberts and Parsell, 1989a).

Qualifications earned by age 16 proved excellent predictors of the samples' likelihood of remaining in full-time education and the types of courses they would take, and also of their chances of obtaining employ-

Table 6.4   Older Cohort

| | Autumn 1985 | | | | Spring 1987 | | | | Spring 1988 | | | |
	Sw	Sh	L	K	Sw	Sh	L	K	Sw	Sh	L	K
Education	45	40	47	61	33	29	28	32	15	21	22	29
YTS	18	38	34	21	3	14	18	18	—	1	1	4
Full-time jobs	28	10	8	6	52	31	30	34	73	50	45	48
Part-time jobs	5	2	2	4	2	4	3	2	4	7	7	3
Unemployed	3	10	9	4	9	21	20	14	4	18	22	13
Other	1	—	—	1	1	1	1	1	3	3	4	3

Types of education

Higher		9	15	10	19
Other		7	6	12	10

Types of employment
R/G Classes

1.	2	1	1	1
2.	14	10	10	13
3a.	40	38	48	37
3b.	18	20	21	18
4.	23	28	18	28
5.	2	3	1	4
n =	372	285	234	279

ment and avoiding unemployment whether they entered the labour market at age 16 or later, and whether they sought jobs immediately or proceeded through the YTS. Unemployment, needless to say, was highest among the least-qualified. The vast majority from the best-qualified quartile who had entered the labour market by spring 1988 were in employment. Indeed, at this stage in their careers the proportion from this entire qualification-band that was in employment, 41 per cent, was not far short of the 48 per cent among the least-qualified, most of whom had completed full-time education over two years previously. There were huge differences in the unemployment rates of groups with different levels of qualifications. The maximum rate of unemployment recorded among the best-qualified quartile outside summer vacation periods was just 4 per cent, whereas over a third of the least-qualified were unemployed from the point when rates of joblessness rose as youth training was completed until the occasion of our spring 1988 survey.

Needless to say, the better-qualified respondents had tended to obtain the higher-status jobs (see Table 6.3). The better their qualifications, the greater their likelihood of entering non-manual employment. The best-qualified quartile was under-represented in all types of manual employment, while the least-qualified was over-represented in the non-skilled grades.

Where they lived made a huge difference to the samples' prospects whatever their qualifications, but especially for the less-qualified. The stay-on rate in full-time education was highest in Kirkcaldy (see Table 6.4). At age 16 this would have been partly due to the relatively large number of Scottish pupils who complete the fourth year prior to reaching the statutory leaving age (see Raffe and Courtenay, 1988). By the second post-compulsory year Kirkcaldy's stay-on rate had fallen to roughly the same level as in the English areas. However, a much larger proportion of the Kirkcaldy sample, 29 per cent against 15 to 22 per cent elsewhere, were continuing in full-time education another year on. This was mainly due to the larger numbers in Kirkcaldy who had entered higher education (19 per cent compared with 9 to 15 per cent in the English areas). Scottish and English secondary schools prepare their pupils for entirely different examinations. Scottish Ordinary Levels are normally taken at age 15–16, like GCSEs in England, but thereafter Scottish students can take up to five Highers in just one further year, then proceed immediately to higher education. However, students in Scotland may spend more than a single year studying for Highers, and may enter higher education with passes in less than five subjects. Our evidence suggests that the more flexible Scottish examinations allow a higher proportion of young people to remain in the academic mainstream. In England this usually depends on obtaining sufficient passes in appropriate grades at 16-plus to complete at least two, and preferably three A-levels within another two years.

The differences in average attainments and stay-on rates between the English areas are interesting. The Swindon sample come from the most privileged home backgrounds in terms of parental occupational status. So it is unsurprising that the Swindon sample was also the best-qualified at age 16 (see Roberts and Parsell, 1989a). Within all areas, remaining in education, especially in the academic mainstream, was related to qualifications already obtained, and to social class backgrounds. However, among the English areas Liverpool had the highest overall stay-on rate at 16, and both Liverpool and Sheffield maintained clear leads over Swindon in enrolments in full-time education (22 and 21 against 15 per cent) up to spring 1988, when those who had proceeded down the academic mainstream at the normal pace were in their first year of higher education.

Young people's likelihood of proceeding to the next stage of post-compulsory education at age 16 or 18 has always depended on their previous attainments. However, during recent years it has also depended on the levels of unemployment in their areas (see Raffe and Willms, 1989). The relatively high enrolment rate in full-time education in Liverpool at age 18–19 was not due to the local schools' success in preparing pupils for higher education. At this age there were more full-time Liverpool students outside than in higher education (see Table 6.4). We have no doubt that many of these young adults would have been in employment, had jobs been easier to obtain locally.

Our evidence suggests that young people's progress in education beyond age 16 depends partly on the provisions of their local education authorities. Whether post-compulsory students were being catered for in schools or colleges appeared to be making less difference to our samples' progress than the kinds of courses that were available in their home areas. In Sheffield post-compulsory education seemed to be geared closely to A-levels, and at age 18–19 this city had a higher proportion of its sample in higher education than either Liverpool or Swindon. Liverpool and Kirkcaldy appeared to be making more full-time provisions outside the academic mainstreams than either Swindon or Sheffield, and were retaining far higher proportions of the post-compulsory age-group on 'other' courses.

Apart from rates and types of educational participation, the other glaring difference between the areas was that Swindon's young people were the most likely to be employed. This was the case in both cohorts, and within the older cohort at age 16, 17, and 18–19. In Swindon 28 per cent of the older sample were already in employment by the autumn following completion of the fifth form. The number of 16 year olds who made 'traditional transitions' in Swindon vastly exceeded entrants into the YTS. In all the other areas, in contrast, far more 16 year olds went into the YTS than into employment. Living in Swindon was proving an advantage in the job market whenever individuals entered, at age 16 or later, and whether they sought jobs immediately on leaving education or after passing through the YTS. Sheffield had the highest YTS intake at age 16, but had a lower proportion of the age-group on the scheme eighteen months later than either Liverpool or Kirkcaldy. The most likely explanations are in terms of the greater need for, and availability of bolt-on second year places in Liverpool, and the higher stay-on rate in education leading to more late-entries to the YTS in Kirkcaldy.

Swindon had the lowest unemployment, while Sheffield and Liverpool had the highest rates at all ages. Kirkcaldy stood midway, not because its young people were more likely to be employed than in Sheffield and Liverpool, but on account of their higher stay-on rate in education. It is interesting that the areas with the highest unemployment, Liverpool and Sheffield, also had the highest proportions in part-time jobs, indicating perhaps that these were not taken in preference to full-time jobs so much as to avoid unemployment.

There were inter-area differences in the types of jobs that the samples had entered, presumably reflecting differences in the local employment opportunities for beginning workers. By spring 1988 Swindon and Kirkcaldy had higher proportions of their 18–19 year old employees in upper and intermediate-level non-manual occupations (16 and 14 per cent respectively) than either Sheffield or Liverpool (11 per cent in both these areas). Liverpool had the highest proportion in the lower non-manual grades (48 per cent of all jobs compared with 37–40 per cent elsewhere). There was little difference between the areas' proportions of employment

Table 6.5   Main position October–December 1985

Jan–March 1987 Main position	Full-time job	Unemployed	YTS	Full-time education
Unemployed	3	62	32	23
YTS	1	9	—	—
Education	2	1	—	—
Full-time job	90	18	66	69
Part-time job	1	5	2	8
Other	2	5	—	—
n =	167	66	247	191

Spring 1988				Left after 1 post-compulsory year	Later
Unemployed	8	50	20	14	16
YTS	—	—	—	—	—
Education	1	1	—	—	—
Full-time job	86	34	74	81	76
Part-time job	2	13	6	5	7
Other	2	—	—	—	—
	168	64	315	201	217

Types of employment
Spring 1988

All with YTS experience

R/G Classes					
1.	2	—	1	1	1
2.	17	10	9	12	16
3a.	25	19	39	57	50
3b.	29	26	23	15	10
4.	25	35	26	23	21
5.	3	10	4	2	1
n =	149	31	402	189	248

in skilled manual occupations (18–21 per cent everywhere), but Kirk-caldy and Sheffield had higher proportions in non-skilled jobs (32 and 31 per cent) than either Liverpool (19 per cent) or Swindon (25 per cent).

Career Routes from Age 16 to 19

In addition to analyzing how the samples' chances of reaching different destinations varied according to their educational qualifications, gender, and where they lived, our evidence allows us to plot the routes that they followed, and assess the extent to which different groups' future prospects were affected by where they placed their first steps after completing the fifth form in England and the fourth year in Scotland. Table 6.5

groups the total sample according to their main positions during autumn 1985, separating those who made successful 'traditional transitions' straight into regular jobs, those who were unemployed, those who had entered the YTS, and those who were continuing in full-time education. The table then gives the proportions from each of these groups who had progressed to various positions fifteen months later between January and March 1987, then another fifteen months further on in spring 1988. For those who were in full-time jobs and unemployed during autumn 1985, everyone's positions at the later points in time are included, whereas only those who had left the YTS or full-time education then entered the labour market are in the percentages. So the clearest direct comparisons in Table 6.5 are between those who had left full-time education and had either obtained jobs or remained unemployed in autumn 1985 on the one hand, and those who were then continuing in education or who had entered the YTS on the other.

There are two striking contrasts in Table 6.5. One is between the outstanding success not only in retaining employment, but also in the quality of the jobs entered by the young people who made successful traditional transitions, and the acute difficulties that those unemployed in autumn 1985 had obviously experienced in attempting to break into any employment. Of all those who had obtained jobs in autumn 1985, 90 per cent and 86 per cent respectively were still in full-time employment fifteen and thirty months further on. At every point in the entire cohort's career development for which we have information, that is, up to age 18–19, the young people who made successful traditional transitions had higher employment rates than any other groups, including those who progressed through the YTS or post-compulsory education before entering the labour market. Moreover, the quality of the jobs held at age 18–19 by the young adults who made successful traditional transitions at age 16 compared favourably with the occupational attainments of all the other groups. In spring 1988 the former had the highest proportions of employees in upper and intermediate non-manual plus skilled manual occupations. According to our evidence, during the late 1980s employers were continuing to recruit 16 year olds jobs at all levels in their workforces. Those 16 year olds who were able to make, and who embarked on successful traditional transitions may have received less 'systematic training' than those who proceeded through the YTS, and they may have been less successful in obtaining further 'recognized qualifications' than those who remained in full-time education, but the former were not being excluded from 'good jobs'.

In stark contrast, the 16 year olds who tried to make traditional transitions at age 16 but were unsuccessful — those who quit full-time education and did not enter the YTS even though they failed to obtain jobs during autumn 1985 — continued to face severe difficulties in obtaining any employment throughout the next thirty months. Just 18 per cent were in full-time jobs early in 1987, and only 34 per cent by spring 1988. Moreover, the quality of the employment of those who obtained jobs was inferior to the groups' who followed all the other routes. Forty-five per cent of the jobs held in spring 1988 by individuals who began their working lives in unemployment were non-skilled, compared with no more than 30 per cent in any other group.

The second direct and informative contrast in Table 6.5 is between individuals who remained in post-compulsory education after age 16 and those who entered the YTS. The evidence in Table 6.5 shows that on eventually entering the labour market those from post-compulsory education had the higher employment rates and the lower unemployment rates early in 1987 and again in spring 1988. However, there were even more glaring differences in these groups' types of employment. The post-compulsory students were the more likely to have obtained white-collar jobs, particularly lower-level non-manual occupations, and were less likely to have entered skilled manual employment than individuals who followed any other career routes. According to our evidence, during the late 1980s remaining in full-time education beyond age 16 was still tending to mean forgoing the chance of craft apprentice or equivalent training. The YTS was much more likely to lead to this type of employment. However, the post-compulsory students were just as likely as to have ended up in non-skilled manual jobs as individuals who passed through the YTS and those who made successful traditional transitions into employment at age 16.

Table 6.6 contains the same information as Table 6.5 except that this time the groups occupying each position in autumn 1985 — employment, unemployment, YTS and education — are sub-divided according to their educational attainments at that time. This enables us to check, for example, whether the overall superior employment chances of the young people who stayed in full-time education vis-à-vis those who progressed through the YTS were due wholly or partly to the former's better qualifications already held at age 16, and whether the continuing difficulties of those who began their working lives in unemployment were due to their lack of credentials.

Qualifications already possessed at age 16 were related to individual's chances of progressing to employment whether they started out unemployed, on the YTS, or as post-compulsory students. With qualifications already held taken into account, the clear advantage of post-compulsory education against the YTS route disappears. In general, those who passed through the YTS were the quickest to obtain employment, but by age 18–19 their lead had disappeared. By then the educational route was leading to the better employment chances for the less-qualified, and the YTS for the better-qualified prior to entry. Also, with entry qualifications held constant, the differences between the types of employment obtained following post-compulsory education and youth training

Table 6.6   Main positions October–December 1985

Educational Attainments	Unemployed		Full-time job			
	Bottom quartile	Other	Bottom quartile	2	3	Top quartile
Positions in Jan–March 1987						
Unemployed	74	46	6	4	2	–
YTS	3	18	–	4	–	–
Education	–	4	–	–	4	8
Full-time job	13	25	94	92	89	87
Part-time job	8	–	–	–	4	–
Other	3	7	–	2	2	4
n =	38	28	35	51	55	23

Educational Attainments	YTS				Education			
	Bottom quartile	2	3	Top quartile	Bottom quartile	2	3	Top quartile
Positions in Jan–March 1987								
Unemployed	49	28	20	24	52	24	25	7
YTS	–	–	–	–	–	–	–	–
Education	–	–	–	–	–	–	–	–
Full-time job	44	71	80	76	34	65	70	86
Part-time job	7	–	–	–	14	11	5	7
Other	–	–	–	–	–	–	–	–
n =	68	94	61	21	23	37	73	56

Table 6.6   (Continued) Main positions October–December 1985

Educational Attainments	Unemployed		Full-time job			
	Bottom quartile	Other	Bottom quartile	2	3	Top quartile
Positions in Spring 1988						
Unemployed	60	38	17	12	4	—
YTS	3	—	—	—	—	—
Education	—	3	—	—	2	4
Full-time job	23	48	83	84	87	91
Part-time job	14	10	—	2	5	—
Other	—	—	—	2	2	4
n =	35	29	36	51	55	23

Types of employment, Spring 1988	Unemployed		Full-time job			
R/G Classes						
1.	—	—	4	2	—	4
2.	—	18	7	7	19	39
3a.	14	24	14	26	23	44
3b.	14	35	21	42	29	13
4.	57	18	43	23	27	—
5.	14	6	11	—	2	—
n =	14	17	28	43	52	23

Table 6.6 (Continued) Main positions October–December 1985

Educational Attainments	YTS				Education			
	Bottom quartile	2	3	Top quartile	Bottom quartile	2	3	Top quartile
Positions in Spring 1988								
Unemployed	40	19	6	4	32	15	17	10
YTS	—	—	—	—	—	—	—	—
Education	—	—	—	—	—	—	—	—
Full-time job	49	77	88	96	65	76	77	84
Part-time job	11	4	6	—	3	9	6	6
Other	—	—	—	—	—	—	—	—
	n = 85	123	83	23	31	78	140	168

Type of Employment Spring 1988	YTS				Education			
R/G Classes								
1.	2	2	—	—	—	—	—	3
2.	9	5	17	15	4	7	18	16
3a.	25	42	38	55	31	41	42	59
3b.	22	22	25	15	27	18	14	7
4.	36	25	21	10	39	34	23	14
5.	7	5	—	5	—	—	3	1
	n = 59	101	77	20	26	73	141	197

disappear. Among the groups who followed each of these routes, the better their initial qualifications, the greater the individuals' chances of proceeding into non-manual jobs, and the lower their chances of entering non-skilled manual occupations.

Those who embarked with good qualifications were more likely to have escaped from early unemployment than the unqualified and poorly-qualified. And when the former did escape they tended to obtain the better jobs. Individuals who made successful traditional transitions into jobs at age 16 had generally remained in employment irrespective of their prior educational attainments, but these were strongly related to their types of employment. In Spring 1988, 87 per cent from the best-qualified quartile who made successful traditional transitions and were in any employment, held non-manual jobs, while 75 per cent of the least qualified's jobs were manual occupations. However, the overall success of the group who made successful traditional transitions in terms of avoiding unemployment and the quality of their employment was in no way due to their being particularly well-qualified. Indeed, at age 16, on average, they were far less-qualified than respondents who stayed on in education, and slightly less-qualified than YTS entrants.

Poor qualifications had remained a handicap whichever routes individuals took at age 16. Poorly-qualified respondents who obtained jobs at age 16 were the most successful in avoiding future unemployment, but only at the expense of entering jobs of generally inferior quality to those obtained by young people with equally poor qualifications at age 16 who proceeded through the YTS or into post-compulsory education. According to our evidence, which steps forward they took at age 16 had made the greatest difference over the next three years to the labour market prospects of the least-qualified

Well-qualified 16 year olds had good employment prospects whether they sought jobs immediately, proceeded through the YTS, or through post-compulsory education. In general, qualifications held at age 16 were very good predictors of the sample's prospects. If the well-qualified quit education at age 16 and experienced early spells of unemployment, their educational attainments increased their likelihood of escaping from the predicament. By age 18–19, the employment rates of well-qualified respondents who had been through the YTS or post-compulsory education equalled those of the group who made successful traditional transitions. But the latter had not been overtaken either in their employment rate, or their quality of employment.

This is a highly significant finding. Some of the unskilled jobs occupied by our 18–19 year olds who left full-time education after one or two post-compulsory years will no doubt prove temporary stations. In time the occupational attainments of these groups may pull well ahead of the young adults who obtained jobs at age 16. However, a plain fact of the shorter-term situation was that many young people who opted for the

YTS and post-compulsory education derived no immediate returns on their sacrifices and investments, if they could have obtained regular jobs at age 16. So when 16 year olds have the option of immediate employment, embarking on further education or youth training will be risky strategies, especially for the better-qualified. Additional passes in examinations that are normally taken at age 16 can be devalued by the extra time spent earning them (Roberts *et. al.*, 1987). So-called vocational qualifications often carry little weight when employers recruit from external labour markets. Of course, this varies from employer to employer, and may depend on the qualifications. Certificates in office skills seem to be a definite asset, whereas the vocational returns that can be expected from general-level BTECs and lower-grade City and Guilds certificates, not to mention the Certificate of Pre-Vocational Education, are far less certain (Raffe, 1989; Roberts *et. al.*, 1987).

Out of Recession?

The 'raw' unemployment figure of 22 per cent among our older Liverpool respondents in spring 1988 (see Table 6.4) is an extremely conservative estimate of the real level of joblessness. Three or four per cent should be added to take account of selective non-response. It can also be argued that the 1 per cent who were still on training schemes, and the extra numbers in part-time jobs and non-advanced further education compared with Swindon, should really be added to the Liverpool total who would have been in full-time paid occupations, had any been available. These adjustments bring the proportion of the 18–19 age-group in Liverpool estimated to be unemployed in spring 1988 to 35 per cent. It can then be argued that the base population used to calculate the unemployment *rate* should not be the entire age-group, but only those in the labour market. With this adjustment, the apparent level of unemployment among Liverpool's 18–19 year olds in 1988 rises to 44 per cent.

Which is the true figure? The blunt truth is that it is really impossible to condense a complicated situation into any single statistic. Even so, no-one is likely to dispute that the local labour market entered by our Liverpool sample remained severely recessed in 1988. Local levels of unemployment had fallen since the mid-1980s, as throughout the UK. We have no reason to doubt that the job prospects of Liverpool's young people were improving during the years leading up to 1988, but only to a level which left 18–19 year olds in the local labour market facing near-evens chances of being unemployed. And the local situations were little better in Sheffield or Kirkcaldy. It would have brought little comfort to these areas' young unemployed if they could have been told that they belonged to smaller proportions of their local age-groups than the jobless earlier in the 1980s. The young adults who remained unemployed in 1988 could surely be excused if they had failed to notice any economic revival.

Since the late-1970s around a quarter of young people in Liverpool have passed into their twenties without establishing themselves in the paid workforce. This build-up of an 'underclass' was continuing in the late-1980s after almost a decade of continuous national economic growth, and despite the new demographic trend. What will happen not if, but when the UK economy is battered by the next recession? Despite the general growth scenario of the late-1980s, in areas such as Merseyside that had become peripheral in the UK economy, less-qualified young people, even those who volunteered for further education or training, were still competing for jobs with excessive numbers of other teenagers, and adults also.

Just 4 per cent from Swindon's older cohort were unemployed in spring 1988. Even after all upward adjustments, the rate would remain a single digit, close to the level now considered full employment. During and following the 1979–81 recession, youth unemployment became a problem throughout Britain. Of course, there were huge regional variations in the scale of this problem, but it required special measures in all parts of the country. Regional inequalities were still vivid at the time of our research and, if anything, had become even more dramatic in so far as economic growth and the new demographic trend, combined with the educational and training measures introduced in the early-1980s, appeared to have all but eliminated youth unemployment in Swindon. By 1988 there must have been many other parts of south-east England where shortages of labour and the diminishing numbers of newcomers to the local labour markets were rightly perceived as the over-riding issues. The situations in Liverpool, Sheffield and Kirkcaldy were not just quantitatively but qualitatively different.

There have been competing explanations for the concentration of youth unemployment among the less-qualified. One suggestion has been that the least-qualified are being left behind and rendered obsolete by economic and technological trends. An alternative view, however, is that beginning workers are arranged in a metaphorical queue headed by the best-qualified who are preferred by employers with scope for choice, and that the least-qualified remain out-of-work only when their local labour markets are too depressed to offer employment to everyone. The near-elimination of youth unemployment in Swindon where economic growth was strongest, and where labour demand was expanding most rapidly, suggests that even the least-qualified still become employable, just as they were in the 1960s, when employers need their services. We are not disputing the persistence of pockets of high unemployment in either Swindon itself, or in other generally prosperous parts of England. Fourteen per cent of the least-qualified quartile in Swindon were unemployed at age 18–19. As in the 1960s, the inability of certain groups to establish

Table 6.7   Main positions by Educational Attainments in Swindon and Liverpool
(Older cohort)

Main positions: Spring 1988	Lowest Quartile	Swindon Ed. Quals		Highest Quartile
	1	*2*	*3*	*4*
Education	—	3	5	34
YTS	—	—	—	—
Full-time jobs	79	84	85	59
Part-time jobs	5	—	6	4
Unemployed	14	7	2	1
Other	2	6	1	3

Main positions: Spring 1988	Lowest Quartile	Liverpool Ed. Quals		Highest Quartile
	1	*2*	*3*	*4*
Education	2	9	20	49
YTS	3	1	—	1
Full-time jobs	35	59	60	36
Part-time jobs	8	7	4	2
Unemployed	51	22	13	5
Other	2	2	3	7

themselves in their local workforces despite conditions of full employment is likely to be due to a combination of a lack of qualifications, their
attitudes and behaviour when in employment, and an inability or unwillingness to settle in any structured situations (Baxter, 1975). Such groups
exist in cities such as Liverpool, but are submerged by the much larger
numbers who are kept out-of-work by a straight-forward shortage of
jobs.

Better-qualified young people's prospects seem far less dependent on
the state of their local labour markets. This is because, wherever they
live, they can continue along the academic mainstreams, maybe into
higher education, whereupon they become part of a national labour
market. If they remain in their relatively depressed home areas, the
better-qualified may have to trade-down, but they will still stand reasonable chances of employment because of their positions at the head of the
job queues. Also, it is young adults who can offer qualifications plus
some work experience who are the most able and likely to migrate
(Furlong and Cooney, 1989; Roberts *et. al.*, 1987). They are the most
likely to be offered jobs elsewhere with rewards that justify the costs of
resettlement. The least-qualified are the most dependent on their local
labour markets in which, as our evidence confirms, levels of demand for
labour still vary considerably.

Comparing the progress of young people with similar qualifications
in Swindon and Liverpool is instructive (see Table 6.7). In all attainment
bands, the Swindon respondents were the most likely to be employed in

spring 1988. In Liverpool the better-qualified half were more likely than in Swindon to have remained in full-time education. Local unemployment would have been among the incentives for those with the necessary ability to stay-on to earn all possible qualifications. Levels of unemployment were higher in Liverpool than in Swindon in all attainment bands, but especially among the less-qualified. In Liverpool only 5 per cent of the best-qualified quartile were unemployed in spring 1988 compared with 51 per cent of the least-qualified. Liverpool's youth unemployment was concentrated among the less-qualified, as was Swindon's, but at a much higher level in the former area. In spring 1988 there was one-and-a-half times as much unemployment as employment among Liverpool's least-qualified quartile, whereas in Swindon there were over five times as many from this same attainment band in employment as were unemployed. The least-qualified young people in Liverpool were the group who would have had the strongest incentive to swap their place of residence, had they been able. In practice, however, poorly-qualified teenagers, with more experience of unemployment than employment, are the group with the least opportunity to migrate.

Trajectories?

From an earlier analysis of this research's 1987 findings (Roberts and Parsell, 1989a), we have already argued that 16 year olds' scope for choice in Britain's education, training and job markets is heavily circumscribed, and that their initial steps forward are highly predictable from their structural locations, especially their qualifications and places of residence. It is true that virtually all 16 year olds now have the option of continuing in full-time education, and that even if they cannot obtain any employment they can usually be offered a choice of training schemes. Or they can 'opt' for unemployment, though without any social security entitlement in most cases since 1988. It is also true that 16–19 year olds move between 'main' positions in a bewildering variety of sequences. Nevertheless, a blunt fact is that the scope for choice open to less-qualified 16 year olds, especially in Britain's more depressed regions, may amount to little more than a variety of ways of postponing their unemployment. Conversely, the well-qualified, especially if they live in the more prosperous parts of the country, can expect decent jobs whether they seek employment at 16, after gaining further qualifications in education, or proceeding through the YTS. The best-qualified have always had the widest range of options, but their alternatives have always been arranged in so clear a hierarchy as to resolve most dilemmas. Very few well-qualified 16 year olds in Swindon had exercised their right to opt for unemployment, or even for youth training. The poorly-qualified's scope for choice, needless to say, does not extend to proceeding along education's prestigious academic routes. Nor had they stood much chance of immediate employment in Kirkcaldy, Liverpool or Sheffield.

In our view, all the connotations of the trajectory concept are realistic. With each successive step beyond age 16, different groups' most likely destinations become increasingly probable. Young people's prospects appear indeterminate only when undue significance is attached to choices that are really inconsequential. It may make less difference to their prospects whether 16 year olds continue in full-time education or enter the YTS, than the particular courses they take if they remain full-time students, or the particular schemes they join if they become youth trainees. Some types of youth training are far more likely than others to lead directly to employment. Employer-led schemes offer the best job prospects. Other schemes are most numerous in areas where labour demand is weakest, and in all areas it tends to be the 16 year olds with the poorest qualifications who are excluded from the better schemes, whereupon their risks of subsequent unemployment increase (Roberts and Parsell, 1989b). Once the appropriate distinctions between different kinds of positions in education and training are recognized, structured links between young people's points of departure at age 16, the next steps that are open to them, and their subsequent employment prospects, are thrown into sharp relief.

A Permanent Reshaping of the Transition?

Our evidence offers no clear answer as to whether the new pathways into Britain's labour markets that were created by the educational and training initiatives of the early-1980s were locked securely in place by the time of our fieldwork. The new routes had certainly become extremely broad. Only a half of the 16 year olds who remained in full-time education took traditional sixth-form courses leading to the credentials normally required for higher education. In Kirkcaldy, Liverpool and Sheffield far more 16 year olds who left full-time education entered the YTS than obtained jobs immediately. Furthermore, by the time that the older cohort became eligible to leave full-time education in 1985, the new routes were attracting better-qualified entrants than some traditional options. The new routes were certainly not just mopping-up the residue.

Even so, our evidence gives three grounds for suspecting that the new routes could be easily undermined. Firstly, the 16 year olds who stayed in full-time education to take 'other' courses were not as well-qualified as those who remained on academic mainstreams, and up to age 18–19 it was impossible to identify any clear and general advantages gained on entering the labour market from qualifications earned after age 16 (see Roberts and Parsell, 1989a). If progress beyond age 16 along

Britain's educational mainstreams that lead to higher education became less selective as a result of reforms in academic curricula and examinations, or if strengthened labour demand led to a wider choice of jobs at 16, 'other' full-time courses could be vacated rapidly. Secondly, the YTS places offering the best prospects in terms of access to subsequent jobs were being used by firms as the initial stages in longer-term training and employment (Roberts and Parsell, 1989b). The bulk of YTS places were not offering this advantage, and could easily be left empty if the option of employment, even in non-skilled occupations, was restored to more 16 year olds. Thirdly, the new routes were carrying the smallest proportions of young people in Swindon, the area where unemployment was lowest. If and when economic recovery and the new demographic trend make a comparable impact throughout Britain, the new measures could be rolled-back rapidly.

Chapter 7

Part-time Employment, Dual Careers and Equal Opportunity

Michael Maguire

Introduction[1]

Traditional theoretical perspectives on the relationship between gender and employment have been criticized for failing to recognize the ways in which gender enters into the organization of production (Beechey and Perkins, 1987; Walby, 1986). Beechey and Perkins (1987), for example, have argued that it is not a matter of contingency that married women dominate part-time employment. Evidence from their study of part-time work in Coventry shows that it was not the case that employers used sex-blind criteria in their hiring practices, or in their selection of people for training schemes, or in their definitions of what constitutes skill or appropriate qualifications — but that they held very definite conceptions relating to gender. Gender, they argue, has been built into the nature of the work.

Davies and Rosser (1986) have outlined a number of ways in which gender is 'written in' to a job. A gendered job, they suggest, is one which capitalizes on the qualities and capabilities a woman has gained by virtue of having lived her life as a woman. Second, a woman's place in an organization becomes forged in relation to their lifecycle stage in a way that a man's does not. Other writers have focused more specifically on the links between home and work. Buswell (1987 p. 81) argues that labour markets which recruit part-time female labour are structured around the assumed dependency of women within a family context. She argues that part-time wages are low because it is further assumed by employers that women belong to a household where the main expenses are borne by a higher wage earner.

The purpose of this chapter is to explore the concept of 'gendered jobs' in relation to women's employment in the Northern Ireland retail trade and to examine the implication of this for the contemporary employment of women. The retail trade epitomizes what Catherine Hakim (1979) has termed horizontal and vertical segregation. On its own retailing is the fifth largest employer of women in Northern Ireland. In 1986 there were 45,500 people employed in Northern Ireland retailing, 60 per cent of whom were women; 12 per cent of the total female workforce. Despite their numerical importance in the industry women are concentrated, however, in the lower paid, lower status jobs while men dominate managerial and professional occupations. Thus, although women comprise 60 per cent of all employees in the industry they provide less than 30 per cent of professional and managerial staff. The extent and intensity of occupational segregation in retailing reflects the wider occupational segregation of women in society (see Martin and Roberts, 1984; Martin and Wallace, 1984).

What is interesting about the retail trade in Northern Ireland, however, is the way sex segregation in employment developed and has been maintained. Until the 1960s in Northern Ireland there were more men than women employed in the retail trade. The large scale recruitment of women in the industry was a response to the competitive pressures within the trade. There was primarily a desire among retail employers to reduce costs (wages) and increase flexibility. Women were specifically recruited to part-time low-paid, low-status jobs. The unequal position of women's employment in retailing is reinforced by the existence of a dual career structure. A structure which divides the bulk of women's shopfloor jobs from the majority of male managerial careers.

The chapter is divided into six parts. Section one examines the changes which have taken place in the organization of work in Northern Ireland retailing since the 1960s. A primary feature of this change has been the pervasive influence of multiple stores and multiple techniques of retailing. The large-scale recruitment of women into the industry was directly connected with attempts by retail employers to restructure the organization of work. The employment of women, especially on a part-time basis, was a key aspect of firms' competitive strategies. The growth of female employment is considered in section two. Section three considers the idea of 'gendered jobs' in retailing and attempts to answer the question as to why women came to dominate part-time retail employment. Sections four and five consider the *structure* of female employment in the Northern Ireland retail trade. It is argued that the industry exhibits a dual career structure. Finally, section six considers the theoretical implications of the data for the concept of gendered jobs and outlines the main policy issues of relevance to female retail workers.

Changes in the Organization of Work

The 1960s saw important changes in the nature of retail businesses and in the organization of work. In Great Britain the period was characterized by the growth of retail multiples whose market share increased from 28 per cent in 1961 to 36 per cent in 1971 (Lewis, 1985). In a highly competitive industry multiple stores — with the emphasis on centralization and innovation — developed major advantages over other forms of retailing. Over the period there was an average increase in store size as multiples developed the successful 'supermarket' techniques of price cutting, no credit, careful presentation and selection of goods and most importantly self-service methods. As a consequence of the increased competition, the period also saw a decline in the number of smaller retailers, co-operatives and local independents (Bamfield, 1980; Lewis, 1985; Sparks, 1983; Alexander and Dawson, 1979).

The rapid expansion of multiple stores was a reflection of the 'methodical' way they approached the retail business, their flexibility and their continued adoption of new forms of retailing (Bamfield, 1980). Particulary important was the introduction of 'self-service' selling. This was a major factor in containing labour costs (Lewis, 1985). Self-service retailing reduced the specialization required previously in shop assistants' jobs (for example, knowledge of goods sold) and reduced the bulk of the tasks to routine shelf filling and till operation (Sparks, 1983). Stores could recruit labour for occupations demanding little or no specialized knowledge and easily acquired skills (Robinson and Wallace, 1973).

The deskilling of the retail labour process facilitated, accentuated and reinforced a further key feature of employment in the period — the growth of female part-time employment. Self-service selling combined with part-time labour eased the problems associated with matching labour with fluctuating daily and weekly trading levels. Much greater flexibility was attained with the deployment of large numbers of part-timers (Robinson and Wallace, 1974; Sparks, 1982; Lewis, 1985). The trend towards larger more concentrated stores, which required less specialized and skilled staff, allowed the substitution of part-time staff for full-time employees. This represented an attempt by retail employers to further reduce labour costs (Pond, 1977).

Between 1961 and 1976 in Britain, total employment in the retail trade fell by 19 per cent. There was however a dramatic rise in part-time employment at the expense of full-time employment (Sparks, 1984). The numbers of full-time female workers, for example, between 1972–5 fell from 5.45 million to 5.42 million; while the numbers of part-time staff increased from 2.8 million to 3.5 million (Sparks, 1982 p. 18). Similar trends in the retail industry also occurred in Australia (Alexander and Dawson, 1979) and the United States (Bluestone and Stevenson, 1981).

In Northern Ireland retail trends have followed closely those of Britain, although more slowly and not to the same degree of intensity. Overall the period from the 1960s to the present witnessed a growth in the number of multiples, a decline in the number of smaller retailers, surburban shopping centres, and increased female participation rates and

Part-time Employment, Dual Careers and Equal Opportunity

Table 7.1   Employment in Northern Ireland Retail Distribution 1950–86

	Men	Women	Total
1960	26049	21520	47569
1962	26953	21953	48906
1964	26355	21870	48225
1966	25218	23317	48535
1968	22366	22900	45266
1970	20936	22017	42953
1972	19110	20590	39700
1974	18750	21700	40450
1976	18960	22150	41110
1978	19570	23770	43340
1980	21000	25710	46710
1982	19760	25720	44890
1984	19340	25510	44850
1986	18090	27290	45380

Source: Census of Employment; data supplied by Northern Ireland Economic Research Centre (NIERC) (1980 SIC).

self-service retailing. In employment terms, Northern Ireland has exhibited very similar patterns to those in Britain. Between 1961 and 1971 total employment in the industry fell by 17 per cent, from 68,359 to 56,497 (Census of Employment). This sharp decline in employment can largely be accounted for by the fall in the numbers of self-employed; a decrease of 18 per cent over the ten years. In this period newly established supermarkets replaced many local independents (NIEC, 1985). The number of employees in the industry fell by 11 per cent.

The Growth of Female Employment

Table 7.1 outlines the main employment trends in the industry between 1960 and 1986 in Northern Ireland. Overall, total employment has remained remarkably stable, declining by only 4.6 per cent over the twenty-six year period.

As can be seen, however, the composition of the labour force changed dramatically. (See Figure 7.1). Between 1960–86 male employment in the industry decreased by 30 per cent from 26,049 to 18,090. In the same period female employment increased from 21,520 to 27,290, a rise of 26 per cent. Until the mid-1960s there were more men than women employed in the Northern Ireland retail trade. In 1959 for example, women represented 43 per cent of the total retail workforce (Census of Employment). By the end of the 1960s women represented 52 per cent of the retail workforce.

The rise in female employment in retailing occurred much later in Northern Ireland than in Great Britain. In 1950 women represented

129

Figure 7.1   Northern Ireland Retail Employment 1959–1986

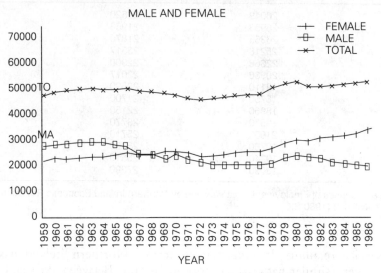

Source: Census of Employment

48 per cent of the British retail workforce, by 1974 this had risen to 56 per cent (Pearson, *et al.*, 1974 pp. 12–13). The increase in the number of female employees in retailing in Northern Ireland did not occur until the mid-1960s.

A second feature of the rise in female employment has been the dramatic increase in the number of part-time workers. Although part-time employment data is not available for the entire period, Table 7.2 gives an indication of change in the 1970s. Between 1971–7 both male and female full-time employment decreased (by 8.4 per cent), although a slight upturn is evident from 1978 onwards. In the seven year period however, part-time employment rose by 47 per cent. The most dramatic increase being in female part-time employment. In 1971, 21,350 women were employed in retailing, 22 per cent of whom worked part-time; by 1978 this had increased to 39 per cent. The trend has continued upwards. In 1984 the Census of Employment recorded that 45 per cent of female retail workers worked part-time.

From the perspective of the retailer the rationale for part-time employment comes from a number of sources. Part-time employment increases the flexibility of the retailer to be able to respond to the fluctuations in weekly and daily trading patterns. Peak trading periods of early mornings, lunchtimes, late afternoons and weekends in addition to the more recent development of late night shopping, must be covered with

Table 7.2   Full-time and Part-time Employment in Retail Distribution 1971–8

	Male		Female		Total
	Full-time	Part-time	Full-time	Part-time	
1971	18580	1070	16650	4700	41000
1972	18020	1090	15870	4720	39700
1973	17570	1240	15780	5800	40390
1974	17250	1500	14780	6920	40450
1975	16710	1820	14340	7940	40810
1976	17140	1820	14070	8080	41110
1977	16660	1760	13800	8280	40500
1978	17780	1790	14460	9310	43340

Source: Census of Employment (1980 SIC), data supplied by Northern Ireland Economic Research Centre.

appropriate numbers of staff. In a highly competitive industry retailers are under constant pressure to reduce costs (labour wages comprising the largest overhead). It now makes economic sense in the retail distributive trade to employ part-timer workers (Sparks, 1981; Sparks, 1982). As stores increase in size so too does the propensity to employ part-time labour (Sparks, 1983).

There are additional factors, however, which need to be considered in the discussion of the development of part-time work. While the above argument represents an economic case for the employment of part-time labour it should not be assumed that such a trend is inevitable. Although the retail trade in many countries (for example, Australia and the United States) has developed along similar lines to that in Britain the pattern is by no means universal. France, for example, has a much lower proportion of part-time workers employed in retailing than Britain. In food retailing there, only 23.3 per cent of the workforce works part-time compared to 44.3 per cent in Britain (Gregory, 1987). The slow development of part-time work in France has been attributed to a reluctance to change work organization by employers and to a reluctance to employ low skilled part-time workers. It has also been attributed to the operation of the social security system and other thresholds which up to 1982 penalized the use by employers of part-time workers (Gregory, 1987 p. 3).

In Britain other factors were important, in addition to the economic arguments, in influencing the development of large scale part-time employment in the retail trade. In particular, changes in employment legislation in Britain further reinforced the trend towards part-time work. National Insurance legislation allows for the differential treatment of groups according to the number of hours worked (Mallier and Rosser, 1980; see also NIESR, 1986 p. 43). Craig and Wilkinson (1985, p. 45) note in their study of pay and employment in the retail trade that the majority of small businesses surveyed fixed their part-timers' hours so that most of them were paid below the level at which national insurance became payable.

Gendered Jobs in Retailing

The question remains as to why women came to dominate part-time employment in the industry. Lewis (1985) argues that the operation of the selective employment tax in Britain (from which employees working less than twenty-one hours a week were exempt) and the raising of the school leaving age to sixteen in 1973, reduced the pool of cheap unskilled labour and increased the competition among employers generally for women's labour. This left retailing:

> ... a traditionally low paying industry, unfavourably placed to compete with the expanding office sector in particular, which paid higher wages to women and was located in the same central city areas. The relative spatial immobility of retailing, reflecting its dependence on close geographical promixity to large markets, led to a situation in which, if the industry was to reduce labour costs and at the same time overcome labour shortages, it needed to secure a particular 'niche' or segment of the labour market which was both relatively cheap and available in large numbers. Part-time married women came increasingly to serve this role (1985, p. 178).

Conventional wisdom in the retail trade concerning the employment of married women refers to a mutually acceptable relationship between employee and employer. As Mallier and Rosser (1980 p. 26) note the 'retail sector has long ago sought to tap the potential labour services of mothers with school age children'. The lower rate paid to many part-timers (see Robinson and Wallace, 1974) was therefore justified on the grounds of a less instrumental attitude to work they were seen to hold:

> Many managers believe pay levels are of relatively less significance to part-time employees than to full-time staff. Pay levels are relevant; but for part-time staff the convenience of the employment, the work environment and the job tasks are of more significance than they are to full time employees (Mallier and Rosser, 1980, p. 27).

Undoubtedly, 'supply-side' factors are important in explaining the growth of part-time work. Among the 100 part-time women workers interviewed for this study there was a strong link between work and the home. The most common reason for taking part-time employment referred to the suitability of part-time working in relation to domestic responsibilities. Seventy-one out of the 100 women part-time workers interviewed stated that they would not take a full-time job if offered one; either with their present employer or elsewhere.

These views have to be considered, however, within the broader context of labour market change and in relation to the jobs available to married women. Evidence from other studies of the retail trade (Gregory, 1977), for example, suggests that in some cases the needs of working women with children were barely given consideration when designing work schedules. Hurstfield's (1977) study of part-time retail assistants found that changing working hours and excessive overtime were very inconvenient for women with childcare responsibilities. Gregory (1987 p. 23) in her study of retail part-time employment in Britain and France notes:

> It must be concluded from the case studies that, while employers had to a greater or lesser extent given consideration to women's needs before initiating changes in working hours or asking for overtime, these aspects of the flexibility in working hours once again almost exclusively benefited the employer.

The growth of part-time jobs in retailing is not therefore primarily a response to demands by women for employment more 'appropriate' to their domestic needs. Olive Robinson (1988, pp. 117–18) has recently argued that:

> When people working part-time represent the sole form of employment growth, as has been the case in Britain for three decades, it seems reasonable to infer that the change in employment structure stems ... from forces originating on the demand side of labour markets as from the socio-economic aspirations which shape the work-hours preferences of married women.

The starting point for part-time employment rests in the desire of the firm to reduce labour costs and to increase flexibility and productivity. In Northern Ireland the rapid increase of female employment was a direct consequence of increased competition in retailing brought about by the changing structure of retail organization. The employment of women (particularly married women) was an essential component of firms' competitive strategy. Women were specifically recruited to low paid low status jobs in retailing.

All of the managers interviewed for this study perceived part-time work as essentially for women. The most frequent reason was that it was seen to suit the domestic responsibilities of married women. Furthermore, one manager commenting on the recruitment of middle-aged female part-time labour stated that employers had a pool of:

> ... cheap, available and flexible labour. These women are not going to be too concerned with their employment rights. For many they are anxious to return to work for social contact. They are often very anxious to please.

The dramatic increase in female retail employment came at a time of — and was directly connected with — considerable change in the Northern Ireland retail trade. A primary feature of this change has been the pervasive influence of multiple stores and multiple techniques of retailing. For example, self-service selling combined with part-time labour eased the problems associated with matching labour with fluctuating trading levels. Women, partly because of their domestic commitments, came to be viewed as a pool of potential cheap labour. First, retail employers felt that part-time work would be more suitable for their domestic situation. Second, the fact that many married women are perceived as contributing a second income to the household economy meant that lower wages could be offered to potential employees, and finally, married women offered employers a more stable and mature workforce. In the early 1970s when a high proportion of young people were employed in the trade it was characterized by a high degree of labour turnover. The trend away from young people to married women in UK retailing is well established (see NIESR, 1986, Maguire; 1989). This was especially the case in relation to the growth of female part-time work.

Managerial Careers and Equal Opportunities

The most significant feature of female employment in retailing is the extent to which women dominate particular jobs. Some indication of the jobs undertaken by men and women in the retail trade can be found in the 1981 Census of Population (Northern Ireland). In 1981 58 per cent of all retail employees were women according to the Census, yet women were under-represented in managerial and professional occupations. As Table 7.3 shows, in 1981, 29 per cent of all retail managers were women and only 24 per cent of professional workers. The majority of women were concentrated in the category of 'other' employees, which comprised mainly sales and ancillary staff.

The Census reveals that 81 per cent of all sales workers in the retail trade were women. Table 7.3 also shows that between 1971 and 1981 there was little change in the occupational profile of female retail employees. In 1981 women remained as they were in 1971, at the bottom of

Table 7.3   Occupational Change in the Northern Ireland Retail Trade 1971 and 1981 (Employees only)

	1971 Male	1971 Female	% Female	1981 Male	1981 Female	% Female
Managers	2102	1125	35	3374	1373	29
Professional workers	155	66	30	251	78	24
Foremen/Supervisors	349	334	49	609	800	57
Family workers	49	58	54	—	—	—
Apprentices	715	99	12	655	28	4
Other employees	11719	19697	63	10219	18893	65
Total	15090	21651	59	15108	21172	58

Source: Census of Population 1971 and 1981 (Northern Ireland)

the retail occupational ladder. In fact the percentage of women managers and professional workers decreased from 34 per cent to 28 per cent in the ten year period. The only significant change in female occupations was an increase in the proportion of female 'supervisors' from 49 per cent of the total in 1971 to 57 per cent in 1981.

The occupational profile derived from the Census has been confirmed by the 1985 Labour Force Survey for Northern Ireland. Of the 240 women employed in retail distribution in the survey, 15.8 per cent were managers or proprietors of retail establishments, 6.7 per cent were in clerical and related occupations, and 59 per cent were in sales jobs. Of the 158 men covered in the survey employed in retail distribution 31 per cent were managers or proprietors, 17 per cent were in sales or related jobs, 10.8 per cent van salesmen/van roundsmen, and 7 per cent butchers and meat cutters.

The results of the PRI Employers' Survey suggest an even greater imbalance in the structure of employment between men and women. The survey found that 64.8 per cent of the 1,822 employees were women; 48 per cent of whom worked part-time. Part-time employees represented 36.8 per cent of all retail workers, 83.7 per cent of whom were women. The most common occupations found in the survey were those associated with 'sales', 56 per cent of all workers were located within this category. The second most common occupational category was that of 'managers', providing 19 per cent of all employees.

The survey once again confirms the important differences in the occupational profile of men and women's jobs in the retail trade (Figure 7.2). Of the 653 men covered in the survey 38 per cent were 'managers', 31 per cent sales staff, 15 per cent 'other' employees (this included such jobs as bakers, butchers, drivers etc....), 7 per cent professional staff, 5 per cent trainees and 4 per cent supervisors. For the 1,169 women in the survey there was a much greater concentration in sales occupations; 70 per cent of all female workers in the survey were located in this occupational category. As Figure 7.2 shows, a further 10 per cent were

Figure 7.2 Occupation of Male and Female Workers in Northern Ireland Retailing

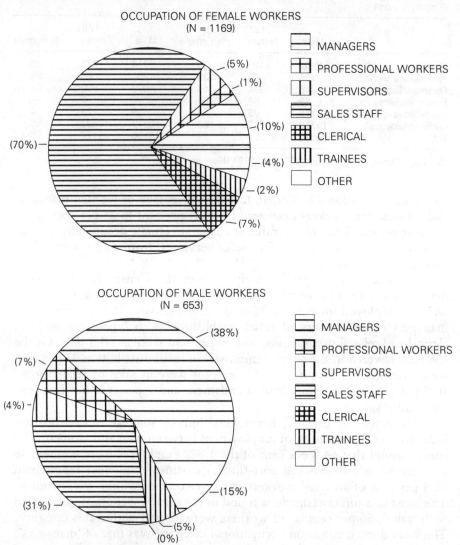

OCCUPATION OF FEMALE WORKERS
(N = 1169)

MANAGERS
PROFESSIONAL WORKERS
SUPERVISORS
SALES STAFF
CLERICAL
TRAINEES
OTHER

(5%)
(1%)
(10%)
(70%)
(4%)
(2%)
(7%)

OCCUPATION OF MALE WORKERS
(N = 653)

MANAGERS
PROFESSIONAL WORKERS
SUPERVISORS
SALES STAFF
CLERICAL
TRAINEES
OTHER

(38%)
(7%)
(4%)
(31%)
(15%)
(5%)
(0%)

Source: PRI Employers Survey

'managers', only 1 per cent professional workers, 5 per cent supervisors, 7 per cent clerical employees, 2 per cent trainees and 4 per cent 'other' employees.

Table 7.4 provides a more detailed occupational breakdown of male and female retail workers from the survey. As can be seen, the most common occupational category of 'sales' was dominated by women, who

Table 7.4   Retail Occupations for Male and Female Employees in Greater Belfast Area

	Male		Female		% Female
	Full-time	Part-time	Full-time	Part-time	
Managers	238	8	115	2	32.2
Professional workers	36	11	15	2	26.5
Supervisors	28	1	53	6	67
Sales	134	67	344	473	80
Clerical	1	—	50	33	99
Trainees	25	9	18	9	44.2
Other	82	13	11	38	34
Total employed	544	109	606	563	64

Source: PRI Retail Employers Survey, 1988.

provided 80 per cent of all sales staff. The majority of female sales workers also worked on a part-time basis (57.8 per cent). This represents a sizeable proportion of the total female workforce employed in retailing. The majority of male sales staff on the other hand were employed on a full-time basis, which implies an important difference in the employment conditions and opportunities of female and male retail workers.

Of the total male workforce in the survey only 16 per cent worked part-time compared to the 48 per cent of female workers. Men dominated the occupational categories of managers (68 per cent male), professional workers (73 per cent male), trainees (56 per cent male) and 'other' employees (66 per cent male). In addition to sales occupations, women were concentrated in clerical jobs (99 per cent female) and supervisory posts (67 per cent female).

It will be apparent from the above profile of women's employment in Northern Ireland retailing that a serious imbalance exists between men and women in terms of their representation in managerial positions. Men dominate full-time employment and are disproportionately represented in managerial and professional occupations. Women, on the other hand, dominate part-time employment and are concentrated in sales jobs.

Explanations for the under-representation of women in managerial and professional positions — among male retail managers interviewed for the study — rested on traditional sexist assumptions as to the role and capabilities of women. Thus the qualities of a 'good' manager (aggressiveness, ambition, drive, competitiveness) were seen to be more suited to men than women. Moreover just as some managers deemed women suitable for some jobs because of their domestic responsibilities (for example part-time sales work) they were felt to be unsuitable for managerial positions because of the same domestic responsibilities (see Maguire, 1989).

The trend within retail employment over the past twenty-five years has been to produce a segmented workforce. Males dominate full-time managerial employment with opportunities for career progression, while women are confined to the lesser skilled jobs, have less access to training and lower earnings (Bluestone and Stevenson, 1989). Sparks (1983 p. 64) commenting on the employment trends within the retail trade notes:

> the rationalization and specialization within the retail structure has led to the polarization of the labour force, with a numerically small band of specialized managers on the one hand, and the larger army of day labourers on the other.

Such trends are apparent in the Northern Ireland retail trade, moreover, they are likely to intensify. As one Belfast manager stated:

> You are going to get two main categories of staff. On the one hand a massive number of largely female part-time workers. On the other hand, a small number of key personnel who make all the decisions.

Evidence for the existence of an internal dual career structure can be found if we examine the system of training followed by some of the larger stores in the industry. Those managers I interviewed confirmed that there was very little movement of staff between the shop floor and management. Training systems had developed which reflected and reinforced the duality of career opportunities. Shop floor staff received, for the most part, training which was job specific. Promotion prospects were limited to that of supervisor (supervising other women) or department manager. The latter might require some specialist knowledge or skills (for example, in the grocery trade knowledge of provisions, meat etc.). While these jobs did carry a degree of responsibility, it was the general opinion of those interviewed that they existed outside mainstream management.

Training for management positions had an entirely separate structure. Junior managers were recruited usually with A levels (aged 18–21), although some firms did recruit graduates. Training was both formalized and 'on the job'. In the case of the latter it was usual company policy to move applicants to a new store with each promotion. In this way the manager received a variety of work experience (with varying degrees of responsibility) in a number of different locations. Management training was therefore entirely independent from that of the shop floor. In some cases experienced female supervisors and sales staff would train junior male management (known as 'the suits' in one store) in their first jobs. Thus the contribution of women workers to the existing managerial structure often went unrecognized by management in a formal way.

The problems facing female retail managers have to be placed, therefore, in a much wider context. For the majority of female sales workers a managerial career is not an option. They have a different set of priorities.

Employment Conditions in Northern Ireland Retailing

The large scale recruitment of women into retailing, as a response to the competitive pressures within the industry, has had a number of implications for the current structure of women's retail employment. As outlined earlier a significant feature of female employment is the extent to which women dominate part-time employment. In 1984 there were 13,598 part-time workers employed in retail distribution (32 per cent of all retail employees), 84 per cent of whom were women. Just under half of the female workforce (45 per cent), according to the 1984 census of employment, worked on a part-time basis, compared with only 15 per cent of males.

In food retailing (the largest sector of female employment), CTNs, footwear, filling stations, and specialized (non-food) retailing there were more women working part-time than full-time. The concentration of women in part-time retail employment in Northern Ireland has been confirmed by other studies. In the 1985 Labour Force Survey 240 women were employed in retail distribution, of whom 48 per cent worked part-time.

The massive growth in the number of female part-time workers generally has given rise to concern over the terms and conditions under which they are employed (Beechey and Perkins, 1987; Robinson, 1988). The PRI survey of 205 women retail employees revealed important differences in the employment conditions of full-time and part-time employees (see Maguire, 1989 for a more detailed analysis). On a wide variety of dimensions the terms and conditions of part-time workers were inferior to those of their full-time colleagues. Part-time workers were, for example, less likely to have itemized pay statements, to be covered by a company sick or pension scheme, to receive pay for unsocial hours, commission and bonus payments. They also had fewer holidays and less training while at work. For part-time workers employed for less than sixteen hours per week (16 per cent of the sample) employment rights are substantially reduced. There did not seem, however, to be any substantial difference in the actual jobs done by both sets of workers; although part-time workers were located within a narrower range of jobs.

The study confirmed the status of retail work as one of the lowest paid sectors in Northern Ireland industry (see Table 7.5). The average gross weekly pay for female workers in the sample was £91.39. This compares with the New Earnings Survey (NI) average for the Distributive Trades of £97.65. The earnings of sales staff were even lower. The gross weekly pay of sales staff in the survey was £80.18 for full-time employees and £45.58 for part-time workers. Although overall averages can be misleading (wages in larger stores were higher than this) 47 per cent of full-time workers in the survey were paid less than £86 per week (gross). The full extent of low wages become clearer when we examine

Table 7.5   Gross Weekly Earnings of Full-time and Part-time Employees

£ Per week	Full-time (%)	Part-time (%)
Less than £30		20
£30–49	7.1	36
£50–69	15.7	32
£70–85	24.3	8
£86–100	28.6	2
£101+	24.3	2
Average Gross weekly pay £	91.39	48.10
Total N	70	50
Average Hours worked	38.54	20

Source: PRI Retail Employees Survey, 1988.

the net weekly pay of employees. The average net weekly wage of those working full-time was £72.23; the amount for part-time workers was £43.07. Out of this amount some workers, in addition, had to pay for travel to and from work, and for meals. In Great Britain, the hourly rate of pay for retail workers (food and non-food) for 1988 set by Wage Councils was £2.33 per hour. A substantial proportion of full-time workers and part-time workers (67 per cent of the total who gave this information) were paid below the legal minimum hourly rate in Britain. The average hours worked for full-time employees was 38.5 while that for part-time workers was 20.

The low wages paid to retail employees in Northern Ireland are significant in the context of present Government attempts to abolish Wage Councils in the province. Retail workers are not covered by Wage Council legislation. It is significant that for many workers in the survey, wages were below the minimum rates set for retail work by Wage Councils in Great Britain. Rather than abolishing Wage Councils, and thus exposing those workers presently covered to lower wages, these findings suggest that Wage Council legislation should be extended to cover retail work in Northern Ireland.

Furthermore, as in the case of other low paid workers there were few opportunities for those interviewed to 'top up' their basic pay. Only 9 per cent of those interviewed stated that they worked overtime regularly; for those that did they were paid at their normal rate for the job. In addition only 10 per cent of those interviewed received commission on goods sold and just under half (48 per cent) did not receive bonus payments.

When questioned as to what they liked and disliked in their present job, very few women, however, stated the low nature of the pay as a problem. Is it the case — as has been suggested in the industry — that women come to work for reasons other than money? For many women in the survey social contact at work, for example, was an important consideration. However, while non-instrumental reasons were important for some women in deciding to come to work (as they are for most people who work) the most popular reason for wanting employment was a desire to earn money. How can this paradox be explained?

To begin with there are gender and class based reasons for the apparent disparity. Daly (1985) notes that working-class women do not have access to an industrial culture and resources to deal with poor working conditions. She argues (1985 p. 69) in the context of poorly paid cleaners that:

> In the absence of such consciousness they tend to use the standards and values of their other major role, that of the housewife, where labour is cheap, if not free, to evaluate their work situation.

If we consider the employment experience of the women in the sample we find that over 50 per cent were not in paid employment prior to taking their present job. Thus their expectations of pay are likely to be lower than if they had been in work. Buswell (1987) also notes the impact of government training schemes in Britain (YTS) in lowering the expectations of young people. They were prepared to accept lower than the going rate for the job as this was still higher than the training allowance paid on YTS. In addition, it is important to consider the type of employment experience of women in the sample. Seventy-two per cent who had been in paid employment had worked in some other form of retailing. It was a case of moving from one low paid job to another.

Finally, a high proportion of those interviewed lived in households with another source of income, thus diminishing the full impact of low pay. For example, 49 per cent of the sample were married, and 84 per cent had husbands who were in full-time employment; also a high proportion of workers were relatively young. When questioned as to their status in the household, 48 per cent of full-time workers said they were living at home and contributing to family income. In both cases living costs were subsidized from another source.

Trade unions were, for the most part, of little relevance or protection to the majority of women interviewed in the study. Seventy-three per cent of those interviewed were not members of a trade union. Those that were were mostly located in the larger stores. This contrasts with the high percentage of workers in smaller stores who did not receive basic employment rights. Only 11 per cent of those who said they had written terms and conditions of employment worked in a single retail outlet. Similarly, less than half of those in single shops received an itemized pay statement. Those workers requiring the most employment protection, therefore, were not members of trade unions.

The retail employees survey also considered the nature of training and job recruitment in the industry. The results once again confirm the low status of female retail employment. One third of the total interviewed did not receive any training for their job. The position was worse for part-time workers; 41 per cent of part-time employees did not receive any training, compared with 27 per cent of full-time employees. The most common form of training received by those interviewed was job specific and unstructured. This training provides an extremely weak foundation for career development.

Finally, the survey also considered the nature of recruitment in the retail trade. Those interviewed were asked how they found out about their present job. The answers were divided between formal sources and informal sources of recruitment. Just over one third of those interviewed (35 per cent) stated that they found their job through formal recruitment channels. The most popular method for full-time employees was through a government training scheme, while training schemes and newspaper advertisements were the most common methods for part-time workers. The most common methods of recruitment for both part-time and full-time workers were informal methods — through a local advertisement, through friends or relatives or contacting the employer directly. Overall, 29.8 per cent of those interviewed contacted their employer directly while a further 29.8 per cent found their job through a relative or friend.

The use of informal recruitment methods — by large and small stores equally — suggests that women's employment exists outside the formal career structure. Firms, by not using formal recruitment procedures further undervalue the work done by women. In addition, the existence of informal methods of recruitment provide some indication of the relationship between employer and employee. In the smaller stores especially, informal recruitment methods may mean that those employed feel under an obligation to their employer. Employment in this context is seen as a personal favour. This is certainly the case in relation to informal recruitment in factory employment (see Maguire, 1986). Once the relationship is personalized employees are less likely to complain about abuses in their employment rights. The widespread use of informal sources of recruitment by employers particularly large retail employers — should give cause for concern within the context of equal opportunity policy. The results point to the relative unimportance of official job markets/employment exchanges as a means of finding employment in the retail trade; only 9.3 per cent of those interviewed found their job through this source.

Conclusions

Gender segregation at work has been identified as the most important cause of the wages gap between men and women in Western economies

(Walby, 1986). More generally, it is one of the principal reasons why sex equality legislation has been limited in its capacity to improve the situation of women in the labour market (Beechey and Perkins, 1987; Trewsdale, 1988). Recent attempts to understand the development of sex segregation have focused on the concept of 'gendered jobs'. Davies and Rosser (1986) argue that a gendered job is one which capitalizes on the qualities and capabilities a woman has gained by virtue of having lived her life as a woman. This paper has attempted to examine the idea of 'gendered jobs' through a study of women's employment in the Northern Ireland retail trade.

What is interesting about the retail trade in Northern Ireland are the processes whereby sex segregation in employment developed and are maintained. Until the 1960s in Northern Ireland there were more men than women employed in the retail trade. From the 1960s onwards there were important changes in the nature and organization of retail work. A primary feature of this change has been the pervasive influence of multiple stores and multiple techniques of retailing. The large scale recruitment of women in the industry was a response to the competitive pressures within the trade, primarily a desire among retail employers to reduce costs (wages) and increase flexibility. Women were specifically recruited to part-time low paid, low status jobs. Retail employment capitalized on the dependence of women in the home, their segregated employment histories, and their relation to the adult lifecycle.

It was clear from the interviews that retail employers had entrenched views on the employment of women in the trade. Just as some managers deemed women suitable for some jobs because of their perceived domestic responsibilities (jobs associated with selling) they were felt to be unsuitable for managerial careers because of the same domestic responsibilities. The unequal position of women's employment in retailing is reinforced by the existence of a dual career structure. A structure which divides the bulk of women's shopfloor jobs from the majority of male managerial careers.

It will have become apparent from the above discussion that equal opportunities policies which focus on increasing the number of female managers in retailing will have a limited impact on the overall employment of women in the industry. Women shop workers have a different set of priorities not the least of which is the nature and extent of low pay in the industry. Furthermore the employment conditions of part-time workers are often inferior to those of full-time employees even when doing the same job. In developing strategies for equal opportunities in the industry action on several fronts is necessary. At a basic level the immediate concerns of women shop workers relate to employment protection, pay and conditions. The equal value amendment will have an impact on those women employed in the larger retail outlets. For women in the smaller stores the extension of statutory protection is required. This finding is disturbing in the context of Government attempts to abolish Wage Councils in Northern Ireland. It is an essential first stage that Wage Council legislation is extended to cover retail workers in Northern Ireland. In addition, it is important that women retail workers receive the protection of trade union membership. Most of the women in the survey were not members of trade unions. It was those women who were most likely to have their employment rights abused.

If the current structure of employment opportunities in the Northern Ireland retail trade continues uninterrupted then little improvement in the long term position of women in the industry can be expected.

Notes

1 This paper is based on research funded by the Equal Opportunities Commission for Northern Ireland. The research was conducted between March 1987 and October 1988 and comprised the following methodology:

a A survey of retail employment comprising an occupational profile of 321 retail outlets and a survey of 205 female retail employees;

b Sixteen semi-structured interviews with retail employers and trade unionists;

c A review of the available statistical information on retail employment in Northern Ireland (including — Northern Ireland Census of Employment, Northern Ireland Census of Population, Northern Ireland New Earnings Survey and Northern Ireland Labour Force Survey);

d A review of the literature relating to women's employment in the retail trade.

As the main part of the project was to rest on the survey of retail employees, considerable time and effort was spent to ensure that those workers interviewed were as representatitive as possible of the retail workforce. A two stage methodology was adopted. Firstly, using the Rating Valuation List as a sampling frame, a survey of 321 retail addresses was conducted. On the basis of the information obtained a second survey of 205 retail employees was completed. The main survey was complemented by a series of sixteen semi-structured interviews with retail employers. For full details on the methodology and results see Maguire (1989).

Chapter 8

Gender and Graduate Under-employment

Tony Chapman

The issue of discrimination in the graduate labour market is particularly topical at present because employers have recently been showing unprecedented interest in the promotion of 'equal opportunities' policies. New initiatives tend to concentrate attention on the provision of special employment arrangements which alleviate the problems faced by 'professional' employees with children. Many companies have established schemes which offer women (and sometimes men) career break schemes so that employees are able to return to paid employment after a period of time bringing up children. Other companies are opening, or assisting employees who wish to set up crèches and playschools, offering women subsidies on childminding costs, and are sharpening up anti-discriminatory practices. These schemes are most commonly aimed at professional employees, given the high cost of retraining new staff. (Berry-Lound, 1990; Hibbert, 1989; Rajan and Van Eupen, 1990).

These policies have been instigated largely in response to an expected shortfall in the number of graduates entering the labour market in the 1990s. Due to a fall in the birth rate, the number of school leavers will fall by between 20 per cent and 25 per cent from 1991–5 (Hibbert, 1989). As Mr John Patten, then Home Office Minister, remarked in 1988 'a demographic time bomb (is) ticking away under employers' (Wintour, 1988). Research by the Institute of Manpower Studies shows that the trends of the early 1980s when graduate supply was higher than demand are likely to be reversed in the next decade (Pearson *et. al.*, 1989). Shortages, it has been demonstrated, will be particularly acute in the output of science, technology and engineering graduates, and it is expected that 'non-traditional' entrants to these courses such as women will be encouraged to study.

This chapter aims to assess the extent to which inequalities of opportunity in the graduate labour market currently exist through an analysis of the early careers of a cohort of graduates after three years in the labour market. It will be shown that women are less likely to obtain jobs with higher grade professional status than men, and that women tend to receive lower salaries. One explanation for this, it will be demonstrated, is that men follow those courses which offer the best employment opportunities. It will also be shown, however, that women achieve less well than men irrespective of their course of study.

Explanations for the apparent 'under-employment' of women graduates will be briefly discussed. These are, firstly, that the *educational socialization* of boys and girls at school tends to shape educational and occupational opportunities and expectations. Second, it will be asserted that anticipated and actual *family responsibilities* affect career orientations while thirdly, the persistence of *workplace discrimination* against women graduates by employers and men colleagues further restrict women's opportunities. To conclude the chapter, recent government and employer policies on equal opportunities will be assessed in broad terms. It will be argued that many of the policies do not challenge the fundamental causes of discrimination, which may mean that current improvements in the employment conditions of women graduates can easily be withdrawn.

The Higher Education and the Labour Market Study

Until recently, the British system of higher education was split into two distinct sectors. The independent sector comprised the universities, while the public sector was composed of polytechnics and colleges of higher education. This chapter reports on graduates from the so-called 'public sector' which was controlled at the time of study by local education authorities. On 1 April 1989, this link with local educational authorities was broken and the funding of this sector is now controlled by the Polytechnic and Colleges Funding Council (PCFC).

Throughout their history, college and polytechnic graduates have been regarded as of lower status than their university educated counterparts (Bacon *et. al.*, 1979). In recent years, however, evidence suggests that the benefits of university education on career chances are narrowing (Hollinshead, 1986; Brennan and Silver, 1986). As a consequence, it is felt that the data presented here on polytechnic and college of higher education graduates can be relied upon to be generally applicable to all British graduates (Brennan and McGeevor, 1988).

The Higher Education and the Labour Market Study (HELM) was funded by the Council for National Academic Awards (CNAA) and awarded to a group of researchers at South Bank Polytechnic and Staffordshire Polytechnic. It was initiated in 1983 to provide longitudinal data on a national sample of over 4,000 1982 graduates. The graduates were selected from 122 courses, taken from thirty-three public sector institutions of higher education chosen on the basis of institutional type and geographical spread. Despite the problems of a reduced sample size by the third wave of the study, the advantages of working on longitudinal data over 'snap-shot' data are clear (Gatley, 1988). In Britain there has been a concentration on 'first destination' statistics which are collected only six months after graduation and before many graduates had entered employment (Tarsh, 1988). Such data provide little indication of the long-term relevance of courses graduates had followed (Brennan and McGeevor, 1988).

The Employment of Men and Women Graduates

The Relationship Between Course of Study and Occupational Status

Evidence of inequalities of opportunity by gender in the labour market is well documented (Martin and Roberts, 1984; Dex, 1985; Bradley, 1989). There has been relatively little analysis of the different patterns of occupational achievement amongst men and women graduates in recent years, however, although there is a growing literature on women in professional employment (Spencer and Podmore, 1987; Silverstone and Ward; 1980). Most studies on graduate employment base their analysis on the relationship between the type of degree course undertaken and occupational outcome. There is indeed a good deal of evidence to support the view that studying certain vocational courses enhances opportunities for obtaining employment with high status, pay, employment security and promotion prospects (Brennan and McGeevor, 1988; Gatley, 1988; Hollinshead, 1986).

The inter-relationship between the course of study and employment outcomes is illustrated in Table 8.1. Four 'types' of course are identified in the table to illustrate the extent of vocational orientation. Brennan and McGeevor (1988) have provided the following definitions of the classificatory schema which was generated by the HELM researchers.

Generalists

These graduates are equipped with general skills and knowledge which are of value to employment but are not especially related to any particular occupational role or employment field. Their degrees may have wide value across large parts of the labour market, but for the graduates the process of seeking, obtaining and becoming competent in a job has only just begun at graduation.

Generalists Plus

In addition to possessing general skills and knowledge, these graduates have certain specialist skills and knowledge applicable to work. There is an element of occupational training in this type of degree and

Table 8.1(a)   Actual and Standardized Percentages of Graduates in Occupational Groupings by Course Type: men

	Higher professional	Lower professional	Row percentages Higher grade technicians	Clerical and supervisory workers	Manual & service workers
Generalist					
Absolute	13.1	36.2	10.0	26.2	14.6
Relative	10.1	30.4	8.1	35.0	16.3
Generalist plus					
Absolute	22.0	17.2	30.6	20.6	9.6
Relative	19.0	20.9	26.6	23.3	10.1
Occupational generalist					
Absolute	28.7	36.6	6.9	21.8	5.9
Relative	24.0	32.4	4.5	28.8	10.3
Occupational specialist					
Absolute	81.3	5.6	1.5	7.1	4.5
Relative	70.9	13.1	2.3	9.7	4.0
All occupations					
Absolute	39.6	20.5	13.6	17.7	8.5
Relative	34.0	22.5	11.4	22.5	9.6

Table 8.1(b)   Actual and Standardized Percentages of Graduates in Occupational Groupings by Course Type: women

	Higher professional	Lower professional	Row percentages Higher grade technicians	Clerical and supervisory workers	Manual & service workers
Generalist					
Absolute	4.7	45.0	7.1	26.6	16.6
Relative	4.3	45.4	6.9	27.8	15.5
Generalist plus					
Absolute	11.8	27.9	30.9	15.4	14.0
Relative	15.8	26.9	28.6	16.9	11.8
Occupational generalist					
Absolute	10.8	56.2	0.8	27.3	5.0
Relative	23.7	45.9	2.0	25.7	2.7
Occupational specialist					
Absolute	40.8	45.1	1.4	7.0	5.6
Relative	51.5	34.2	1.0	7.1	6.2
All occupations					
Absolute	16.7	43.3	10.0	19.2	10.7
Relative	22.9	36.5	12.2	18.8	9.7

the prospect of a closer tie-up between course content and job requirements. However, like the generalist, the generalist plus at graduation has only just started the process of seeking, obtaining and becoming competent in a job.

Occupational Generalist

These graduates made the first step towards a particular job with their choice of degree course. However, their ideas may not have been very precise at that stage, relating to a general field of employment rather than a precise occupational role. After graduation the graduate will still face choices about further specialization or about type of employer. However, from the employer's point of view, the graduate has demonstrated commitment to a broad field of employment and has knowledge and skills of specialist value at work.

Occupational Specialist

These graduates have received a partial training for a job and their degree qualification regulates entry into it. Their choice of career occurs at the point of entry to higher education not after it. After graduation there are likely to be clearly defined steps to acquire full professional status and a job.

When these course 'types' were devised by the HELM researchers, it was not considered possible to identify these boundaries as 'rigid'. Rather, 'They reflect differences in emphasis, moving from fairly loose relationships between courses and employment outcomes to increasingly close ones' (Brennan and McGeevor, 1988 p. 4).[1] From Table 8.1 it is possible to identify a tendency for courses with a substantial vocational content to provide graduates with a greater chance of obtaining higher grade professional work. Although it is clear that women do less well than men, even if they did follow the same type of course.

Considering firstly the absolute percentages of men and women graduates as a whole in each type of employment it is clear that more than twice as many men obtained higher grade professional work than women (40 per cent men, 17 per cent women).[2] The table indicates that a similar proportion of men and women were employed in non-professional employment (26 per cent men, 30 per cent women). Clearly, the differences in higher grade professional work are balanced by the over-representation of women in lower grade professional work (34 per cent men, 53 per cent women).

In order to help disentangle the extent to which the type of course undertaken affects employment outcome, Table 8.1 compares 'absolute' levels of recruitment into each of the occupational status groups, with 'relative' levels. The latter percentages reflect the proportions of graduates who may have obtained each type of occupation should there have been equal numbers of respondents on every course studied. This hypothetical comparison between 'absolute' and 'relative' percentages suggests that about 4 per cent more women and 4 per cent fewer men might have been expected to obtain higher grade professional jobs; and that 5 per cent fewer women and around 4 per cent more men would have obtained lower grade professional jobs. The proportion of men and women in non-professional work is similar, except that about 5 per cent more men may have been employed in clerical jobs.

Although this analytical exercise does not claim to *predict* the impact of equity in course recruitment on occupational outcomes, it does help to show that if more women undertook occupational generalist and occupational specialist courses the proportion of women in the higher grade professions would increase. Perhaps more importantly, these statistics indicate that even if parity were obtained at the level of recruitment on degree courses, a very substantially larger proportion of men would continue to obtain higher grade professional occupations.

Adopting the same principle of analysis for each of the course types identified, it is clear that only amongst the occupational generalists and occupational specialists would parity on courses increase the proportion of women in higher grade professional work. In the case of occupational specialists more than a 10 per cent increase in the number of higher grade professionals might be expected among women, and an increase of over 12 per cent of women occupational generalists.

Although these calculations must be treated with caution, an interesting issue is raised: that it is necessary to begin to speculate whether the relatively low percentages of graduates from generalist disciplines who obtain higher grade professional work might be explained not only by employer's reluctance to offer higher grade professional work to generalists but that employers discriminate against women *per se* — as is the case elsewhere in the labour market.

The Quality of Graduate Work

One of the problems with adopting occupational status scales for the purposes of analysis is that it remains unclear what extra benefits a higher grade professional occupation may offer to graduates. One useful way of identifying such benefits is to consider the salaries of men and women three years after graduation.

From Table 8.2, it is clear that the type of degree respondents obtained had an important impact on salary levels. In general terms, the evidence suggests that generalists and generalist plus graduates were less likely to obtain as high wages as occupational generalists and occupational specialists. It would not be wise to draw too strong conclusions from these data at this stage, however, as anomalies do arise. For example,

Table 8.2   Pay of Men and Women Three Years After Graduation According to Degree Type

Pay	Generalist Men	Generalist Women	Generalist Plus Men	Generalist Plus Women	Occupational Generalist Men	Occupational Generalist Women	Occupational Specialist Men	Occupational Specialist Women
Under £7,000	42.6	41.6	20.7	42.3	11.3	29.6	13.9	38.0
£7,000 to £9,999	39.3	44.0	45.2	38.5	43.3	44.3	45.5	42.3
£10,000 to £12,999	9.8	12.0	24.5	16.2	27.8	20.0	29.9	14.6
£13,000 to £15,999	3.3	1.8	3.4	1.5	9.3	2.6	9.1	1.5
£16,000 and over	4.9	0.6	6.3	1.5	9.3	3.5	1.6	3.6
N =	122	166	208	130	97	115	187	137

(Column percentages)

Table 8.3   Pay of Men and Women Three Years After Graduation: standardized data

	MEN Actual %	MEN STD %	WOMEN Actual %	WOMEN STD %
£7,000 and under	21.5	22.1	38.3	37.9
£7,000 to £9,999	43.8	43.4	42.3	42.3
£10,000 to £12,999	23.8	23.0	15.3	15.7
£13,000 to £15,999	5.9	6.0	1.8	1.9
£16,000 and over	5.0	5.5	2.2	2.3

men generalists and generalist plus graduates were about as likely to obtain jobs with salaries exceeding £16,000 a year. Indeed, men occupational specialists were very unlikely to obtain such a salary after three years in the labour market, although they were much less likely to earn less than £7,000 a year than generalists or generalist plus graduates.

What stands out most clearly from these data is the relatively poor pay of women in comparison with men with the same kind of qualification. Amongst occupational generalists, for example, only about half as many women as men had salaries of £10,000 or more. Indeed, only among generalists were women equally as likely as men to obtain salaries at this level. Given that many fewer women had generalist plus or occupational specialists degrees, and were also over-represented in generalists disciplines, it is useful to standardize these data according to the method used in Table 8.1. Table 8.3 shows that even when these data are standardized, (that is, as if the same number of men and women undertook each course type) women would still be very much less likely than men to obtain the higher levels of pay.

A consideration of salaries is a useful measure of the quality of work graduates do, but it is clear that this should not be the only consideration. Assessing the appropriateness of qualifications for employment is another useful measure of the quality of work. Table 8.4 shows that amongst higher grade professionals the vast majority of graduates (81 per cent men and 87 per cent women) feel that their qualifications are appropriate for

Table 8.4   Perceived Appropriateness of Graduate Qualifications for Current Occupation According to Occupational Status

	Column percentages							
	Higher grade professional		Lower grade professional		Clerical and other non-manual		All graduates	
	Men	Women	Men	Women	Men	Women	Men	Women
Over qualified	13.6	13.1	32.8	31.2	63.2	69.7	26.6	33.4
Qualification about right	81.1	86.9	63.7	66.8	28.1	28.1	68.5	65.0
Under qualified	5.3	—	3.4	2.0	8.8	2.2	4.8	1.6
N =	286	122	262	346	57	89	606	557

the job. Only a relatively small proportion of these graduates feel that they were over-qualified (about 13 per cent of men and women).

Lower grade professionals were much more likely to feel over-qualified. Some 33 per cent of men and 31 per cent of women felt that this was the case. Nevertheless, about two-thirds of men and women lower grade professionals did feel that their qualifications were appropriate, and it seems reasonable therefore, to maintain the argument that lower grade professional work should be regarded, on the whole, as graduate level work.

It is abundantly clear, though, that clerical and other non-manual workers did not consider their work to be appropriate: over 63 per cent of men and 70 per cent of women felt that they were over-qualified.

Although it has been shown that there is a close relationship between job status and the appropriateness of qualifications for both men and women, it is essential not to lose sight of the initial findings of this study — that very few women obtain higher grade professional work in comparison with men. It is surprising, then to note from Table 8.5 that women, overall, seem to be equally confident of achieving their career aims. This may provide some room for optimism for women who do achieve higher grade professional status jobs, although it remains to be seen whether their expectations are the same as men's and, if they are, whether they will be able to achieve them. As the HELM study proceeds, more light may be thrown on this issue — but at present it is a matter for informed speculation.

The Under-employment of Women Graduates: Explanations and Policy Implications

From the data presented in this chapter, it is now necessary to speculate briefly why women graduates are more likely to be under-employed than men;[3] and to assess, in the broadest of terms, recent industrial and

Table 8.5 *Confidence of Getting a Job Appropriate to Qualifications*

	Very confident		Confident		Row percentages Not very confident		Not all confident		N =	
	Men	Women	Men	Women	Men	Women	Men	Women	Men	Women
Higher grade professionals	32.1	31.2	62.4	62.4	4.4	5.5	1.1	0.9	271	109
Lower grade professionals	23.0	21.1	56.1	58.6	14.3	15.8	6.6	4.6	249	304
Clerical and other non-manual	5.5	2.6	52.7	48.1	30.9	39.0	10.9	10.4	55	77
All graduates	25.6	20.4	58.8	57.8	11.2	17.1	4.4	4.7	570	490

governmental policies on discrimination in light of anticipated shortages in the graduate labour market in the 1990s.

Educational Socialization and Choice of Course in Higher Education

There is in existence a great deal of evidence to show that school education helps to channel boys towards the study of scientific, mathematical and technological disciplines while girls are discouraged. (Moore, 1987; Kelly, 1985, 1988) Historical analysis of the curriculum shows that the close gender association with disciplines has been consciously manipulated by educationalists and governments (Dyhouse, 1981, 1984; Burstyn, 1980; Bryant, 1979). The basic philosophy behind gender segregation in subject choice derived from ideological pressures which distinguished between men's and women's adult roles. Men were clearly expected to participate fully in the professional world of industry, commerce, science and government; while women's 'proper' sphere of interest was thought to be household and family.

There has been a number of campaigns since the last war to break down this traditional delineation between male and female subjects, but resistance from parents and teachers, and of course children, has been substantial (Orr, 1985; Kelly, 1985; Griffin, 1985).

Amongst the graduates surveyed in the HELM study, to which this chapter refers, it is clear that traditional demarcation between men's and women's disciplines are maintained:

> Women were more than four times as likely to hold sub-degree qualifications in domestic science or secretarial studies, while men were similarly over-represented in subjects of a predominantly practical orientation such as woodwork, technical drawing, metal work and applied mechanics. More importantly, very strong gender differences occur in pass rates of academic studies. Women were very much more likely to hold qualifications in psychology, sociology, classics, human biology, European studies or languages. Men on the other hand, were more likely to have passes in the hard sciences, mathematics, accountancy, economics, British government, and geology (Chapman, 1989, pp. 91–2)

Although research material on women's under-representation in science and technology disciplines has been available for some time, government policy has consistently failed to encourage more girls and women to opt for these courses in the 1980s — despite severe problems in the recruitment of sufficiently large numbers of qualified students into higher education (Pearson *et al.*, 1989). Given the present government's preoccupation with 'matching' student numbers with labour market needs, (P. Scott, 1988; Moser, 1988; Barnett, 1988), it is surprising that it seems reluctant to take the appropriate steps.

Recent decisions on the national curriculum for GCSE by the former Education Secretary, Kenneth Baker, show that the recommendations on the issue of increased 'compulsory' science education for boys and girls of his own specially appointed advisors have been largely ignored. In broad terms, advisors suggested that more compulsory science should be introduced at GCSE level to meet national needs. However, Mr Baker dropped this idea, which means that boys will continue to dominate in this area.

Further problems arise in response to the Government's stated aim to introduce student loans. The evidence collected in the HELM study on women's employment status and salaries raises serious questions about the advantages of higher education courses for women. Many women consider it to be unwise to use 'top up' loans. According to the Government's stated policy, graduates will be expected to pay back loans provided that they earn over 85 per cent of average earnings. Given that women graduates tend to earn considerably lower wages than men, many women may fall into a kind of 'debt-trap' in the sense that loan repayments may represent a heavier penalty for women than men.

These comments are, of course, entirely speculative. Nobody yet knows how the introduction of a national curriculum and top-up loans will affect graduate employment. Certain contradictions in Government policy are apparent, however, in that sweeping assertions are made about the value of attracting more women into higher education, whilst financial disincentives are actively pursued. Government employment and family policies may further discourage women from entering higher education or graduate level employment given the problems women with children may face in relation to financial and practical childcare support.

Family Socialization and Family Life

Many writers have emphasised the importance of family socialization on expectations about adult roles. (Oakley, 1974, 1981; Sharpe, 1976; Finch, 1984; Finch and Groves, 1983) Child socialization in the family clearly reinforces the pressure on young people to conform to societal expectations. It could hardly be expected that graduates could become immune to such pressures. As a consequence, it is not surprising that graduates behave in socially prescribed ways in their own relationships with partners and children.

Evidence from the HELM study shows that three years after graduation 37 per cent of men and 53 per cent of women were married or living in permanent relationships. At this time only a relatively small proportion of graduates (about 10 per cent of men and women) had actually started a family. However, about a quarter of respondents intended to do so in the near future. Most respondents were married or cohabiting with highly educated partners, but women were more likely to marry men of a higher occupational status than themselves. One consequence of this was that women perceived their career opportunities to be diminished to some extent as their husband's job was likely to be regarded as the 'primary' occupation of the partnership. Indeed, the HELM study shows that married men graduates were more positive about their careers than other men, *especially* if they had a family.

It is clear that having a family was not the only factor which affected married men's and women's career development. The HELM study shows that amongst graduates generally, women were much more likely to take on the bulk of the responsibility for household cleaning, laundry, cooking and childcare. Only in the case of household maintenance was it obvious that men took on most of the work. Similarly, men were more likely to be assisted by their partner in work related tasks — even if their partner was of the same occupational status. (Chapman, 1989, pp. 106–110; see also, McRae, 1989). It is hardly surprising, therefore, that married women graduates considered that their prospects for career development were more limited than single women's and men's. Indeed, some 29 per cent of married women were not very, or not at all, confident about getting a graduate status job compared with only 12 per cent of married men (Chapman, 1989, pp. 111–14).

From these findings, it is tempting to lend support to Finch's view that for many married women:

> Marriage is the most economically viable option ... because a higher standard of living can be gained over a lifetime by being a wife than most women could achieve in their own right. In those circumstances, it may well seem that the most sensible economic option for a wife is to invest her energies in her husband's work, thus promoting his earning potential, rather than pursue her own (1984, p. 152).

Recently developed equal opportunities programmes in industry are now helping to reduce what Whyte (1986) has defined as the 'wastage of womanpower'. But the Government has been slow to realize the importance of easing the burden of family responsibility on women who choose to follow a career. Although ministers are now considering new policies to encourage women to return to work after having children (Smith, 1989; Berry-Lound, 1990), the Government's record has been poor to date. Britain now has the worst record in Europe for childcare provision, and as a consequence, many women are likely to continue to under-utilize their professional skills. Britain remains the only European Community state which does not provide statutory maternity rights for all working women, and very few incentives are provided for working mothers (Hibbert, 1988; Moss, 1988). It must, though, be stressed that even if Government policy was oriented in such a way as to fully encourage women who have higher educational qualifications to pursue careers, it is still unlikely that equal opportunities could be achieved given the deeply-rooted prejudices which continue to persist against women in the professions.

Sex Discrimination in the Professions

There are now very few professions from which women are barred. The fact that women are represented in most of the professions does not, however, necessarily mean that they have been fully integrated. Research evidence shows that despite the existence of sex discrimination law, in most professions women are still discriminated against at the point of recruitment, and in terms of career development (Curran, 1987; Collinson, 1988). Much of the discrimination against women in the professions centres on the commonly held belief among senior men professionals that women cannot, or are not prepared to commit themselves fully to a career because of actual or potential family ties. Women are also often thought not to be as well suited to professional life, and as Kanter (1977) has argued, male professionals accuse women of 'abuse of power', as being 'over concerned with detail', 'jealous', 'personal', dictatorial' and so on. Even more seriously, women are often evaluated first by their 'sexual attractiveness' to men, rather than by their performance as professional colleagues (Spencer and Podmore, 1987, p. 123).

Ironically, if women do behave in the same way as men professionals, they are further criticized. In law, for example, as Spencer and Podmore have shown, 'if they do possess such qualities women show them at their peril. Indeed, the very qualities looked for in men lawyers arouse intense suspicion when encountered in women.' (1983, p. 7)

An important consequence of such attitudes is that women tend to be channelled onto the margins of the professions (Elston, 1977; Spencer and Podmore, 1983, 1987). Because women professionals are excluded from the mainstream of professional life, it is hardly surprising that many feel isolated from their men colleagues.

Although the HELM study did not explore the issue of discrimination against women in the professions in any detail, in a follow up study, based on graduates from Staffordshire Polytechnic, it was shown that discriminatory practices strongly affected women graduates' experience of work. Many women graduates were actively seeking a new job because of discrimination. Some 13 per cent of women cited sex discrimination, and 10 per cent cited sexual harassment as being reasons of great importance in their wish to leave their present job (Gatley and Chapman, 1989, p. 55).

Conclusion

Clearly, equal opportunities can only be achieved when similar numbers of women and men are recruited to and fully incorporated into professional life. This, in turn, could only occur if notions of careers were transformed substantially to incorporate the idea of men and women sharing family responsibilities. Many of the praiseworthy policies which have been established recently make little attempt, however, to challenge fundamentally traditional views about women's roles.

The problem centres on the fact that careers continue to be defined as unbroken and unfettered by interference from family life. Providing nursery facilities and career break schemes *is* important, but this does not necessarily challenge the traditional model of a career unless they are genuinely open to both women and men. Instead, most policies merely attempt to 'fit' women in to the 'male-as-norm' model of career building. This philosophy is aptly illustrated by Employment Minister, Patrick Nicholls recent remark that 'The Government is encouraging employers to *adapt* traditional working practices to *accommodate* the needs of women.' (*Employment Gazette*, February 1990, p. 56. my emphasis).

The evidence presented in this paper provides a strong indication that even if women do obtain the same types of qualifications as men, and if they are enthusiastic about pursuing a career, they are likely to be swimming against a tide of discrimination which is founded on the misconception that men have no major role to play in the day to day care of the household and childcaring. Only if the issue of men's and women's family and employment roles is successfully challenged can equal opportunities be achieved.

This is not to argue that recent policy developments are without value. Indeed, some organizations are encouraging men to break out from traditional views about the merits of pursuing a career to the exclusion of all else (Foster, 1989; Nollen, 1989). Innovative managerial strategies such as these are still, unfortunately comparatively rare. Nevertheless, the very fact that women are becoming more 'visible' in the professions, and that women are contributing an increasingly large proportion of family income will help to challenge traditional views on family responsibilities and the 'male-as-norm' conception of career building.

Notes

1 The subject groupings are composed as follows: *generalist*: humanities, English literature, geography, communication studies, social studies, inter-faculty; *generalist plus*: modern languages, economics, mathematics, science, chemistry, biology, computer science, environmental science, fine arts; *occupational generalist*: business studies, environmental planning, hotel administration, textile design, three dimensional design, graphic design; *occupational specialist*: librarianship, law, clinical psychology, urban and estate management, civil engineering, production engineering, pharmacy, accountancy, nursing.

2 Data on respondents' occupational status in this paper are based on the Hope Goldthorpe (1974) thirty-six category scale. The categories are formulated as follows: *higher grade professionals*, cats. 1, 2, 3, 4 and 7; *lower grade professionals*, cats. 5, 8, 10, 12, 14 and 16; *higher grade technicians*, cat. 6; *routine non-manual workers*, cat. 21; *manual and service workers*, cats. 22–3, 25–6, 29–36. *Higher grade technicians* in the Hope Goldthorpe scale are included in *lower grade professionals*. This occupational status category is separated in Table 8.1 to highlight the large number of graduates in this type of work, especially from technical degree courses. Illustrative jobs include 'work study engineers, computer programmers, draughtsmen, laboratory technicians' (Hope and Goldthorpe, 1974, p. 134). For a full discussion of these distinctions, see Chapman, 1989.

3 There is no space here to develop fully these explanations — see Chapman, 1989, pp. 6–12, on professions; pp. 80–93 on educational socialization; and pp. 92–114 on family life.

Chapter 9

Gender and Patriarchy in Mining Communities

Sandra Hebron and Maggie Wykes

This paper contains some preliminary findings from 'Coal and Community', a research project funded by the ESRC and carried out in the Department of Communication Studies at Sheffield Polytechnic between November 1986 and December 1988. A full analysis can be found in Waddington, Wykes and Critcher (1990). The purpose of the study was to assess the social consequences of the 1984–5 coal dispute in three mining communities. The three communities were selected so that they should be broadly comparable in terms of demography, but differed in their response to the dispute. The research attempted to look at all areas of life within each community, and covered the following: the concept of community; patterns of paid and domestic work; family and social networks; leisure; attitudes to and experiences of the strike; opinions about the police; attitudes towards the media; political beliefs and activities; prognoses for the future.

One obvious and important consideration which cut across all the research areas was the extent to which experiences and attitudes are differentiated by gender. Miners have entered the popular consciousness not only as 'archetypal proletarians' (Campbell 1984), but also as a peculiarly enduring breed of male chauvinists. We were interested to explore how far this assumption was borne out in reality and to assess the way that the nature of mining communities and the roles of men and women reproduced traditional gender norms. Of particular interest, given the overall brief of our research, was the question of how far women's — and men's — experiences during the strike have affected gender relations within each community, especially in terms of the division of paid and unpaid work.

Methodology

The previous experience of the research team led to the adoption of a combination of quantitative and qualitative techniques as the most useful exploratory methods. In-depth qualitative interviews with key members of each community (some eighty individual and group interviews across the three communities) were followed by a survey which attempted to establish how far the experiences and attitudes of the interviewees were generalizable to the broader population in each community. A questionnaire was administered to a quota sample, based on gender, age and employment in the coal industry. The questionnaire covered broadly similar areas to the interviews, though obviously in much less depth. In all, 400 survey questionnaires were administered. The relationship between the qualitative and quantitative data was always intended to be complementary, and as far as possible the following discussion attempts to integrate the two. A more detailed account of our methodology appears in our end-of-grant report of May 1989.

The Selection of the Three Communities

The three communities were selected using data from the 1981 Census to ensure that they were as similar as possible in terms of size and other key characteristics. We were particularly concerned that the proportion of men employed in the mining industry should be comparable, and also that the proportion of women in paid work should correspond. We took into account the degree of geographical isolation of each village, although in this respect our communities are not as perfectly matched as we should have liked.

Yorkshire supplied us with our first village, a community where all but a small minority of the workforce were on strike for the duration of the dispute. Our second village, where the workforce was split almost equally for and against the strike, was geographically within Derbyshire but is part of British Coal's Nottinghamshire area. Our third village, with only a small proportion of strikers, was in Nottinghamshire. All of the communities were fairly easily accessible from Sheffield, although not particularly well served by public transport. In order to preserve the anonymity of our interviewees, the communities are referred to throughout as Yorksco, Derbyco and Nottsco.

The Fieldwork

Although the interview schedule and survey questionnaire were the research tools proper, the researchers also gleaned a good deal of information about gender relations from their experiences of carrying out the research. This was particularly the case with the in-depth interviews. Our interviewees were selected on the basis of their belonging to one of our target groups. Our original research framework identified a broad range of individuals and groups as 'key informants'. These included both people directly involved in the dispute. (the NUM, the UDM, women's support groups, the police and British Coal) and also those more indirectly involved (political and community activists, parish and district councils, MPs, clergy, local traders, GPs, health workers and district nurses, social workers, and teachers).

One of the issues which had concerned the research supervisors was how successful a female researcher would be at gaining access to some institutions which, if not exclusively male, were predominantly so. In fact this was not a problem although there was surprise from some quarters that a woman should be carrying out research into a major industrial dispute. Despite women's very active participation in the strike, matters relating to the strike were often seen to be of little interest to women and because the research was perceived within the village as being 'about the strike' it was sometimes fairly difficult initially to persuade women to take part, not surprisingly they were not keen to be asked questions which they felt they would not be able to answer. However, this was a problem which was more or less overcome by word of mouth about the interviews. There was, in many of the interviews, a very clear gender division in terms of areas of interest or perceived experience. Male interviewees were sometimes unwilling to comment on family life or domestic routines, and referred the researcher to their wives, mothers and so on. Similarly, women did not feel able to comment on the coal industry, nor on the broader political issues. This was not always because they were less informed than the men, who on the whole did not share their reluctance!

Some responses to the presence of a young, woman researcher were telling about local gender roles. Many of the interviewees expressed surprise that the researcher should be in her mid-twenties, yet unmarried with no children. This clearly fell outside the social norms and expectations of the villages. These expectations are certainly not restricted to mining communities. Nevertheless, they serve to illustrate the degree to which we encountered quite clearly prescribed and demarcated gender roles within all three of the communities.

The Strike

Much of the writing about women's experiences during and since the strike seemed to assume that a large number of women who had suffered a particularly repressed existence prior to the strike had shaken off their shackles and become equal with their male counterparts. In fact this tends to obscure the fact that even within the very 'male' structures of mining communities, there have always been a small but active number of women who have taken a role in the running of their communities. While the close links between the worlds of the pit, union activity and politics serve to exclude the majority of women, each of the villages do have women who are active, particularly at the level of parish and local council work.

As Sheila Rowbotham has pointed out 'I think there are many forms of organizing — welfare organizing, voluntary groups — which aren't seen as political' (1973, p. 112) and it is precisely in these areas that women are likely to be active. One of our Yorksco interviewees recognized this as 'political' activity:

> The ladies have tended to be more politically active, tended to be more concerned about the community and personally I was a bit amused by the media presentation of so many of the miners' wives support groups. It was almost as if, suddenly, the wives of miners, who'd been beaten and bullied and kept down had been released by the circumstances to start taking a part in their communities.

In Derbyco for instance, the core membership of the women's support group pre-dated the strike. They were a group of local Labour Party members who had been actively involved in a by-election in a neighbouring area.

One of the members commented on how patronizing she had found much of the discussion of the role of women in the strike: 'It was as if we were all totally illiterate, that we'd come from behind the sink and we'd found this freedom, we were all ready for the revolution.'

In each of the villages we looked at, we found that the core members of the women's support group were already likely to have been active within the community in one way or another, often in local politics. Alternatively, they were the wives of active and politicized men. Of course not all the women's support group members can be categorized in this way, but these women were important in the early stages of getting organized.

Although a lengthy industrial dispute, with the protection of jobs and communities as its motivation, provided a set of exceptional circumstances, these were not sufficiently exceptional to cut across existing gender divisions. In each of the communities the relationship between the women's support group and the local NUM suffered from some degree of friction. In Yorksco in particular, women criticized local officials for being backward-looking and for failing to see that women had any part to play in the strike. In Yorksco and Derbyco the NUM funded strike kitchens which were staffed in the main by women who worked in the pit canteens. These were completely separate from the women's support groups, and branch officials were able to keep a much closer eye on the kitchens than they could on the activities of the support groups.

Whilst the post-strike consensus is that the women's support groups did vital work, some of the older branch officials in particular did not see it as appropriate that women should be involved in this way. Even when there was a recognition that as much support as possible was needed, there were clear gender-based distinctions about what form this support should take. When women started to take on the role of providers of food, either food parcels or meals, this was generally approved of (by supporters of the strike). This was much less the case if women wanted to go picketing, or particularly if they wanted to travel away from the villages for fundraising. For some women, conflicts arose not only about the nature of the activities which they were involved in, but also over the amount of time they were spending on them. Certainly the majority of women in the women's support groups were women who were not in paid work prior to the strike, so their prolonged absences from home, however justified, undoubtedly came as something of a shock to their families. Some women did face overt opposition from partners, and some did acquiesce. A number of interviewees, both men and women, said that as far as they were concerned the most important role for women during the strike was in keeping their own homes together and their families fed.

Changing Roles

A major cause for speculation at the end of the strike concerned the extent to which women's lives would change as a consequence of their experiences during the strike. We found no clear consensus as to whether or not substantial changes had occurred. In terms of direct, observable change our discussion of the domestic division of labour (below) would indicate that any changes were fairly slight. But the interviews provided a whole range of answers on perceptions of change:

> One or two of them, before the strike, were very quiet and submissive and never used to offer any points of view. And now they're always questioning, and one or two have gone on to get part-time jobs. One of them is hoping to apply to do CQSW at Sheffield.

> A lot of them have got young families and they still feel guilty going out to work because they've got young families. But I

think the benefits are going to be long term benefits, because when their children get into junior school especially, they are going to start branching out. It's opened horizons for them, whereas a few years ago they would probably just have got a part-time job working at the local factory.

All of a sudden we've realized we're somebody and it's a funny feeling. Everybody was grateful at the end of the strike for what we did and we wanted to carry on. A lot of women I think are dominated by their husbands, and daren't.

... even with the people that were on strike, while the women proved that they were equal to the men then, it is slowly going back to where the women belong at home and it's just the men that go out and arrange things.

There certainly has been no massive change in women's consciousness. I mean I would argue that there hasn't been in other areas either, but at least there has been some manifestation of it.

Obviously the number of women who were active in women's support groups varied from community to community, in line with the degree of general support for the strike, but the over-riding impression in all the communities is of a small core group with a larger number of women around the periphery. When we asked questions about how far women's lives have changed since the strike it was almost always assumed that it was support group activists who we were referring to, rather than women in general. The typical pattern, which held true in each of the communities, was of a handful of women who could clearly be seen to have become more active locally. This activism took a number of forms: joining the Labour Party or other political parties; joining anti-apartheid or other campaigning groups; working to raise funds for sacked miners; standing as candidates in local council elections.

Gender Relations Now

Most women in mining communities, as elsewhere, tend not to be involved in political activism or campaigning. We were interested to get a picture of the nature of gender relations across the whole of each community, as far as this was possible, therefore we have to take account not only of the structure of these communities, but also of the prevailing attitudes within them. Obviously it is only in this broader context that we can hope to assess how far the strike has changed things.

At the outset of the research we were interested in the opportunities for employment which are offered by communities which are still organized around the centrality of the pit. We found remarkably similar patterns across the communities with regard to women's employment. Prior to the strike only 39 per cent of the women we surveyed said they did some paid work. In 1988 this had been reduced to 29 per cent, compared to the national average of 50 per cent of women working outside the home (Martin and Roberts 1984). More than 50 per cent described themselves as housewives rather than 'unemployed' indicating that for many women paid work is not even part of their self-perception. The few women in employment typically worked in factories (each community had one or two small clothing factories) or shops, with a smaller proportion doing office work or domestic work. One woman described her experiences of paid work:

> I worked in the Co-op. There's not very much round here, even at that time, twenty odd years ago there wasn't much. It was either the factory, we've got two or three factories, or shop work, or if you could do it, secretarial work. But even then you'd got to move out, there were nothing here.'

A local welfare rights worker summed up the current situation, telling us 'The employment opportunities for women in particular are dire' and in one of the other villages: 'There's the clothing factory, there's the pit canteen, cleaning, shops and YTS.'

Most of the women with jobs work in their own village. Women's work is usually part-time, less than twenty hours a week. As the wealth of available literature on women's employment will testify, this kind of women's work is likely to be low paid and insecure, and heightens women's economic dependence. In each of the villages a small number of women work at the pit either as cleaners or canteen staff. At the time of the interviews, the Yorksco women were campaigning to be paid in line with their male colleagues who do comparable work. As Campbell (*op. cit.*) points out, the highest paid women at the pit are likely to be paid less than, and receive the same percentage bonus as, the lowest paid men.

The lack of employment opportunities for women as confirmed by Allen (1989) is a major reason for women in the communities not taking up paid work but this lack is integral to the structure of the coal industry which concurrently imposes other restrictions on women. Mining is man's work, literally and exclusively, with women excluded from the camaraderie and support of work-mates. The system of shifts effectively curtails women from seeking their own career, it is difficult to negotiate in terms of a marital relationship and near impossible in terms of child-care. As the norm of mining is masculine so the norm for mining women is domestic and familial with both in turn ultimately serving the needs of capital. Within such structures partriarchal ideology becomes naturalized for lack of any alternative.

Women's economic dependence perpetuates traditional definitions of appropriate masculine and feminine behaviour. While the majority of people we interviewed think these definitions are breaking down, especially amongst the younger members of the communities, any observable evidence of this is somewhat thin on the ground. Men and women do have clearly distinct areas of experience and expertise. With very few exceptions, women's primary role is in servicing the family. Mining is acknowledged to be arduous and frequently unpleasant work, and consequently miners are seen to be entitled to be well looked after. One Yorksco political activist (male) described the gender relations in his village as typical of any community with a heavy industrial base:

> You see the mining communities have always been male oriented environments, but it's like steel, any heavy industry, it always tends to be like that. Woman plays her domestic function not by desire, but by necessity. You know, shift work, heavy industrial work, men don't have enough energy really to carry out any other function than just working. And of course new technology taking the real hard work out and shorter hours and more leisure time obviously forces women to start to reconsider their position: 'Am I continually working seven days a week and he's getting more and more leisure time?' And there's a challenge comes from the women, which of course has already taken place away from the heavy industrial areas.'

A defining characteristic of mining communities has traditionally been their close knit and stable family networks. While all our communities had high percentages of long term residents, the percentages for men were higher than for women. This seems to be largely due to women moving to their partner's communities when they marry. Ninety-one per cent of the Derbyco women were married or had a partner, as were 75 per cent of the Nottsco women and 65 per cent of the Yorksco women. Judging from the people we interviewed and from their perceptions, it seems that in each of the communities women are still likely to marry young and to have children young. A Derbyco community worker commented:

> You've got to have a man about, even if he's a real shit, you've got to have him. They'll complain that he thumps them and that he thumps the kids and all this sort of stuff, but there is more stigma attached to not having a man, so they will stick with him

until someone else comes along who is probably as bad. There doesn't seem to be anything else to do, I mean having children seems to be a major occupation for most of the young girls.

There is also quite a high incidence of young unmarried women having children, although in Yorksco and Derbyco a proportion of the single mothers are women from outside the villages who have been rehoused in council accommodation there. Larger than average families were reported to be the norm:

Three or four kids would be average. Often women will have three kids by the time they're in their twenties. There's still the old tradition of having big families. They will still think about three or four children as the norm. And again, many of them still have the old tradition that the wife's business is in the house, she doesn't go out to work. There's a strong feeling about that, although it's breaking down with the younger ones.

One of our major interests was the whole area of the domestic division of labour, given the fact that during the strike some men undoubtedly did become more involved with the day to day affairs of home and family. We asked men and women if they 'normally do' a range of domestic tasks. The following figures are averages across the three villages.

	men	women
washing dishes	85 %	97 %
cleaning	75 %	98 %
laundry	35 %	98 %
cooking meals	76 %	96 %
shopping for food	77 %	90 %
gardening	58 %	84 %
repairs/diy	80 %	34 %
childcare	36 %	58 %

The percentage differences between the villages are fairly small, the main difference being a lower proportion of Derbyco men who reported doing any domestic tasks, including the traditionally masculine work of repairs and DIY. Amongst mining households, men were the most frequent reporters of change in domestic routines since the strike. In Yorksco, 28 per cent of men and 15 per cent of women reported changes; in Derbyco the figures were 37 per cent of men and 30 per cent of women and in Nottsco the figures were 50 per cent and 44 per cent. Even where changes after the strike were reported, more women than men felt that things have returned to their former patterns now. On average across the communities around 80 per cent of the women said this is the case:

'*Yes, domestic routines have returned to the old way now*'

Yorksco men	50 %
Yorksco women	83 %
Derbyco men	58 %
Derbyco women	78 %
Nottsco men	28 %
Nottsco women	80 %

There is clearly a difference in perception between men and women about the current division of labour. While comparatively high percentages of men claim to be doing more housework or childcare, these percentages do not tally with the percentages of women who say they are doing less. It seems unlikely that this difference could be explained by an overall increase in the amount of housework and childcare being done, and is more probably attributable to over-reporting on the part of the men.

Aside from the predominantly short-lived effects on the domestic division of labour, the strike certainly seems to have had other effects on family life. The survey data shows Yorksco reporting the most instances of change, followed by Derbyco and Nottsco. The most usual responses were that extended families had provided important financial help and support, that families had become closer through their shared beliefs about the strike (highest in Yorkshire and Derbyshire) or that families had been divided over strike related issues (highest in Derbyshire and Nottinghamshire). These findings bear out comments made in the interviews. Some families, particularly but not exclusively in Derbyshire, continue to be divided. For the purposes of this chapter our interest lies in how far gender relations within households were affected. Within each community, interviewees reported a small number of marital breakdowns arising from the strike, but these were attributed more to the financial stress suffered by striking families and difficulties pre-empting the strike than to disagreements over the strike or to changed expectations about male and female roles. However, in Yorksco we were led to believe that women's involvement in the strike had caused some tensions within relationships. A local teacher explained,

> In families, some things have changed quite drastically in terms of relationships and roles. I think there's been an increasing awareness amongst women, and rejection of their role ... I also think there's a lot of tension amongst men who can't cope with the sort of shifting role that some women are expecting, and are deeply distressed and concerned by it. Not, I believe, in a sense of wanting to restore the power base, but of just coping with it and adjusting to it.

And in Derbyco:

> Some women have been much more determined and immediately
> after the strike, well for the following few months, I perceived,
> maybe it was just me, an increase in people phoning up and
> saying 'I'm leaving him. I've been through all this and I'm not
> going back to that. What do I need to do?' (social worker)

The police and social services informed us that incidences of domestic
violence are high in each of the communities. However, it was impossible
to ascertain whether this form of violence has increased since the strike.
Health care professionals reported that domestic violence is generally
perceived to be normal, with new generations being socialized into its
acceptance. The police also treat it as commonplace, with call-outs to
'domestics' being one of the mainstays of their work, along with car
thefts and burglaries.

One final area in which we were interested was the degree to which
leisure and social life is structured along gender lines. The previous work
of two of the researchers (Clarke and Critcher, 1985; Green *et. al.*, 1987)
led us to predict that men and women would have substantially different
experiences of leisure. What emerged from the interviews with mining
households was a high degree of gender segregation. Men tend to pass a
good deal of their spare time with other men, often but not always their
workmates. Women have less leisure time, but are likely to spend what
time they do have with other women, either friends or family.

One Yorksco man described how he and his partner spend nights
out: 'She likes to go out with her mates, I like to go out with mine and
maybe meet up in the pub at the end of the night'.

Whilst one Yorksco (married) woman told us: 'The women aren't
expected to go out at all, not to have any interests.'

A second woman from the same village, newly separated since the
strike told us about her recently improved social life:

> I go to the Labour Party meeting on a Tuesday, stay in on a
> Wednesday, the Miners' Welfare on a Thursday, we go to Har-
> worth on a Friday and then the Tickhill Working Men's Institute
> on a Saturday, that's a good night there. Sunday we stay in and
> Monday we go to the Labour Club, country music night, a
> lovely night. And that's it, we stay in Wednesdays and Sundays.

She is fortunate in having her daughter available as a companion for
nights out, and also in having her own car.

In the survey, we asked about favourite spare time activities. Across
the communities as a whole, women's favourite activities are sport/keep
fit (17 per cent), watching television (14 per cent), gardening (13 per

cent), going to pubs and clubs (12 per cent), reading (11 per cent) and crafts (11 per cent). However, going to pubs and clubs is the favourite activity of Yorksco women (18 per cent), whereas for the Nottsco women watching television was their favourite activity (19 per cent). Men's favourites are similar, but more narrowly concentrated: sport (36 per cent), gardening (19 per cent), going to pubs and clubs (12 per cent) and watching television (7 per cent). Again, the proportion of men who prefer going to pubs and clubs is highest in Yorksco, whereas sport is more popular in Derbyco and Nottsco. Overall, the findings bear out existing research which shows women's leisure to be more home-centered than men's. Not surprisingly then, men were more likely than women to say that the strike had affected their social life. There was some slight variation between communities, with Derbyco having the highest percentage reporting change, followed by Yorksco and Nottsco in that order. The most usual consequences were avoiding 'scab' families (32 per cent), avoiding 'striking' families (19 per cent, mostly Nottsco) and staying at home more (27 per cent).

Conclusion

Overall, we found surprisingly little difference between the communities in terms of changed gender relations since the strike. As we might have expected, any changes which did occur were within striking households. Although women were on the whole supporting the strikers through traditionally 'feminine' work, they were organizing collectively to do this. While some husbands or partners welcomed this support, others felt that it was inappropriate, that a woman's primary concern should be with her own family. In most households where women were actively involved in strike activities, this obviously disrupted normal routines. Nevertheless, any long term changes — particularly for instance in the domestic division of labour — have been restricted to a small minority of households. There do seem to be more widespread changes in attitudes to gender taking place, and perhaps the greater confidence which many women gained as a result of their competence in organizing during the strike is speeding up this process. What emerges clearly from the research is the conflict generated by women's questioning of their position in the light of their strike experiences.

Given that women's structural position is, by and large, unchanged since the strike, it is not surprising that most women's lives are now not noticeably different from their lives prior to the strike. In economic terms the position of women in mining communities seems even to have become more restricted since the strike. The continuing decline of the coal industry has reduced even the ill-rewarded potential for traditional women's work servicing the pit, cleaning or in the canteen. Higher unemployment amongst miners has apparently impeded women even further in two obvious ways. Culturally, mining men are reluctant to tolerate their wives as breadwinners, and this tradition persists according to our data and in any case women's work becomes less viable still if it results in reductions of state benefit.

Where changes in gender roles are perceivable they appear as shifts in male attitudes which relate to broader social norms. As elsewhere, men in the mining communities no longer feel ashamed to be seen (occasionally) pushing a pram and many mentioned with pride the 'feminine' domestic roles they undertook. On the whole however women seemed less aware of claimed masculine contributions to domestic and family chores than was suggested by male evidence. Structurally defined gender norms relating directly to the economic organization of mining continue in the culture as a legacy even as the centrality of the pit diminishes. Common sense definitions of men and mining persist to define women's potential for work, leisure and self-perception even as the coal industry declines.

For those women actively involved in the strike there is now the added burden of living with a new understanding of their oppression and an apparently reducing potential to act on it in terms of becoming economically independent. However, Joan Witham takes the view that,

> What is of fundamental importance is that they may do very much the same things as before the strike, but they will never again think in the same way. Their new knowledge is indelibly impressed on their consciousness, their awareness and understanding heightened and extended and their self confidence assured.' (1986 p. 217)

What still remains to be seen is how far this will empower more than a tiny minority of women to change their lives within the fundamentally unchanged patriarchal structures of their communities.

Chapter 10

Economic Change and
Employment Practice:
Consequences for Ethnic Minorities*

Nick Jewson and David Mason

This chapter aims to identify and analyze some of the implications of economic change, changing labour markets and developments in employment practice in the 1980s for conventional recommendations in the field of equal opportunities. Specifically, it is argued that these recommendations do not take adequate account of the reality of much day to day recruitment practice and that they are often out of touch with the trends in management strategies and the labour market in the 1980s. The chapter draws on the results of recently completed research in order to illustrate some of the processes involved.

The Research

The research on which this chapter is based was commissioned by the Department of Employment. Its aim was to build upon historical sources of evidence with a view to documenting the impact of changes in employment practice on the position and opportunities of ethnic minorities within the labour forces of six major British companies. The most important of these sources was a series of case studies of seven major companies (undertaken by the Department itself and published as *Take 7*, 1972) and Dennis Brooks, *Race and Labour in London Transport* (1975).

The focus of the research was the need to explore and explain the processes responsible for changes in the occupational distribution of ethnic minority employees. The aim was to relate changing patterns of ethnic minority employment to changing employment practice. In

---

* Any views in this chapter are those of the authors and do not necessarily represent those of the organizations involved.

particular we were directed to test a number of hypotheses, the most important of which was:

> ... ceteris paribus, the greater the degree of formality existing in recruitment, promotion and upgrading procedures, the greater the likelihood of ethnic minority employment and occupational advancement. (DE specification, August, 1985)

We took formality to refer to the specification of procedures and practices in written form. Formalization, then, refers to the process whereby employment practices and conventions are specified, defined and regulated by means of codified rules expressed in documentary form. Informal practices are not necessarily unstandardized or inconsistent. They do, however, take the form of custom, convention and unwritten understanding. Other hypotheses directed us to examine the structure of internal labour markets and the role of seniority in promotion.

Participating companies were selected, and research access was negotiated, by the Department of Employment. The fieldwork was conducted between May 1986 and July 1987. In each organization a maximum of sixty, one-hour interviews with management and supervisory staff was agreed. In practice this number was exceeded in some companies. Representatives of trade unions were also interviewed. In a number of sites it was also possible to interview a small number of shopfloor workers. These could, however, never be more than a supplementary source of information. Respondents were selected with a view to providing a coverage of different operations, departments and divisions. The character of the research access was such as to focus interviews primarily on management and supervisory staff. The majority of respondents were white males though there was considerable variation between organizations. Wherever possible attempts were made to ensure that ethnic minority respondents were included in the sample; they were, however, always in a small minority. Five of the organizations are referred to in our report by means of pseudonyms. Attempting to maintain anonymity would clearly have been disingenuous in the case of our sixth organization, London Regional Transport, and it was, with agreement, referred to by name.

Given that there was an almost complete absence of data in the participating companies on current and past patterns of distribution of ethnic minorities it was not possible to chart processes of change over time in any systematic way. We relied on historical sources of information and the reports and recollections of our informants. Within these limitations, we sought to establish an overall picture of the operation of detailed employment practices in their specific organizational settings and to locate ethnic minority employment, in its various aspects, within this context.

We should note, at this point, that in conducting the analysis we made use of a distinction between suitability and acceptability selection criteria. Jenkins makes a distinction between technical ability to do the job (suitability) and 'the likelihood that the person will fit into the organization without creating any problems' (acceptability). In selection processes, suitability is commonly assessed in terms of educational, technical or other particularistic qualifications (such as experience or physique) which are relevant to the performance of the occupational task. Acceptability, by contrast, is usually evaluated in terms of matters such as appearance, manner, attitude, maturity, age, marital status, personality and 'gut feeling'. (For a further discussion of these and related issues see Jenkins, 1986; 1988).

In what follows, we draw on the results of our research to develop an argument about how recommendations in the field of equal opportunities might respond to, and indeed make use of, what we identify as key trends in the contemporary labour market. In doing so, we have not attempted to incorporate detailed evidence in the form of quotations from our respondents, or other qualitative data. In a paper of this length it would clearly be impossible to do so systematically and the result would be both tokenistic and open to the charge of excessive selectivity. Moreover, the nature of case study evidence is such that any attempt to proceed in this way would be misleading. By its very nature, case study evidence cannot conclusively establish the *generality* of the trends identified in this paper. Nor can it conclusively validate its suggested policy implications, rather, our case study evidence provides clues to the operation of the labour market. It suggests, on the basis of analysis of everyday practice in a small number of examples, trends, the existence of which needs to be verified and tested by other research. Accordingly, we have in this paper sought to draw out what we take to be some of the implications of our research for equal opportunities as we enter the 1990s. In support of our arguments we adduce our reading of evidence which is presented much more fully in the report of the project (Jewson, Mason, Waters and Harvey, 1990).

Formality and Conventional Recommendations

The centrality of the question of formalization in the research brief appears to mirror a number of aspects of the recommendations of statutory and other bodies in the area of equal opportunities policies. It is obviously possible to read the codes of practice of both the Commission for Racial Equality (CRE) and the Equal Opportunities Commission (EOC) in a number of ways but there is a clear emphasis on the formalization of procedures (CRE, 1983; EOC, 1985).

A theme in both Codes is the suggestion that consistent criteria for recruitment, promotion and redundancy will drive out subjective and unfair decision making at the work place (EOC Code, para. 11; CRE Code, para. 4). A moment's thought will clearly show that consistency alone is not enough. Many of the specific proposals seem to indicate that, in practice, what is meant by consistency is, in fact, formalization; that is, the specification, definition and regulation of employment practices by means of codified rules expressed in documentary form. (This notion of the importance of formality and formalization is further developed in Collinson, 1988).

It might be argued that there are other themes underlying the recommendations of the Codes such as positive action and clear-cut lines of management responsibility for equal opportunities matters. Even these, however, appear to be grounded in assumptions about centralized and formalized management structures. Moreover, it was clear from our interviews with managers that they perceived the emphasis on formality to be the key element in the Codes.

It is interesting to note that these assumptions lying behind the codes were developed in an era when social democratic theories of modernization, managerial efficiency and organizational effectiveness all pointed towards increasing concentration, formalization and professionalization of enterprises. In the 1960s and 70s all political parties, to a greater or lesser extent, advocated planning, economies of scale, rational management structures and scientific practice in programmes for the modernization of the British economy. These were reflected in many of the realities of business organization and concentration in this period. Personnel practices were heavily influenced by a trend towards professionalization and this coincided with corporatist inspired changes in employment legislation. Put another way the codes reflect the heritage of an era in which corporatism and centralization held sway in a number of areas.

Formalization: The Evidence from Two Case Studies

The thrust of our chapter will be to suggest that these aspects of the CRE recommendations fail to address many of the trends which currently dominate the British economy and labour market. Before we turn to this point, however, we wish to acknowledge that, in the appropriate circumstances, these recommendations may offer a positive way forward. Indeed, some of the organizations which participated in our study might appear, at least for part of their history, to illustrate the effectiveness of CRE recommendations. The London Underground railway and National Retail might appear to be cases in point.

Available evidence suggests (Brooks, 1974–5; 1975; Jewson, Mason, Waters and Harvey, 1990) that not only were there high levels of ethnic minority recruitment to London Underground during the post-war period but there have also been substantial levels of ethnic minority promotion into supervisory grades. Brooks's research explains this pattern of ethnic minority employment largely in terms of the formalized and centralized character of managerial and organizational structures. While arguing that his approach is not one of technological determinism, Brooks emphasizes the influence which the technical requirements of railway operations have traditionally had on the character of employment practices and work patterns within London Underground. He notes that the work practices required to provide a large scale transport service demand both a high level of attention to time keeping and highly predictable behaviour by all staff across the system. Furthermore the needs of safety also demand closely prescribed behaviour and a quasi-militaristic discipline from the workforce. Brooks argues that, in these circumstances, the organizational response was one of developing detailed, comprehensive and formalized sets of rules which specified precisely how equipment was to be used and how staff were to behave. The coordination of activities across the system was similarly achieved by bureaucratic means, resulting in hierarchical and centralized organizational structures. Thus, Brooks concludes that in a number of respects London Underground 'accords closely with Weber's ideal type bureaucracy' (1974–5 p. 38).

Brooks argues that many aspects of this centralized and bureaucratic environment proved to be conducive to both the selection and advancement of ethnic minority employees. Thus, the recruitment process was very formalized and incorporated a number of standardized tests. The scope for arbitrary and capricious decision making based on racial stereotypes was strictly limited by reliance on measurable criteria of suitability. Furthermore, the recruitment process was highly centralized, being based at one major centre and three subsidiary offices. Centralized recruitment made for a greater degree of professionalization in selection and reduced the possibility of localized variation in recruitment practices. Brooks does not argue that the formalized and centralized character of recruitment totally precluded the possibility of unfair discrimination but he does suggest that it made such discrimination significantly less likely to occur.

In a similar vein, Brooks draws attention to the implications of formal training for patterns of promotion within the organization. He suggests that where work is closely prescribed by the demands of formal rules and technical requirements, training becomes a prerequisite for much advancement, especially into supervisory posts. Thus, for many positions, promotion on the Underground entailed attainment of formal and measurable standards of task performance, as indicated by tests conducted at the end of training courses. These provided criteria of promotion that were relatively objective and free of racial stereotypes.

Seniority also played an important part in the promotion process. Brooks describes how for many posts, up to and including inspector (roughly equivalent to foreman status), seniority was used as a device which determined eligibility for training courses. Moreover, once the inspector grade had been achieved promotion up to station master was almost entirely by seniority. Brooks argues that seniority is an impersonal promotion criterion which leaves little room for managerial or supervisory caprice.

It is possible to read the history of London Underground as something other than solely the triumph of rational, technologically oriented bureaucracy. Indeed there is evidence in Brook's own analysis which would support other interpretations, and our own research suggests that events in the 1980s are radically restructuring many aspects of London Transport and challenging many features of its traditional work culture. This is not the place to explore these issues although they are dealt with at length in the full report of our research (1990). Instead we turn to another organization which may be said to provide an example of the operation of centralized structures and procedures, much in line with CRE and EOC recommendations.

National Retail was one of the UK's largest chain store companies. It had had a formal equal opportunities policy since 1967 and had collected returns on ethnic minority representation in the workforce since that time. Following the 1981 riots, and partly as a response to them, the company revised its policy, set up an Equal Opportunities Unit at Head Office, developed its own code of practice and formulated five year action plans with respect to gender and racial equality. National Retail was a highly centralized organization with a fairly rigid rule structure governing procedures in almost every aspect of the business. It appears well suited, then, to the implementation of an equal opportunities policy which closely followed many of the recommendations of the CRE and EOC codes of practice.

National Retail had what was probably the most developed and responsive equal opportunities programme we encountered. Much of its effectiveness, however, flowed from the way in which formalized procedures and targets went together with informal means of implementation. A case in point was company practice with respect to low levels of application from ethnic minority candidates. A lack of suitable applicants was not accepted as a valid reason for managers' failure to meet centrally set targets. The generation of applications was also a responsibility of managers and they were encouraged to use informal as well as formal means to fulfil it. Thus local ties, contacts, relations with community groups and straightforward word-of-mouth recruitment of black people were all used to meet targets. In this critical case, then, formality and informality went hand in hand as conscious instruments of policy. There was thus no straightforward contradiction between the existence of a highly formal policy and the utilization of informal means of implementation.

Another lesson of National Retail is that formalization of monitoring procedures and lines of responsibility is not a sufficient condition for the operation of an effective equal opportunities system. What was also critical was a clear and well-understood commitment to equal opportunities objectives from those with power in the organization. In the case of National Retail, a paternalistic organizational culture facilitated the exercise of personal authority by key senior figures committed to equal opportunities issues. An explicit attempt was made to incorporate equal opportunities objectives into the traditional culture of the organization.

The two cases so far reported might be taken as lending at least conditional support to the view that formalization and centralization have positive effects on ethnic minority employment. We have argued elsewhere that formalization does not necessarily produce fairness (Jewson and Mason, 1986a; 1986b). In this context we have made a number of points: formalization may incorporate forms of unfair discrimination; even when fair, formal procedures may be circumvented or manipulated; the nature of many positions is such that suitability criteria cannot be of great significance. These points could be substantiated with respect to the cases already discussed but we do not wish to reiterate the arguments in detail here. Rather we wish to draw attention to another point: that is that the organizational and managerial structures characteristic of National Retail and London Underground in the period described are increasingly unrepresentative of those prevailing in British industry. These matters are explored in the next section.

The Changing Environment of the 1980s

As our research proceeded it became increasingly clear that changing employment practice could not be understood without considering the context of changes in the broader labour market and managerial strategies within it. In our companies we found evidence of a number of trends which echo developments in the British economy as a whole in the 1980s. These were not uniformly consistent across our organizations but they were threads which ran through, and were repeatedly encountered in many different contexts.

Prominent among these changes was a trend towards devolution and decentralization of managerial power and responsibilities, often taking the form of cost centre or profit centre management. The aim of this development was to make cost-consciousness and financial objectives the main priorities of members of staff at all levels in organizational hierarchies.

Devolution and decentralization of managerial control, especially as it affected the recruitment process, had the effect of shifting the locus of decision making towards lower level line managers/supervisors and of weakening the control of professional personnel specialists. This not only increased the opportunities for capricious and subjective decision-making on the part of individuals but, perhaps more importantly, established the principle of variation in practice and procedure across the units of the organizations. It is important to note that this development is not a contingent side-effect. It is the avowed purpose of decentralized and devolved control. Moreover, cost-centre or profit-centre management has the effect of giving overwhelming priority to financial and budgetary considerations in the calculations of even the lowest level line managers. It is not surprising, therefore, that financial considerations were at the top of the priorities of many of the line managers we interviewed. In the absence of a clear appraisal sanction or budgetary implication for non-compliance, equal opportunities is likely to have a low priority.

Several of the organizations we studied were characterized by new kinds of labour contract (such as temporary and part-time). In addition there was a demand for an increasingly flexible core labour force with emphasis being placed on multi-skilling and the breakdown of lines of traditional demarcation.

One of the implications of this was an increasing segmentation of internal and external labour markets. In principle, the structuring of internal labour markets and the relationship between internal and external labour markets may be mediated by either formal or informal procedures. In some of the organizations we studied it took the form of formal differentiation of career hierarchies, promotion opportunities, ports of entry and so on. It follows, therefore, that formalization as an equal opportunities strategy does not, of itself, address this issue of segmentation or remove the disadvantage associated with exclusion from some labour market segments.

Another implication of multi-skilling and erosion of demarcation lines was a growing salience of acceptability criteria in recruitment selection and promotion decisions. Other trends reinforced the significance of acceptability. Thus, for example, in many cases labour forces were required to develop skills in the areas of customer care and communication. The context in which many of these changes occurred was a process of changing working relationships within plants. Prominent here was the development of semi-autonomous, self-regulating work-groups, in which flexible working was institutionalized. This was often associated with, but did not depend on, technological change and investment in new plant. In these circumstances judgments about ability to 'fit in' and personality traits became important in determining who was the best person for the job.

Acceptability criteria were further strengthened by the emphasis, in a number of cases, on involvement of the work-force (especially core or

primary workers) on an individual basis, in company culture and identification with organizational goals. This was achieved by developing
intra-plant and intra-organization communications and consultation procedures and institutions. This, in turn, helped to undermine the strength of
trade unions at both local and national levels and facilitated the growth of
local level bargaining and the decentralization of management practice.
Although trade unions have not always been the greatest friends of equal
opportunities, they have had a traditional and well-founded interest in
formal and centralized procedures. The undermining of their influence
has, therefore, obvious implications. This is particularly significant in
an era when many trade unions are increasingly awakening to equal
opportunities issues, notably at the national level.

Managers frequently drew attention to the fact that many of the
processes described above were associated with moves to greenfield sites
and a major spatial relocation of capital. Here the general trend was a
move away from the inner city, with potential implications for access by
ethnic minorities which were frequently invoked by managers as explanations for persistent or increased under-representation of ethnic minority
people in the workforce.

In all the organizations a changing relationship could be discerned
between the internal and external labour markets. The general tendency
was towards the erection of higher barriers. One of the reasons for
managers' perceptions that high barriers were necessary was that most of
the companies studied were recruiting from a plentiful supply of potential
applicants. Indeed, in many cases, mechanisms had to be evolved to deal
with what were described as floods of enquiries. Sometimes this involved
enhanced suitability criteria but there was evidence of much prominence
being given to acceptability. In these circumstances, companies were not
ignoring technical qualifications but there was a tendency to regard these
as screening devices and to rely upon acceptability criteria in making final
selections. The prominence of acceptability criteria was observed in both
high- and low-tech environments. Much research, such as that of Jenkins
(1986 pp. 80–115), has shown how acceptability criteria and racial stereotypes interact in managerial practice. There was considerable evidence,
in our research, of similar negative stereotypes among managers and
supervisors responsible for selection decisions.

High levels of application relative to the number of vacancies was
also invoked, in most organizations, as reason for a general move away
from formal, external advertising. Instead, there was a continuing or
enhanced use of in-house methods of attracting applicants or a reliance on
speculative callers.

Ironically, this deformalization of channels used to generate applications was by no means incompatible with, and sometimes actually went
hand in hand with, increased formalization of recruitment procedures at
later stages of the selection process. This highlights the way in which

management strategies respond to a variety of imperatives and are built upon the principle of utilizing the most effective perceived means of achieving objectives. Managers, therefore, perceived no incompatibility between formality and informality at different stages of the process nor did they believe their practices to be inconsistent. In these circumstances a recommendation for global formalization of the recruitment process may be perceived as unrealistic because it fails to recognize financial constraints in a period when all managers are being sharply reminded of them and increasingly judged on their performance relative to targets.

It should also be noted here that the use of formalized recruitment procedures was by no means incompatible with a high degree of significance given to acceptability criteria in reaching selection decisions. Thus, even in areas where formalization had been institutionalized it had by no means displaced practices which are often held to be conducive to unfair discrimination. Indeed in some cases the specification of acceptability criteria was itself formalized, not least because they were perceived to be critical to job performance.

In some organizations the changes described above were a response to a declining market situation. In others they were associated with attempts to exploit technical and commercial advantages with respect to competitors. In both cases there was much emphasis on the institutionalization of change and a future commitment to continuing processes of innovation rather than fixed bureaucratic codes. Achievement of performance targets rather than adherence to rules of procedure was increasingly becoming the measure of efficiency and competence.

It is not our argument to suggest that the culture of change simply or unequivocally demanded or produced informality across the board. Rather, it appeared that managers were prepared to adopt formal or informal practices in a pragmatic fashion as and when they appeared appropriate in the light of organizational objectives. Blanket appeals to formalization were, therefore, likely to be perceived as unrealistic and out of touch with the realities of the commercial environment. At the same time, at the highest levels of companies, there was a perceived need to respond to the threat of legal pressure from bodies such as the CRE. This often led senior managers at the centre to formulate equal opportunities policies as insurance against possible legal action. Local managers tended to perceive these as merely token or symbolic gestures. In such circumstances, equal opportunities programmes were unlikely to be seen as central to organizational culture and integral to everyday activities.

Automated Production Ltd

Some of the key aspects of the labour market changes described above, are well illustrated by another of our case studies: that of Automated Production Limited.

Automated Production was owned by a multi-national group which operated a number of light engineering manufacturing plants throughout the UK. In the seven or eight years prior to our research, the group had rationalized its UK and overseas operations. This had involved the closure of a number of unprofitable, technologically outdated plants and the up-dating, reorganization or building of new plants. A measure of the scale of the rationalization was the decline in the group's UK workforce from 34,000 in 1979 to less than 16,000 by mid-1986.

Following sustained losses, the factory studied in *Take* 7 was closed in 1982. It had been located in the inner-city close to a large ethnic minority residential area. At the time of *Take* 7, 21 per cent of the work-force was said to be 'coloured'. In later years, when the work-force reached its maximum, the ethnic minority composition was estimated to have been approximately 40 per cent. The plant's operations were characterized by: a rapidly dating technology; fragmented, low skill, labour-intensive work practices; and traditional skill demarcations.

In 1978 the Group opened a new factory on a greenfield site on the outskirts of the same Midlands city and adjacent to a number of large, predominantly white, housing estates. It was this site which was the subject of the research reported here. In contrast to the situation obtaining in the old plant, at the time of our research only 5.8 per cent of the new plant's work-force of 513 were of ethnic minority origin. All were employed on the shopfloor and none held a supervisory post. The ethnic minority population of the city was in excess of 20 per cent.

The new plant, one of the largest of its kind in Europe, incorporated the latest flow-line technologies, 'open' management styles and methods of group working necessitating a multi-skilled and highly flexible work-force. Its opening was associated with several other developments. Among the most important were: increasing devolution of managerial responsibility to plant level within the company as a whole; greater emphasis on in-plant communication, and shift level group participation, which to some extent served to marginalize trade unions; and an increased emphasis on flexible working, multi-skilling and open promotion channels. Labour turnover in the plant was minimal, reflecting high salaries and attractive fringe benefits. Permanent vacancies, therefore, were rare and, since the company operated an internal promotion policy, tended to occur in the lower grading levels.

The environment of the new factory was perceived by management to require a particular kind of employee. As a result there developed, at the new plant, strong boundaries between the internal and the external labour markets. Crossing them required not solely, or even mainly, the possession of particular skills. Rather what was required were what were judged to be appropriate attitudes and aptitudes. Complex and formal procedures were developed to assess applicants. Although a minimal level of relevant prior skill and/or perceived mechanical aptitude was sought, assessment was principally in terms of acceptability criteria. These referred to such notions as 'flexibility', 'the right attitude' and willingness to 'fit in'. They were assessed in terms of: personal presentation; attitudes and indications of character; hobbies and life styles; age; and family commitments. The process of generating applications was itself essentially informal with little recourse to external advertisements or the services of the Job Centre. At the same time procedures for processing applications became increasingly complex, demanding and formal. Thus the increasing formalization of selection procedures coincided with a decrease in the proportions of ethnic minority workers in the labour force.

The internal labour market itself exhibited a high degree of openness. There were examples of managerial staff having worked their way up the hierarchy, while the principles of flexibility and mobility were central to management's labour strategy. The plant had a highly formalized appraisal system that resulted in a number of employees being earmarked and developed for future promotion. Here again, however, the right attitudes and personality were the keys to the selection process. The possession of these characteristics was a matter for the judgment of supervisory staff whose reports and assessments were central to the promotion process.

Despite highly formal selection and assessment procedures, then, the criteria employed were essentially those of acceptability. The character of the judgments required, and the way in which they were arrived at, were such as to allow at least the possibility of abuses, including unfair discrimination of various kinds. In this context it is necessary to record the presence of negative stereotypes of ethnic minority (and female) workers at various levels in the factory.

Conclusion

The main objective of our paper is to argue that effective equal opportunities recommendations have to address contemporary developments in business objectives, management strategies and employment practices generally. The patterns of managerial strategy which our research highlighted appear to be leading employment practice in directions which run counter to conventional policy recommendations in the area of equal opportunities. These recommendations often urge management to formalize and centralize. Our evidence points to tendencies towards deformalization, decentralization, the devolution of managerial responsibilities, increased use of acceptability criteria and the institutionalization of a culture of change. In these circumstances policy effectiveness depends upon developing recommendations which are congruent with current management strategies and organizational contexts.

We should note that our research did not suggest that there is a single formula for employment practice which can be said to guarantee either the fair and equal operation of procedures or equality of distribution of members of different ethnic categories in the workforce. This is not merely to make the trite observation that every organization is different. More importantly the principle of devolution and decentralization requires that recommendations in the field of equal opportunities address the inevitability that there will be significant variations in procedure and practice across the units of any organization. The demand for consistency, which is central to the Codes, is in principle, out of touch with the intention of the strategy of devolved and decentralized management.

This is not to say that the Codes were totally ignored within organizations. Indeed, their existence appears to have been important in helping to stimulate some policy developments. However there was a clear indication that many of these responses were perceived by managers and supervisors as unrealistic and were, therefore, treated as no more than token or symbolic. Furthermore many equal opportunities policies adopted a minimalist strategy and had clearly been developed with a view to providing a source of defence in the case of legal challenge. We take the implication of this to be that the potential influence of the Codes of Practice should not be underestimated and that spending time to update and revise them to meet modern conditions would be a worthwhile activity.

A comparison of the companies in our research made it very clear that the key to securing policy objectives in the area of ethnic minority employment, as elsewhere, is power. That is to say, commitment at those levels of the organization where business objectives are determined is crucial to developing management strategies which are both sensitive to issues surrounding ethnic minority employment and tailor-made for the organization concerned.

It is possible to conceive of a strategy for establishing and achieving equal opportunities objectives which makes use of the tendencies described. A small centralized unit or group of personnel managers might exercise monitoring functions over devolved and localized departments and operations. Such a unit would need to be tied closely to the locus of effective control over business objectives and management strategies. Such arrangements would not interfere with the autonomy of local management. They would, however, enable personnel to incorporate equal opportunities objectives into the targets which local management is set. In these circumstances, equal opportunities would become one of a series of issues such as health and safety, industrial relations and cost control, in terms of which managers were appraised (and rewarded or sanctioned). It will be seen then that targets or objectives are a central element of our recommendations and should not be regarded as an optional extra with rather radical overtones. Indeed we might note that targets are often conceived in a very limited way and are often misrepresented as quotas.

There are, however, a variety of ways in which targets can be understood. They may, for example, be set in terms of the provision of opportunities rather than simply in term of outcomes — e.g. training places, access courses, career development opportunities. In whatever terms they are set, it is critical that targets comprise measurable objectives.

The arrangements outlined might facilitate the elimination of some tiers of formal regulation. Providing the policy has secured commitment from senior institutional power holders and targets have been set for local units, organizations can be expected to devise their own localized and specific mechanisms for the achievement of objectives without necessarily conforming to preconceived notions of formalized procedure. In other words we are emphasizing a more precise specification of formal performance indicators and less emphasis on the degree of formalization of procedure. This is not an argument for totally abandoning formality, nor does it imply that formalized procedure is always an inappropriate strategy. Rather the absence of formal procedure, or the difficulty of generating it in decentralized organizations, does not rule out effective equal opportunities policy. Our recommendations here are designed to respond to, and make use of, current trends in the labour market and managerial strategies rather than seeking constantly to swim against the tide. Put another way we might argue that turning the routine operation of existing recruitment practice towards equal opportunities objectives is a more realistic way forward, in many instances, than attempting a wholesale reconstruction of the employment practices of British industry and commerce. It should also be made clear that the policy strategy we outline can be perfectly consistent with existing legal provisions. It does not imply or require illegal positive discrimination. For example one way in which informal mechanisms might be used to meet targets is in generating applications from otherwise under-represented groups in circumstances where they were not otherwise forthcoming.

Decentralization might even facilitate the pursuit of equal opportunities objectives by making it clear where problems were to be found and specifying who was responsible for rectifying them. Such arrangements could only operate effectively where there were explicit — and hence possibly formal — lines of control and responsibility. Formalization of these arrangements would enable central units to make their control over devolved departments a reality. None of this prejudges the principles on which policy would be founded or the methods used to meet targets. It should be made clear here that a distinction can be made between the formalization of the processes by which policy objectives are specified and the formalization of the processes by which objectives are achieved. Our recommendations crucially depend upon adherence to the first. However, all changes in management strategies and organizational patterns reviewed in this chapter would suggest that the extent to which procedures for the achievement of policy objectives should, or can, be formalized is a contingent matter to be decided in the light of the circumstances of particular organizations. There is no reason in principle why highly informal means should not be used effectively to secure equal opportunities objectives.

Chapter 11

Gatekeepers in the Urban Labour Market: Constraining or Constrained?

John Wrench

The word 'gatekeeper' is used to describe those individuals who by virtue of their position within organizations have direct control over entry to employment or other opportunities. This paper considers the role of the Careers Service in the processes leading to the opening and closing of 'gates' to employment and training for ethnic minority school leavers. The paper draws on research on racial inequality and the youth labour market carried out in the mid-late 1980s, with particular reference to youth training, the Careers Service and racial discrimination by employers (Lee and Wrench, 1987; Wrench, 1987; Cross, Wrench and Barnett, 1990). Although the Careers Service is not a gatekeeper in the sense of having direct control over entry to employment opportunities within a particular company, careers officers often work closely with those who do operate the 'gates', and have a great deal of influence on which individuals are initially pointed in their direction.

The Careers Service is a department of the local education authority whose main aim has been described as 'to help individuals leaving full-time education to make a satisfactory transition from school or college to work.' ('A Career as a Careers Officer' — Careers Service Training Council). However, the work of a careers officer is more than this. Not only are they engaged in matching school leavers to appropriate vacancies, but they also maintain a longer term counselling role with some clients over a number of years. Careers officers also work with schools and colleges, supporting their work in careers education,and guidance; they work with the unemployed in activities such as job clubs, and even get involved in adult guidance. They liaise with the Manpower Services Commission (MSC, now the Training Agency) over the provision of the Youth Training Scheme (YTS). Employers and YTS managing agents contact the Careers Service with their job or placement vacancies, and the Service will maintain contact with and advise employers on, for example, new developments in education and training.

The British Careers Service has been described as 'unique'. Whereas those in other countries are either wholly located within the educational system or in the labour market, the British Careers Service operates in both spheres, functioning as a bridge between school and work (Maguire and Ashton, 1983, p. 87). It is both a provider of vocational guidance in schools and a labour market placement agency. Careers officers have been described as 'oddly placed', having two masters (Cockburn 1987, p. 54). The minister responsible for the service is the Minister of State at the Department of Employment, but each local careers service is based under the local education authority, which is responsible for its running.

Literature on the recent history of the Careers Service invariably employs the phrase 'the Cinderella service'. It was long seen as a backwater, manned by well-meaning but unexciting people, generally ignored by others in the local authority but often criticized by employers and young people alike. (Lee and Wrench, 1983; Sillitoe and Meltzer, 1985; YETRU, 1986; Cockburn, 1987). However, recent years have seen a shift in the profile of the service, and a number of developments, particularly the advent of the Youth Training Scheme (YTS), have thrust the workings of the service more visibly into public view. In 1988, around 90 per cent of YTS recruitment took place via the Careers Service. The Manpower Services Commission/Training Agency has seen the operation of the Careers Service as central to the viability and success of YTS. The government has reflected this greater interest through a 1987 joint initiative by the Department of Employment, the Department of Education and Science and the Welsh Office in which every local education authority was asked to review its existing careers education and guidance policy and provision, and instructed to inform the Secretaries of State of progress by October 1988.

Equal Opportunities and the Careers Service

The issue of race and equal opportunity should be an important one for the Careers Service. For one thing, the service sits in the middle of a set of processes which eventually lead to many ethnic minority young people *not* making a satisfactory transition from school or college to work, even when they have the same level of objective educational attainment as their white peers. Unemployment among Afro-Caribbean and Asian people remains obstinately higher than it should be, with the differential unemployment rate between white and ethnic minority young people being greater than for any other age group (see Newnham, 1986). If this were not justification enough for concern by careers officers, evidence shows that ethnic minority young people seeking work in fact are more reliant on the careers service than are their white counterparts (Brooks and Singh

1978; Lee and Wrench 1983; Sillitoe and Meltzer 1985; Verma and Darby 1987).

There are two issues here. The first is that reliance on the careers service as a method of job seeking in itself may be disadvantageous in relation to other methods, such as direct application to employers from advertisements, following up word of mouth information from family and friends, and so on. Careers officers themselves have recognized this:

> The reason why a lot of black kids won't make the grade is because they are totally dependent on the Careers Service. Many white kids have got a social network they can use. (Careers officer, Lee and Wrench, 1983, p. 38)

If this is true, then any upgrading of the careers service role and importance in the labour market ought to benefit ethnic minority young people. The second issue is whether the careers service itself deals fairly and professionally with ethnic minority youngsters. The quality of their encounter with the service is going to be very important, given that they are so reliant on it. It is therefore a matter of concern if, as some have suggested, agencies such as the careers service 'operate to stereotyped and naive assumptions about the careers choices of ethnic minorities' (see Verma and Darby, 1987, p. 74).

In the past, both careers officers and teachers have been accused of prejudice and ignorance. (See Eggleston *et al.*, 1986, p. 205). Fenton *et al.* (1984, p. 28) noted occasions when careers officers and others 'made judgements regarding the range of (YTS) schemes considered appropriate for ethnic minority youngsters which were based on questionable, though common, assumptions', such as a belief that ethnic minorities were reluctant to travel. Evidence of the same (unreasonable) assumption amongst careers officers was found by Ballard and Holden in their study of graduate job seekers (1975, p. 329). Stereotyping can affect the work of careers officers as much as other professionals in this area, and the combination of ethnocentrism and colour blindness can seriously damage a young person's prospects. There is the danger of misjudgments of the abilities and aspirations of ethnic minority young people, with a corresponding undervaluing of their potential (Ali *et al.*, 1987, p. 76). Sillitoe and Meltzer found a divergence in the assessments of careers officers of the job suitabilities of whites and equivalent Afro-Caribbeans, officers being less likely to approve of the job aspirations of the latter. (1985, p. 41) Similarly Brown (1985, p. 679) found evidence of a dismissive view of Asian aspirations within the service that he researched.

Eggleston, Dunn and Anjali (1986) wrote to Principal Careers Officers (PCOs) in every local education authority with an ethnic minority population of 10,000 or more seeking information on their use of statistics on ethnic minority young people. The replies suggested that some local careers services were quite unaware of any practical implications for their work of racial inequality. Since the time of the work by Eggleston and his co-researchers the issue of equal opportunities has been raised higher on the careers service agenda. In 1986 a Careers Officers Working Group began working with the Commission for Racial Equality (CRE) to produce discussion papers to assist the careers service to develop and implement equal opportunity programmes (LGTB/CRE, 1988). For a number of years now there have been individual local services which have been active in their concern for properly organized and implemented equal opportunities work. Developments of recent years suggest that now this awareness may be spreading more generally throughout the service, and that the stance of 'colour blindness' is increasingly being questioned. However, there remains a danger that within an expansion of equal opportunity work the specific problem of racism in the labour market may still remain underplayed. A concern with equal treatment in the counselling provided by careers officers may not be enough. As Eggleston *et al.* (1986, p. 184) write:

> The distinction between equality of opportunity and equality of outcomes applies particularly to the work of careers officers. Officers may offer interviews equally to black and white young people of equivalent qualifications, but employers may accept them unequally. The careers service is offering equality of opportunities, but not providing equality of outcomes.

There exists a range of issues that could be taken on board by a careers service with a progressive interest in equal opportunities. These might include training sessions on areas such as the avoidance of cultural stereotypes, the particular sensitivities needed by careers staff when interviewing some ethnic minority young people or when talking to their parents. Other topics might include policies to encourage the recruitment of more ethnic minority careers staff, special careers conventions directed at ethnic minority school leavers who are aiming to challenge occupational stereotypes, as well as providing new role models, working with schools and colleges to promote multi-racial careers education programmes, outreach and community work to establish working links with key community groups, and so on. However, there are a number of reasons why a service apparently concerned with equal opportunities may nevertheless underplay the factor of external racism, and this may have serious implications for the workings of an apparently comprehensive equal opportunity policy.

The 'Awareness' of Racial Discrimination

Research in the early 1970s revealed a belief current amongst careers officers (then called 'youth employment officers') that racial discrimination did not affect the opportunities of school leavers (Fowler *et al.*, 1977; Eggleston *et al.*, 1986; p. 33). More recently, Eggleston, Dunn and Anjali identified careers officers with a lack of awareness of, or an unwillingness to acknowledge, the problem of racial discrimination in the labour market, and a failure to use statistics in a way which would have served to highlight it for them. Similarly, in interviews conducted with careers staff between 1984–7 the present researcher found that despite the accumulated years of evidence from academic research, industrial tribunals and CRE reports, there were still careers staff who apparently had not considered the practical implications of racial discrimination in their locality.

In the following section extracts are quoted from tape recorded interviews with careers officers and employment officers (a more junior grade of careers staff) who were all located in offices serving multi-ethnic areas and personally dealing with significant numbers of ethnic minority school leavers. These interviews revealed that there was still a core of staff within the careers service who subscribed to the 'no problem/colour blind' school of thought — for example, the officer of more than thirteen years service who dismissed the idea of any local problems of resistance by employers to ethnic minority youngsters: 'If the young person has the right qualifications, motivation and personal qualities, they have the same chance as others'. Careers staff could still be found who were not only unaware of current debates such as that on inequality on YTS, but who were also ready to make ethnocentric generalizations about why ethnic minority young people were not doing so well: 'Its more likely to be attitude ... and other things — bad timekeeping. They stay off work because Grandad is ill'.

Corresponding with this ignorance of the issue of racial inequality on the part of such respondents was an ignorance of the procedures to follow in the event of a racist instruction by an employer, or a suspected incident of racial discrimination — procedures which are set out in the careers service manual. 'I know where to find them, but I don't think I know what they are'; 'To be honest with you, I don't have much knowledge of the procedures — partly from not having gone through it'.

'Ignorance' might not always be the right word to use, as the impression was gained that some staff didn't *want* to know about racial discrimination. The following comments are from three officers from the same service where little practical consideration had been given to the issue of equal opportunity and racial inequality. Officers in this service consistently volunteered the view that racial discrimination was not a problem for them. The interviewer suggested that perhaps there might be a problem 'out there' that they were not picking up on. One said

> It's that that worries me — the fact that there may be all this going on outside and we don't know anything about it ... it may well be that we are totally missing what is going on anyway.

Another felt that they had such a superficial level of relationship with employers, they didn't know what was going on 'out there'. '... With regard to what's happening at street level, I think it's probably easier to just pull the blinds down a bit'. The third remarked

> In a way, if you are the sort of person who tends to want everything to be equal and play it equal yourself, you're not looking for it. Perhaps you should be, I don't know.

This chapter identifies some of the reasons why careers staff might find it easier to 'pull the blinds down a bit' in the course of their work. This analysis starts from the assumption that it is indeed valid to question the 'no problem' view. Such questioning does not only spring from common sense — in other words, the fact that any well informed observer would find it hard to believe that 'racial' problems do not exist in areas where large numbers of ethnic minority young people are seeking work in competition with their white peers. It is also apparent from an examination of stories in local newspapers, or the annual reports of local Community Relations Councils, that there are many who would not describe these localities as characterized by an absence of 'racial' problems.

The most pertinent grounds for questioning the 'no problem' view come from evidence from other careers staff, amongst stories told to the researcher over something like four years of conversations and tape recorded interviews with managing agents, CRE personnel, careers officers and other careers staff in different parts of the country. Unlike their more blinkered colleagues, many careers staff recognize that discrimination is a fact of life in the labour market, and some could point to examples in areas where other careers staff had assured the researcher that there was 'no problem'.

A few illustrations of this material are included below. So as not to interrupt the flow of the text other examples are included in the Appendix: these are all taken from direct transcriptions of tape recorded interviews with careers staff. Although such qualitative evidence is not intended to demonstrate the *extent* of discrimination, it does illustrate the forms it takes, and how it affects careers service work. Specific incidents of racial discrimination may only intermittently break the surface and cause ripples — it nevertheless remains a perpetual undercurrent whose effect is always there to be felt.

Examples of Racial Discrimination by Employers

An ethnic minority specialist careers officer described a recent occurrence in her office: when dealing with a vacancy for a sewing assistant, a member of careers staff was told by an employer that she 'didn't want to see any Asians'. It was referred to the ethnic minority specialist careers officer who, on ringing the employer back, was told 'If we trained Asians they would go off and start their own business. I couldn't work with them — they make me sick.' When informed of the Race Relations Act the employer replied 'I can take on who I like'. The careers officer informed the CRE, who asked for an apology; none was received. Meanwhile the employer had turned down two Pakistani girls who had replied to her newspaper advertisement saying 'Why don't you go to your own?'. The CRE ultimately instigated tribunal proceedings. It was thus quite a straightforward case of direct and open racial discrimination — as the careers officer remarked, 'I never thought I would get such a blatant case'.

In this sense this case was unusual, precisely because it was so blatant. Many careers officers made the point that for those individuals who are inclined to take action, cases such as this one are less of a worry. More problematic for the Service are those more subtle cases when discrimination is operating at a level which makes it harder for a concerned officer to take action, or easier for a less concerned officer to live with.

There are many occasions when officers have their suspicions aroused, but have nothing really tangible to go on. As one employment assistant said, 'Employers are now a bit more clued up and wise to what they can get away with.' Racism was less likely to be blatant, now more subtle — '"I only want someone from (...), a white area. Or a certain school."' Respondents noted that 'white kids get picked up quicker' than ethnic minority young people. One remarked 'They take longer to place ... there are several very good Asian girls who have been on the register for months, which is unusual'. Officers noted that some firms never recruit an ethnic minority youngster 'and its not for the want of submitting them'. One remarked 'There will be those where we give the names to employers and the the white kids actually get interviewed, while the Asian kids just have their name and address taken. That has happened'. Sometimes there might be 'coded messages' from employers — 'you know the sort of person we are looking for'. Most common of all seemed to be the feeling gained in telephone conversations with an employer that he or she was not going to recruit an ethnic minority young person, due to a noticeable change in tone of voice when an Asian name was mentioned.

> You can tell when you speak to them over the phone — the change in voice when you mention a name ... You can hear them back off mentally. But they still say 'Send them along'.

As one employment officer put it 'So its very subtle. And you get to the stage when you think "Is it just me imagining it?"'
  Sometimes a bit of effort and detective work could show up a racist employer when otherwise it might have been easy to let it pass.

> I've had one case which we actually took further — she didn't receive a fair interview; she came back in and told me. She said 'it wasn't an interview, he had the television on during it, and he didn't even ask me any questions about my experience. Then he told me that the job had been filled the day before'.

This employment officer got in touch with other young people who had been for an interview 'and then we'd got him over a barrel'. The white applicants had been given proper interviews, only the Asian girl had not, and the employer was shown to have lied when he had said that the job had been filled.
  A final example is that of an employer with a bakery shop who had walked into the careers office to notify a vacancy. He told the employment officer that he wanted a counter assistant but 'didn't want any coloureds'. He was told he couldn't say that, and replied 'I know, that's why I'm whispering it'. The employment officer notified her specialist colleague, who was told by the employer, 'I've nothing against them myself, but I'll lose my customers.' The officer gave him a copy of the Code of Practice, told him they couldn't accept the vacancy and reserved the right to notify the CRE. A little later he came back into the office 'ranting and raving', having received a letter from the CRE. He complained that he had come to the careers office in good faith, that he only came in for advice (which wasn't true), and so on. He had been requested to make a written reply to the CRE; the careers officer was uncertain whether it would get to a tribunal stage.
  This example shows how it might be that some 'pressure to discriminate' cases could remain unchallenged by the careers service. In this case the instruction was 'whispered' to an employment officer; had she decided to ignore it, it is possible that no one would have been any the wiser. (In some services this would have happened; in this case the service had recently run training for staff on the appropriate procedures to follow in these circumstances.) However, in reporting it to the ethnic minority specialist officer she thereby created for herself more trouble and work; if

a case goes to a tribunal she will have to testify what happened, undergo a form of cross examination, make sure she has maintained a precise record of what was said. Furthermore, it could be argued that the service has now alienated an employer who may now think twice before using it again. Clearly, some careers staff could be reluctant to challenge discrimination particularly if, as happened in this example, it is only 'whispered'.

The examples quoted above were all taken from careers staff who were aware of the relevant issues and willing to challenge the employer or report the matter to the CRE. This is easier when cases are unambiguous, or even blatant. There are also less clear examples where action is unlikely to follow, where it is more difficult even for 'aware' staff to contemplate action. And there are careers staff, as we have seen, who are not even willing to acknowledge the existence of racism, and therefore will not even pick up on the less ambiguous cases, let alone the more subtle forms of racial exclusion. These are the respondents who were unable to quote any examples of racial discrimination in the locality, and could not describe any tribunal cases as there had been none.

Having said this, the difficulties that face the service in dealing with discrimination should not be underestimated, particularly when, as one officer put it, 'there are employers who are as conversant with the Race Relations Act as we are'. It is difficult for a service to take action when an employer adheres to all the rules but still discriminates:

> They'll say 'Fine, yes, I'll see all those young people' and then at the end of the day they consistently refuse to recruit Asian youngsters. That is far harder.... Quite often you would be sending along youngsters who are of a fairly comparable stand-ard, so you can't say 'Why have you taken the very worst person that we have submitted?' ... So its very difficult to prove.

The Avoidance of Confrontation

Generalizations on careers service practices are difficult because of the immense regional variation in the provisions that local services make for ethnic minority clients, and the variety in the sophistication of individual staff awareness of racial issues. Bearing in mind this complexity, it remains valid to argue that the careers service in general has not been as aggressive in confronting racist employers as it could have been, and that in particular there are pockets of complete passivity on this issue. Many interviewees expressed their frustration on this. An Afro-Caribbean careers officer in the Midlands saw his colleagues as 'ground down by the pressures of institutionalized racism ... the Careers Service gives up too easily the fight on West Indians and Asians'. One result of this was that he felt that some of his colleagues were *anticipating* rejection by certain employers, guiding ethnic minority young people to where they were more likely to be accepted. A number of other careers officers confirmed that this could happen.

> With jobs and with YTS we make the submissions. So if black kids or Asian kids aren't being submitted to those jobs then it's one of two things — either they are not suitable, or its been pre-judged.... in a service like this with so many people and not a lot of checks and balances then I imagine that that goes on in the submission stage. That I get on well with company A, and company A manager has said to me sometime 'Don't send me these sort of people' — then that might impinge on your objectivity in putting somebody forward for that vacancy.

Other officers admitted that 'protective channelling' went on, motivated by a desire to protect the young person from an unsympathetic environment. Its effect is that racial discrimination does not have to break the surface in a form which would necessitate action of any sort.

It is clear that the readiness to tackle racial discrimination could vary according to local priorities.

> We can all spot things that we suspect are going on ... I think its just lack of time, pressure of time. At some stage you have to sit down and decide what your priorities are. I'm not saying that any evidence of discrimination is automatically thrown out of the window, but you have to consider it along with your other priorities.

Officers in the CRE have for years been pushing local careers services for a greater readiness to confront racist employers and notify the CRE, with a view to eventual prosecution. A CRE official recently pointed out that suspensions of YTS managing agents or work placement providers arising from discrimination is almost unknown. Careers officers argue that they have very little power — that if they refuse to action a vacancy the employer can simply fill it elsewhere. A CRE employment officer conceded the there were problems for the careers service and that it had only limited power in relation to employers. However, he felt that such problems are sometimes 'played up' by the service. He could point to cases where careers service action has been effective — for example, a local service suspended vacancies over suspected racism on a YTS scheme in a nationally known High Street clothes store, and the shop stopped recruiting until it was sorted out — and began to negotiate with the CRE on an equal opportunity policy. Some employers are worried about the threat of bad publicity that the careers service can give. 'Simply the fact of saying 'I think I will have to report this to the CRE' can actually persuade employers to do a lot of things.' And the careers service could be a key source of information on employers for the Training Agency regarding Approved Training Organization (ATO) status. Recent developments have enhanced the importance of the careers service role: the increased publicity about discrimination in the youth labour market; more generalized concern about what is happening to ethnic minority young people, and more of an interest being taken by local councillors in what the careers service is doing.

In consequence the CRE argues for internal changes within local careers services. They would like to see properly set out equal opportunity policies covering the range of aspects of careers service work, enhanced training for staff not only on areas such as the reduction of stereotyping and more sensitive careers guidance but also on setting out clear and well rehearsed procedures for responding to incidents of suspected racial discrimination. A careers officer saw such procedures as necessary to help staff resist the pressure to 'take the easy way out and turn a blind eye' to suspected or ambiguous cases of racial discrimination.

> I think if there was a formalized structure, that would be easier, and people would be more likely to pass it on ... Plus there are so many other things to do in the job and you think 'Yes, I should pick up on that' but you maybe let it go. I think the key would be if there was a more formalized structure that you could go through ...

There should also be systematic ethnic monitoring in careers service statistics, so that patterns may show the existence of a problem that may not otherwise be apparent, and action should be taken based on these statistics — for example, visiting employers with persistent imbalances in recruitment, or even setting a form of equality target to be achieved by a certain time.

The traditionally rather weak response of the careers service to incidents of racial exclusion in recruitment, and to 'pressure to discriminate' cases by employers, needs further examination. The most obvious focus of any explanation of careers service passivity would seem to be on the careers staff themselves — their attitudes and personal characteristics, their background and training, and how this is reflected in their daily judgments, practices, and actions — or inactions. It would be strange if careers staff did not contain within their ranks some who exhibited the ethnocentric judgments, stereotyped thinking or racist attitudes which have long permeated British society and culture. Although a researcher with a tape recorder conducting face to face interviews might not expect to hear expressed the worst examples of white British racial attitudes, there was nevertheless evidence from some respondents that there was an 'attitude problem' on the part of some staff in their office. For example, an employment officer lamented the views of some of her colleagues:

It's blatant sometimes. Certainly not in front of the youngsters. But when the youngsters have left the office, there's a (tutting sound). And you can hear it said when a vacancy comes up — 'Well, I'm not sending any Asians for that because they won't like the uniform...'

A careers officer commented 'I think we have people who are quite racist. What they are doing in a job like this I don't know, but I think people do have views'. One way she saw these views demonstrated was in the attitude to those young people who were 'signing on' but who didn't seem to be genuinely interested in looking for a job. Some staff 'seem to get more upset' when it happened to be Asian girls, 'whereas you've always got white kids — punks, whatever — who make themselves unemployable, but they're not given a hard time, because its seen they've opted out'.

And those two groups are treated totally differently. Its fair game amongst a lot of careers staff to give the Asians a hard time ... 'Asian girl, hasn't been in twice, doesn't want to work — hard time — let's come heavy with her'.

There were other examples of careers officers who expressed concern at the views and attitudes of some of their colleagues in the office. It is to be expected that some careers staff would exhibit some of the racist attitudes and stereotypes prevalent in British culture and this will inevitably be reflected in their dealings with ethnic minority young people, whether in the manner of their face to face encounters, in 'labelling' them via stereotypical assumptions, or in attaching a low priority to the confrontation of employers who refuse to recruit them. The effect of such attitudes could be very damaging for a young person. Although some careers officers felt that they had very little power to influence the actions of either school leavers or employers, others recognized the possibly enormous effects of their decisions on the future lives of individual young people.

If you've got a vacancy ... and you think 'Sod it, the Asian girls won't turn up for the interview' — if you've got that attitude you are denying them access to the actual vacancy. There's a lot of power about who goes to a vacancy, rather than at a Job Centre, where someone picks *themselves* out. I don't think people are aware at times how much power they have got on that young person's life, career, earning capacity, and things like that.

Having said this, it would be a mistake to reduce the problem to one simply of the questionable attitudes of some careers staff. There are particular organizational arrangements in which such attitudes are are more likely to thrive, and alternatively, those where they are less likely to cause damage. Correspondingly, the existence of organizational and structural constraints means that the *absence* of such attitudes on the part of careers staff still does not mean that a successful anti-racist approach will be embraced. The interviews revealed many instances of individuals with a critical awareness of racism and a progressive concern for equal opportunities who still did not feel themselves to be in a position to be effectively 'anti-racist'.

Constraints Upon Anti-racist Action

In any consideration of the desirability, appropriateness and effectiveness of equal opportunity and anti-racist measures for careers services there must be an awareness of certain external and historical constraints on the actions of careers officers. These constraints are likely to work against the effectiveness of equal apportunity measures and could diminish the motivation of careers staff to operate them.

The first of these is the fact that careers staff have to work within the context of weak race relations legislation (Lustgarten, 1987). This does not encourage that part of an equal opportunities programme which ultimately relies on a recourse to the law. In their study of race, training and employment Verma and Darby (1987) conclude that the present legal provision to protect young people from ethnic minorities against discrimination by placement agencies or sponsors is not very accessible to the young people themselves, and is often misunderstood and difficult to take action under by officers who might wish to take advantage of it. The fact that such actions are stressful and highly time consuming means that the level of commitment has to be very high if a person wants to go through with it.

A Midlands careers officer sympathized with her colleagues who she felt might 'think twice' before initiating any action which might ultimately lead to legal proceedings by the CRE. For one thing, they could see that even the CRE was not particularly effective in its enforcement policy, as penalties for employers found guilty remained slight. A careers officer attributed the inaction of some of her colleagues to 'fear'.

> ... You can undestand why people 'sit' on worries because they have personal liability under the Act, not like lots of other legislation, where the County Council would be in the dock ... Its a fairly umpleasant business, the idea of having to give evidence, and 'Are you sure that was said' and all the rest of it — and I

think that people need to believe that there is a corporate backing for a stand against a racist employer.

And many careers staff have learned that this 'backing' is not forthcoming from senior management. Some described how they felt disillusioned because on occasions when they had sent reports of 'pressure to discriminate' cases up to their senior staff, and nothing seemed to come of them. A CRE employment officer complained that a local careers service was not passing on cases of pressure to discriminate — they had heard from a menber of support staff in a local office that twenty cases had been referred up to the Principal Careers Officer (PCO) in five months, and the CRE had only got to hear about three of them.

The Balance of Power

The reluctance of many careers officers to initiate a harder line with employers has to be seen in a wider structural context. There exists an imbalance of power in the youth labour market between the buyers and sellers of labour power — or, in the case of the careers service, those involved in advising and assisting the sellers. The nature of the encounter between the careers service and young people is constrained by this imbalance of power and the pressures are there to fall in with the desires and prejudices of employers and managing agents in this unequal operation of supply and demand. This forms the essence of the contradiction in the careers service's position. As Brown (1985) argues, the careers service is part of the state apparatus involved in allocating a 'new' workforce on behalf of capital, but it is also a counselling agency — 'vocational guidance representing the liberal humanist view of pluralistic individual attainment'. This creates a tension in the service parallel with the Great Debate on the nature of education and the extent to which it services the needs of industry.

This contradiction regularly found expression in the statements of careers officers: the careers service 'has such a problem deciding where its client group is, and deciding whether it backs employers or whether it backs kids'.

It's a question of which hat you are wearing. With us it is 'are we on the employers' side or are we on the kids side?' We seem to do so much to lose the trust that young people have in us that some people see us as with the employers. But employers accuse us of 'sending anyone', just trying to get the kids who are no good off our case load. So they see us as with the kids. The job makes you paranoid.

Although this contradiction has always been there for the service in its location between the spheres of education and work, it has become highlighted more in recent years with the increase in unemployment, the advent of YTS, and the strategies and policies of the Conservative government. The fact that the balance of power in the youth labour market has in recent years swung more markedly to the employers' side has had implications for careers service work.

In the early 1970s the careers service crystallized a 'client centred' philosophy involving counselling techniques, non-directive interviewing, psychometric testing and other methods to assist the young person to make the appropriate career choice. Thus a professional philosophy of vocational guidance for young people was emphasized, rather than a narrow matching of individuals to employer needs. As one careers officer put it:

> There is this thing that our primary client is the *kid* and not the employer ... I think most careers officers believe that, very much so — sometimes to the frustration of people like me who work in the Employer Section.

However, as Cockburn writes, it was not long before the 'Great Debate' in education and the 'new vocationalism' were to collide with these liberal principles:

> A right wing view of education and the school-to-work transition, given force by the return of a Conservative government in 1979, defined and limited the boundaries of professional autonomy, whether of teachers or careers officers, and legitimised a new 'industrial needs' emphasis. (Cockburn 1987, p. 70)

A careers officer wrote of the new demands on the service, particularly with the advent of YTS: 'There is enormous pressure from the Department of Employment, the MSC, and managing agents for the careers service to keep schemes fully occupied.' In consequence it was felt that other work of the service — the provision of local labour market information, discussing options, facilitating free decision making and offering non-judgmental guidance — was becoming increasingly impossible for careers workers (LMNI, 1987).

Davies (1985) argues that many careers officers have become disillusioned. The initial response of some within the service was that in the new circumstances the careers service should become a political pressure group, acting on behalf of young people to challenge government policy on youth unemployment. Countervailing political pressure came via Peter Morrison, Minister of State for Employment, addressing the 1983

Annual Conference of the Institute of Careers Officers. He warned that many in authority had come to regard the careers service as dangerous social engineers who were unwilling to help employers by encouraging people to take up places on YTS. He made it clear that the future of the service depended on how they handled YTS (Times Educational Supplement, 7/10/83). The Minister warned that the Rayner Review into the operational efficiency of the careers service would be particularly interested in the service's contribution to YTS. He suggested that the careers service should pay less attention to occupational guidance and more to placing young people into schemes (Careers Bulletin, 1983 pp. 20–1; Davies; 1985, p. 20).

Thus political pressures were added to those arising from economic change for careers officers to underplay the 'professional' part of their work — the vocational guidance interview — and concentrate on work which Davies (1985, p. 15) calls 'sub-professional': obtaining job market information, giving practical advice on job seeking and interview skills, and placing with employers. The erosion of a demarcated area of 'professional skill' has the inevitable effect of reducing the autonomy of an occupational group, and leaving it open to further external pressure.

The overt pressure on the service has been followed by other pressures. The development of YTS into its two year version entailed a bigger role for the service. Careers services themselves argued that they were already fully stretched by the scheme, and were in some places finding difficulty in providing vocational guidance to school pupils. 'They ... cannot see how they could undertake the detailed assessment of 500,000 YTS entrants without considerable expansion of the Service' (TES 12.7.85). Later guidelines from the Department of Employment argued that careers officers should only give guidance to a YTS trainee if the managing agent agreed. The head of a city careers service saw this as undermining the whole basis of the service's relationship with young people: 'The youngsters most likely to need guidance are those who are getting a rough deal from the people who are supposed to be training them: how on earth could we allow those very people to control our access to the youngsters in question?' (TES, 4.10.85). This development can be interpreted as further pressure on careers staff to shift the emphasis of their work away from a client-centred guidance role towards one of servicing employers.

Conclusion

Ethnic minority young people do less well in terms of labour market success than their equivalently qualified white peers; at the same time they are disproportionately dependent on the careers service. Careers service staff have not always been sensitive to these two simple facts. Nor have they always been sufficiently aware of the importance of allowing for genuine cultural differences, whilst avoiding facile stereotyping, when dealing with ethnic minority clients.

More recently there has been a growing race and equal opportunity consciousness in the service, with a more critical questioning of the old 'professional/colour blind' stance. However, the embracing of 'equal opportunities' may not be enough. A point which has so often been made in the sphere of education is equally valid here: it is important to adopt *anti-racist* practices as well as multi-cultural and equal opportunity policies (Troyna and Williams, 1986; Troyna, 1987). One major reason why ethnic minority school leavers do not get the most desirable jobs and YTS places is the operation of racial discrimination by employers and place-ment providers. Yet there exists a great variety between local services in their response to racism, and evidence that racism in its many, sometimes subtle, forms is not always 'noticed' or confronted. Thus it is possible to conceive of a situation where 'equality' exists in the fair and professional treatment of ethnic minority clients by the Service, without any change being effected in outcome in terms of labour market success.

The implications of a lack of anti-racist awareness and practice go further than might be first thought. It has a bearing not only on how careers staff relate to employers, but also on their treatment of the young people themselves. It has been shown that some careers officers are prone to label ethnic minority clients as over-aspiring or unrealistic. But such a generalization may not simply be rooted in a lack of cultural awareness or tendency to think in stereotypes. It may also be related to the knowledge that ethnic minority young people are liable to experience resistance by those employers for whom they aspire to work. The very fact that ethnic minority young people are particularly likely to aspire to 'good' jobs with training and prospects points them towards those scarcer jobs in sectors where they are more likely to meet racial discrimination. Thus part of the 'over-aspiration' labelling process could itself be due to a knowledge of the existence of employer racism — a reaction of officers who are aware of this but who do not feel themselves to be in a position to confront it, and who feel powerless to do anything about it.

Another response that has been identified is that of 'protective chan-nelling', a similar but perhaps more conscious response on behalf of careers staff, where a knowledge of employers who are not sympathetic to ethnic minority youngsters leads officers to direct young people to where it is felt they will have a more sympathetic reception. There is also another 'anticipation' process — that of the young people themselves. Some officers were aware that an apparent reluctance to be submitted to some prestigious employer based schemes was due to the young peoples' fear of unfair treatment. A Midlands PCO confirmed 'We have encoun-tered resistance to YTS from black youngsters who feel their prospects are few at the end of their training and who fear discrimination on schemes'. (Youth Training News 36, February 1987)

Many careers officers will say that racial discrimination is rare. However, the extent of the problem is not identified by how often it breaks the surface. The above phenomena — the deflating of 'unrealistic' aspirations, the protective channelling, and the anticipatory avoidance of racist employers by young people all combine to lessen the likelihood that acts of racial discrimination will *need to* occur. A greater emphasis on anti-racism by the service can ultimately help to reduce the fatalism of both careers staff and young people, and begin to break this syndrome. There needs to be an automatic reaction from staff to pressure to discriminate and racist instructions by employers, a refusal to accept vacancies in such cases, and a readiness to forward details of cases to the CRE for consideration for prosecution. There should be clear office procedures backed up by training for staff at all levels on how to respond in situations of suspected racial discrimination, and disciplinary procedures for any staff found involved in discrimination and racist practices. Careers staff should be sensitive to the operation of quiet and subtle racial exclusion and ready to engage in a little detective work when necessary; there should also be routine monitoring of ethnic statistics on placement and acceptance rates and a willingness to act where statistics show a potentially suspicious imbalance.

The Careers Service and the Enterprise Culture

It has been argued that the careers service has become central to the operation of the youth labour market and figures more prominently in the government's plan for training and employment, with a correspondingly enhanced effect on the futures of ethnic minority young people. At the same time, the government's fostering of the 'enterprise culture' in general, and the more specific pressures to serve uncritically the needs of employers has not assisted those within the service who wish actively to promote racial equality in employment. Economic and political pressures have operated to persuade careers officers that previous professional emphases are now inappropriate, and that servicing the needs of employers and managing agents is paramount. The 1980s saw the further application of free market principles to education, with schools urged to serve more narrowly the interests of industry and commerce. Within this climate, the pressures against effective anti-racism are many. The careers service is the weaker party in the imbalance of power within the youth labour market. The legislative framework it operates within is weak. In one sense its potential power has been further undermined — the service would have been well placed to play a key information role on employer practices where a local authority was operating a policy of contract compliance on equal opportunities. Yet in the late 1980s the Conservative government began to outlaw the practice of contract compliance and emasculated it further via the local Government Act (see IPM, 1987). Many careers services now feel particularly strained with their enhanced duties, yet effective equal opportunity and anti-racist work implies even more of a drain on their limited resources. Those who are involved in anti-racism within the careers service need to be particularly committed in their efforts in order that the momentum of such work is sustained. Anti-racist and equal opportunity work make the lives of careers staff more difficult, and the pressures are there on careers staff for racial discrimination in the youth labour market not to be 'noticed'. The service's power is constrained by the fact that employers can recruit their trainees directly and do not have to use the service. At the outset of YTS it was argued unsuccessfully by the TUC and others that the recruitment of trainees should be the sole responsibility of placing agencies such as the careers service. The fact that employers can go elsewhere for their trainees has undermined the service's potential to apply pressure for change in their YTS recruitment practices.

Thus there are contradictions in the role of the careers service in a decade of enterprise. It has been allocated an enhanced role in the labour market, but at the same time government policies and the operation of the free market have made it harder for those concerned about equal opportunity in careers service practice. However, despite this, there are ways in which the service's potential influence with employers has been enhanced. The shortage of school leavers available for employment in the late 1980s/early 1990s means greater difficulties for those employers traditionally dependent on the recruitment of 16–18 year olds. In the context of labour and skill shortages, the arm of those concerned with equal opportunity has been strengthened, and arguments about the utility of equal opportunity measures have been thrown into sharper relief. There has long been an academic debate on the efficiency or otherwise for employers of equal opportunity measures. One school of thought talks of the inefficiency of racial discrimination in that it prevents employers from drawing on the full range of talent available. Others argue that equal opportunity measures and 'fair' recruitment procedures impose unnecessary costs on employers, who would already have adopted them voluntarily had they been 'efficient' for a firm. As Rubenstein (1987) puts it, sex and race discrimination can often be *rational* behaviour for profit maximizing employer, which is precisely why the problem is so intractable. Having said this, there may well be certain sectors of employment and certain conditions of market or labour supply where economic benefits of equal opportunity practices begin to apply. There has already emerged some evidence to confirm that a bad equal opportunity image can be harmful for an employer who is experiencing difficulties in recruiting workers, even when the existence of job vacancies coincides with local unemployment (Mira-Smith and Ladbury, 1989). Conversely, the Rover Group recently announced that a change in its recruitment and training policies to encourage more young people from ethnic minority communities had resulted in a 10 per cent rise in applications despite a fall in the number of school leavers, reversing a drop in the number of school leaver applications over the previous two years (*Labour Research,* November 1989).

The operation of the single European market in 1992 will raise new issues of labour mobility and supply, and could be a further stimulus for critically raising issues of broader access to vocational training. European Community literature argues for a fight against the under-utilization of resources and places great emphasis on a European 'pool of skills' to take full advantage of the single market, with a 'significant investment' in training and a desire to promote social conditions which enable workers to overcome any lack of prospects for improving their skills and qualifications (Social Europe, 1988, p. 57). It is clear that in the UK those whose resources are most obviously 'under-utilized' are ethnic minority groups. Unrestrained racial discrimination eventually becomes self-perpetuating by discouraging able and qualified young people from putting themselves forward in the first place. There are conditions and circumstances when the racist exclusion of able young people from quality vocational training can be dysfunctional for employer interests. The enterprise culture, left to itself, will not foster progress in this area, and the operation of unrestrained market forces only serves to perpetuate or exacerbate existing structured inequalities. The empowering of an enlightened and anti-racist Careers Service, on the other hand, could form one part of a counter strategy.

Appendix

The following are direct quotes taken from transcripts of tape-recorded interviews with careers officers and employment officers between 1984–7, in response to the question as to whether in the course of their work they had encountered any examples of clear or suspected racial discrimination by employers. Each quote is from a different officer.

> We rang up to submit someone to a vacancy, and everything seemed to be alright, until we mentioned the name, and then it suddenly changed — 'Oh, I'm sorry, the vacancy's been filled'.

> An electrical shop had a vacancy for a sales assistant — they didn't want any Asian girls. 'Its not right for our customers — they don't dress smartly enough'.

The last case of direct discrimination was two years ago with a Japanese company. I was told 'The Japanese don't recruit West Indians'. So the PCO wrote to the Head Office in Japan.

They usually damn themselves out of their own mouths if they are that way, because they speak to you conspiratorially and say 'Not your colonial friends' or something like that.

This recent incident is unusual in that it was so blatant — we had an employer register a vacancy for a motor mechanic, and the employer said over the phone to a careers officer 'By the way, the standard of youngster you are sending to me is appalling — you are even sending me blacks.' I phoned the employer, asked if he would receive a visit from the Race Relations Advisory Service. He was rude on the phone. One black lad who had been turned down at interview agreed to take it further, so the CRE was informed, and it went to a Tribunal.

About a year ago a colleague in this office had a girl who was right for a retail vacancy; phoned up the employer, said 'I've got a girl who would do', and the employer happened to say 'Oh, by the way, she isn't black is she?' He said 'Do you realise you are breaking the law by just asking me that?'. The employer said that they were a fairly high class store and it may affect the selling — he eventually said 'I didn't say anything, thank you very much' and put the phone down.

I've spoken to an employer, and the employer has said to me 'What's his name?' . . . and then 'I've interviewed four now, love, and I think I can make my mind up'. Then I will take the vacancy off immediately, because I think 'Well, you've said it'.

A company that deals in waste paper has said 'We don't want any Asians', and when told that's totally unrealistic — 'Oh no, they don't work,' and using wholesale stereotypes.

. . . 'What's he look like?' or 'Oh, I didn't realize it was an Asian — I'm not being funny and I'm not racist, but he wouldn't fit in' and we have to say 'Sorry, I'm not allowed to discriminate — can we arrange a time for you to see him?' And if you put it like that, they normally catch on — 'Yes, all right then'. It normally doesn't get any further than that.

We had one YTS sponsor, as opposed to managing agent, who wouldn't interview a youngster on the basis of a name, which was obviously Asian. . . . I had another case where an accountant wouldn't consider an Asian youngster, again on the basis of a name, but gave reasons that he had had another Asian before who tried to commit suicide — which didn't really hold water.

We had one last week where we sent a youngster for a vacancy and he was told that there was no vacancy. We had checked an hour before that there was a vacancy and we sent him down. The poor little soul came back out of the snow and said 'Excuse me, have you sent me to the right firm, because they told me that there were no vacancies?' So I rang them up and I said 'Have you interviewed this boy?' and they said 'We took his name and address'. I said 'Did you tell him that there were no vacancies?' and they said 'Oh, just a minute, I will have to refer you to some body else' and that virtually went on all day, backwards and forwards. But that has gone out of my hands now, and we are not putting that back up as a vacancy . . . because I think that is direct discrimination.

I haven't had a case professionally where I have had to do something about an employer being openly racist, but it's something that you pick up from discussions with employers when you are not in your role as careers officer. Some employers will still say 'Well I'm not taking on anyone who is black'. That's unofficially, obviously, and if you try to pin them down on that or repeat it obviously they wouldn't.

When you are out visiting you might get the odd employer who will let something drop: 'Don't let any black kids here'.

Some companies will have a quiet word in you ear and say 'Well I know full well that the manager in the company won't accept them' . . . because 'they tend to leave more regularly' or something. You can only point out that they can't say that. . . . But at the final selection I'm not sure how much power we have.

Acknowledgment

I am grateful to Ken Grainger for advice and comment on this work.

References

ACKERS, P. (1987) 'Review of LD Smith, Carpet Weavers and Carpet Masters' (Tomlinson, 1986), *Business History*, December.

ACKERS, P. (July 1988) 'Changes in workplace industrial relations in West Midlands manufacturing industry in the 1980s', M. Phil Thesis.

ACKERS, P. (1989) 'Workplace benefits: The Human Resources Management revolution', *New Socialist*, April/May.

ALEXANDER, I. and DAWSON, J. (1979) 'Employment in retailing: A case study of employment in surburban shopping centres', *Geoforum* 10.

ALI, N., COOK, J. and RYAN, A. (1987) 'Processing black clients: A Careers Service perspective' in CROSS, M. and SMITH, D.I. (Eds) *Black Youth Futures: Ethnic Minorities and the Youth Training Scheme*, Leicester, National Youth Bureau.

ALLEN, J. and MASSEY, D. (1988) (Eds) *The Economy in Question*, London, Sage.

ALLEN, S. (1989) 'Gender and work in mining communities, paper presented to the British Sociological Association Conference, Plymouth Polytechnic, March, 1989.

AMIN, A. (1989) 'Flexible specialisation and small firms in Italy: Myths and realities', *Antipode*, 21(1), pp. 13–34.

ANDERSON, J. and COCHRANE, A. (1989) (Eds) *A State of Crisis*, London, Hodder and Stoughton.

ASHTON, D.H. and FIELD, D. (1976) *Young Workers*, London, Hutchinson.

ATKINSON, J. (1984) 'Manpower strategies for flexible organizations' *Personnel Management*, August.

ATKINSON, J. (1989) 'Four Stages of Adjustment to the Demographic Downturn', *Personnel Management*, August, pp. 20–24.

BACON, C., BENTON, D. and GRUNEBERG, M.M. (1979) 'Employers opinions of university and polytechnic graduates', *The Vocational Aspects of Education*, 31(80), pp. 95–102.

BALLARD, R.E.H. and HOLDEN, B.M. (1975) 'The employment of coloured graduates in Britain', *New Community*, 4(3).

BAMFIELD, J. (1980) 'The changing face of British retailing', *National Westminister Bank Quarterly*, May.

BARBASH, J. (1987) 'Like nature IR abhors a vacuum: The case of union free strategy', *Industrial Relations*, (Canada) 42(1).

BARKER, T.C. (1977) *The Glassmakers: Pilkington: 1926–1976*, London, Weidenfeld and Nicolson.

BARNETT, R.A. (1988) 'Institutions of higher education: Purposes and performance indicators', *Oxford Review of Education*, 14(1) pp. 97–112.

BASSETT, P. (1986) *Strike Free*, London, Macmillan.

BAXTER, J.L. (1975) 'The chronic job-changer: A study of youth unemployment', *Social and Economic Administration*, 9, pp.184–209.

BECHHOFER, F. and ELLIOTT, B. (1981) 'Petty property: The survival of a moral economy', in BECHHOFER, F. and ELLIOTT, B. (Eds), *The Petit Bourgeoisie: Comparative Studies of the Uneasy Stratum*, London, Macmillan.

BECHHOFER, F. and ELLIOTT, B. (1985) 'The petit bourgeoisie in late capitalism', in TURNER, R. and REISS, A. (Eds) *Annual Review of Sociology 1985*, Palo Alto, Annual Reviews Inc.

BEECHEY, V. and PERKINS, T. (1987) *A Matter of Hours: Women, Part-time Work and the Labour Market*, Cambridge, Polity Press.

BERRY-LOUND, M. (1990) 'Towards the family friendly firm', *Employment Gazette*, February, pp. 85–91.

BEVAN, J., CLARK, G., BANERJI, N. and HAKIM, C. (1989) *Barriers to Business Start-Up, A Study of the Flow Into and Out of Self-Employment*, Research Paper No. 71, London, Department of Employment.

BHASKAR, R. (1979) *The Possibility of Naturalism*, Brighton, Wheatsheaf.

BINFIELD, C. (1982) 'Business paternalism and the congregational ideal', Paper to London Meeting of Historians Study Group.

BLACK, J. and ACKERS, P. (1988a) 'The Japanisation of British industry: A case study of the carpet industry', Paper to 1987 UWIST Conference, *Employee Relations*, 10(6).

BLACK, J. and ACKERS, P. (1988b) 'New patterns of IR practice in West Midlands companies', *Management Research News*.

BLACK, J. and ACKERS, P. (1989) 'Managing organised labour in the 1980s — a tale of two companies', Paper to Aston/UMIST 6th Annual Conference on Management Control, March 1988. Forthcoming in *Journal of Industrial Affairs*.

BLACK, J. and NEATHEY, F. (1989) 'Labour and deskilling, a critique of management control in the glass industry', in *New Perspectives in Management Control*, London, Macmillan.

BLACK, J. and TAYLOR, J. (1986) *Management Control and Work Organization: A Case Study*, London, Van Nostrand and Reinhold.

BLUESTONE, B. and STEVENSON, M. (1981) 'Industrial transformation and the evolution of dual labour markets: The case of retail trade in the

References

United States' in WILKINSON, F. (Ed.) *Labour Market Segmentation*, London, Hutchinson.

BOLTON REPORT (1971) *Report of the Committee of Enquiry on Small Firms*, Cmnd. 4811, London: HMSO.

BRADLEY, H. (1989) *Men's Work, Women's Work: A Sociological History of the Sexual Division of Labour in Employment*, Cambridge, Polity Press.

BRENNAN, J. and McGEEVOR, P. (1988) *Graduates at Work*, London, Jessica Kingsley.

BRENNAN, J. and SILVER, H. (1986) 'A liberal vocationalism? A concept and its policy implications', *Development Services Paper*, London, CNAA.

BRIGGS, A. (1968) 'Birmingham: The making of a civic gospel', in *Victorian Cities*, Harmondsworth, Penguin.

BRIGHT, R. (1987) *Small Business and Nine Years of Entreprise Culture*, London, Conservative Party.

BRITISH COAL ENTERPRISE (1985–6) *Annual Review*, London, BCE.

BROOKS, D. (1974–5) Railways, Railwaymen and Race', *New Community* 4(1) Winter/Spring.

BROOKS, D. (1975) *Race and Labour in London Transport*, London, Oxford University Press.

BROOKS, D. and SINGH, K. (1978) *Aspirations Versus Opportunities*, London, Commission for Racial Equality.

BROWN, K.M. (1985) '"Turning a blind eye": Racial oppression and the unintended consequences of white "non-racism"', *Sociological Review*, 33 (4).

BRUSCO, S. and SABEL, C. (1981) 'Artisan production and economic growth' in WILKINSON, F. (Ed.) *The Dynamics of Labour Market Segmentation*, London and New York, Academic Press.

BRYANT, N. (1979) *The Unexpected Revolution*, London, Heinemann.

BUCK, N., GORDON, and YOUNG, K. (1986), *The London Employment Problem*, London, Oxford University Press.

BULMER, M. (1975) 'Sociological Models of the Mining Community', *Sociological Review*, 23(1), pp. 61–92.

BURROWS, R. (1991a) (Ed.) *Deciphering the Enterprise Culture: Entrepreneurship, Petty Capitalism and the Restructuring of Britain*, London, Routledge.

BURROWS, R. (1991b) 'A socio-economic anatomy of the British petty bourgeoisie: A multivariate analysis' in BURROWS, R. (Ed.) *Deciphering the Enterprise Culture: Entrepreneurship, Petty Capitalism and the Restructuring of Britain*, London, Routledge.

BURROWS, R. (1991c) 'The discourse of the enterprise culture and the restructuring of Britain: A polemical contribution', in CURRAN, J. and BLACKBURN, R. (Eds) *The Future of the Small Enterprise*, London, Routledge.

BURROWS, R. and CURRAN, J. (1989) 'Sociological research on service sector small businesses: Some conceptual considerations', *Work, Employment and Society*, 3(4), pp. 527–539.

BURSTYN, J. (1980) *Victorian Education and the Ideal of Womanhood*, London, Croom Helm.

BUSWELL, C. (1987) 'Training for low pay', in GLENDINNING, C. and MILLAR, J. (Eds) *Women and Poverty in Britain*, London, Wheatsheaf.

BYNNER, J. (1987) 'Coping with transition: ESRC's new 16–19 initiative', *Youth and Policy*, 22, pp. 25–8.

CADBURY, A. (1985) 'Quaker Values in Business'. Unpublished.

CAMPBELL B. (1984) *Wigan Pier Revisited*, London, Virago.

CASEY, B. and CREIGH, S. (1988) 'Self-employment in Great Britain: Its definition in the Labour Force Survey, in 'Tax and social security law and in labour law', *Work, Employment and Society*, 2(3), pp. 381–91.

CATLEY, D. and CHAPMAN, A. (1989) 'Equality of opportunity in the graduate labour market', *Staffordshire Polytechnic Graduate Study Final Report*, Vol. 1, Stoke on Trent, Department of Sociology, Staffordshire Polytechnic.

CAULKIN, S. (1987) 'Pilkington after BTR', *Management Today* (June).

CHAPMAN, A. (1989) 'Just the ticket? Graduate men and women in the labour market three years after leaving college', *HELM Working Paper No. 8*, London, CNAA.

CHILD, J. (1964) 'Quaker employers and industrial relations', *Sociological Review*, NS Vol. 12.

CLARKE, J. and CRITCHER, C. (1985) *The Devil Makes Work: Leisure in Capitalist Britain*, London, Macmillan.

CLARKE, S. (1990) 'What in the F___'s name is Fordism?', in GIBERT, G.N. and BURROWS, R. (Eds) *Fordism and Flexibility: Divisions and Change*, Basingstoke, Macmillan.

CLOUGH, E., GRAY, J., JONES, B. and PATTIE, C. (1988) *England and Wales Youth Cohort Study: Routes through the YTS*, Manpower Services Commission, Sheffield.

COCHRANE, A. and ANDERSON, J. (1989) (Eds) *Politics in Transition*, London, Sage.

COCKBURN, C. (1987) *Two Track Training: Sex Inequalities and the YTS*, Basingstoke, Macmillan.

COLLINSON. D.L. (1988) *Barriers to Fair Selection: A Multi-Sector Study of Recruitment Practices*, London, HMSO.

COMMISSION FOR RACIAL EQUALITY. (1983) *Code of Practice for the Elimination of Racial Discrimination and the Promotion of Equality of Opportunity in Empolyment*, London, HMSO.

CONNOR, S. (1989) *Postmodernist Culture, An Introduction to Theories of the Contemporary*, Oxford, Basil Blackwell.

CONSERVATIVE PARTY (1987) *Small Businesses: The Success Story*, London, Central Office.

COOKE, P. (1989) (Ed.) *Localities*, London, Unwin Hyman.

COYLE, A. and SKINNER, J. (1988) *Women and Work: Positive Action for Change*, London, Macmillan.

CRAIG, C. and WILKINSON, F. (1985) *Pay and Employment in Four Retail Trades*, London, Department of Employment.

CROSS, M. (1991a) *Caribbean Echoes and British Realities: Blacks Asians and the Colonial Encounter*, London, Avebury.

CROSS, M. (1991b) *The Two Racisms: Afro-Caribbeans, Asians and the Class Structure*, London, Unwin Hyman.

CROSS, M., WRENCH, J. and BARNETT, S. (1990) 'Ethnic minorities and the Careers Service: An investigation into processes of assessment and placement', Department of Employment Research Paper No. 73, London, HMSO.

CROW, G. (1989) 'The use of the concept of "strategy" in recent sociological literature', *Sociology*, 23(1) pp. 1–24.

CURRAN, J. (1986) *Bolton Fifteen Years On*, London, Small Business Research Trust.

CURRAN, J. (1987) *Small Enterprises and Their Environments: A Report*, Kingston Polytechnic, Small Business Research Unit Report.

CURRAN, J. (1990) 'The role of the small firm and self-employment in the British economy', *Work Employment and Society, A Decade of Change?* Special Issue, May.

CURRAN, J. and BLACKBURN, R.A. (1990) *Enterprise 2000*, London: Small Business Research Trust.

CURRAN, J. and BURROWS, R. (1986) 'The sociology of petit capitalism: A trend report', *Sociology* 20(2), pp. 265–79.

CURRAN, J. and BURROWS, R. (1987a) 'The social analysis of small business: Some emerging themes' in GOFFEE, R. and SCASE, R. (Eds) *Entrepreneurship in Europe: The Social Processes*, London, Croom Helm.

CURRAN, J. and BURROWS, R. (1987b) 'Ethnographic approaches to the study of small business owners', in O'NEILL, K. *et al.* (Eds) *Small Business Development: Some Current Issues*, Aldershot, Avebury.

CURRAN, J. and BURROWS, R. (1988) *Enterprise in Britain: A National Profile of Small Business Owners and the Self–Employed*, London, Small Business Research Trust.

CURRAN, J. and STANWORTH, J. (1986) 'Trends in small firm industrial relations and their implications for the role of the small firm in economic restructuring', in AMIN, A. and GODDARD, J. (Eds) *Technological Change Industrial Restructuring and Regional Development*, London, Allen and Unwin.

CURRAN, M. (1987) *Stereotypes and Selection: Gender and Family in the Recruitment Process*, London, HMSO.

DAHRENDORF, R. (1987) 'The erosion of citizenship and its consequences for us all', *New Statesman*, 12 June.

DALE, A. (1990) 'Self-employment and entrepreneurship: Notes on two problematic concepts', in BURROWS, R. (Ed.) *Deciphering the Enterprise Culture: Entrepreneurship, Petty Capitalism and the Restructuring of Britain*, London, Routledge.

DALY, M. (1985) *The Hidden Workers*, Employment Equality Agency, Dublin.

DAVIES, C. and ROSSER, J. (1986) 'Gendered jobs in the health service. A problem for labour process analysis', in KNIGHTS, D. and WILLMOTT, H. (Eds) *Gender and the Labour Process*, Aldershot, Gower.

DAVIES, C.P. (1985) 'A study of the factors involved in the occupational aspirations of fifth year secondary school pupils', M. Phil, University of Aston in Birmingham.

DENNIS, N., HENRIQUES, F. and SLAUGHTER, C. (1956) *Coal Is Our Life*, London, Tavistock.

DEPARTMENT OF EMPLOYMENT (1972) *Take 7: Race Relations at Work*, London, HMSO.

DEPARTMENT OF EMPLOYMENT (1986) *Building Businesses ... Not Barriers*, Cmnd. 9794, London, HMSO.

DEPARTMENT OF EMPLOYMENT (1989) *Small Firms in Britain*, London, Department of Employment and Central Office of Information.

DEPARTMENT OF TRADE AND INDUSTRY (1988) *DTI — The Department for Enterprise*, Cmnd. 278, London, HMSO.

DEX, S. (1985) *The Sexual Division of Work: Conceptual Revolutions in the Social Sciences*, Brighton, Wheatsheaf.

DYHOUSE, C. (1981) *Girls Growing up in Late Victorian and Edwardian England*, London, Routledge.

DYHOUSE, C. (1984) 'Storming the citadel or storm in a tea cup? The entry of women into higher education: 1860–1920' in ACKER, S. and WARREN PIPER, D. (Eds) *Is Higher Education Fair to Women?*, London, SRHE/NFER Nelson.

EDMONDS, T. (1986) 'Small firms, background paper', London, House of Commons Library Research Division, June.

EGGLESTON, S.J., DUNN, D.K. and ANJALI, M. with WRIGHT, C. (1986) *Education for Some: The Educational and Vocational Experiences of 15–18 year-old Members of Minority Ethnic Groups*, Stoke-on-Trent, Trentham Books.

ELSTON, M.A. (1977) 'Women in the Medical Profession: Whose Problem?' in STACEY, M., REID, M., HEATH, C. and DINGWALL, R. (Eds) *Health and the Division of Labour*, London, Croom Helm.

EMPLOYMENT GAZETTE (1989) 'Labour force outlook to the year 2000', *Employment Gazette*, 97, 4 April, pp. 159–172.

EQUAL OPPORTUNITIES COMMISSION (1985) *Code of Practice for the Elimination of Discrimination on the Grounds of Sex and Marriage and the Promotion of Equality of Opportunity in Employmemt*, London, HMSO.

FAINSTEIN, S., GORDON, I. and HARLOE, M., (1990) *Divided Cities*, London, Edward Arnold.

FENTON, S., DAVIES, T., MEANS, R. and BURTON, P. (1984) *Ethnic Minorities and the Youth Training Scheme*, Sheffield, MSC Research and Development Paper No. 20.

FEVRE, R. (1989) *Wales Is Closed*, Nottingham, Spokesman.

FINCH, J. (1984) *Married to the Job: Wives' Incorporation in Men's Work*, London, Allen and Unwin.

FINCH, J. and GROVES, D. (1983) (Eds) *A Labour of Love: Work and Caring*, London, Routledge.

FOREMAN, C. (1979) *Industrial Town*, Granada/Paladin.

FOREMAN-PECK (1985) 'Seedcorn or chaff? New firm formation and the performance of the inter-war economy', *Economic History Review* (2nd Series), 38, 3.

FOSTER, H. (1984) (Eds) *Postmodern Culture*, London, Pluto.

FOSTER, J. (1989) 'Balancing work and the family: Divided loyalties or constructive partnership', *Personnel Management*, September, pp. 38–41.

FOWLER. B. LITTLEWOOD, B. and MADIGAN, R. (1977), 'Immigrant school leavers and the search for work' *Sociology*, 11, (2).

FOX, A. (1966) 'Industrial sociology and industrial relations', Research Paper 3, *Royal Commission on Trade Unions and Employers Associations*, London, HMSO.

FRANCIS, H. and REES, G. (1989) ' "No surrender in the valleys": The 1984–85 miners' strike in South Wales', *Journal of Welsh Labour History*, 5(2) pp. 41–71.

FURLONG, A. and COONEY, G.H. (1989) 'Getting on their bikes: Teenagers leaving home in Scotland in the 1980s', Centre for Educational Sociology, University of Edinburgh.

FURLONG, A. and RAFFE, D. (1989) *Young People's Routes into the Labour Market*, ESU Research Paper No 17, Edinburgh, Industry Department for Scotland.

GABRIEL, Y. (1988) *Working Lives in Catering*, London, Routledge and Kegan Paul.

GAMBLE, A. (1988) *The Free Economy and the Strong State: The Politics of Thatcherism*, London, Macmillan.

GANGULY, P. and BANNOCK, G. (1985) *UK Small Business Statistics and International Comparisons*, London, Harper and Row.

GATLEY, D. (1988) 'The Influence of Social Class Origins on the Choice of Course, Career Preferences and Entry into Employment of CNAA Graduates', Unpublished PhD Thesis, Stoke on Trent, Staffordshire Polytechnic.

GEORGE, K. and MAINWARING, L. (1988) (Eds) *The Welsh Economy*, Cardiff, University of Wales Press.

GIDDENS, A. (1984) *The Constitution of Society*, Oxford, Polity.

GOETSCHIN, P. (1987) 'Reshaping work for an older population', *Personnel Management*, June, pp. 39–41.

GOLDTHORPE, J.H. and LOCKWOOD, D. (1969) *The Affluent Worker: Industrial Attitudes and Behaviour*, Cambridge, CUP.

GOODMAN, E., BAMFORD, J. with SAYNOR, P. (1988) *Small Firms and Industrial Districts in Italy*, London, Routledge.

GOODMAN, J.F.B. (1977) *Rule-making and Industrial Peace*, London, Croom Helm.

GORDON, I. and SASSEN, S. (1990) 'The labour market' in FAINSTEIN, S., GORDON, I., HARLOE, M. (Eds) *Divided Cities*, London, Edward Arnold.

GOSS, D. (1990) 'In search of small firm industrial relations' in BURROWS, R. (Ed.) *Deciphering the Enterprise Culture: Entrepreneurship, Petty Capitalism and the Restucturing of Britain*, London, Routledge.

GRAHAM, N. et al. (1989) '1977–1987: A decade of service', *Employment Gazette*, 97(1) pp. 45–54.

GREEN, E., HEBRON, S. and WOODWARD, D. (1987) *Gender and Leisure*, Sports Council.

GREGORY, A. (1987) 'Flexibility for whom? Part-time work in food retailing in Britain and France. With particular reference to the use of part-time work in large-scale grocery retailing', paper prepared for the WYCROW Conference.

GRENIER, G. (1988) *Inhuman Relations?*, Philadelphia, PA, Temple University Press.

GRIFFIN, C. (1985) *Typical Girls*, London, Routledge.

GUEST, D. (1987) 'Human Resources Management and industrial relations', *Journal of Management Studies*, September.

HAKIM, C. (1979) 'Occupational segregation: A comparative study of the degree and pattern of differentiation between men and women's work in Britain, the United States and other Countries' Research Paper No. 9, Department of Employment.

HAKIM, C. (1987) 'Trends in the flexible workforce', *Employment Gazette*, 95, pp. 549–60.

HAKIM, C. (1988) 'Self-employment in Britain: A review of recent trends and current issues', *Work Employment and Society*, 2(4), pp. 421–450.

HALAL, W. (1986) *The New Capitalism*, New York, John Wiley.

HALL, P. (1985) 'The geography of the Fifth Kondratieff cycle', in HALL, P. and MARKUSEN, A. (Eds) *Silicon Landscapes*, London, Allen and Unwin.

HALL, S. and JACQUES, M. (1989) (Eds) *New Times: The Changing Face of Politics in the 1990s*, London, Lawrence and Wishart.

HALL, S. and JACQUES, M. (1983) *The Politics of Thatcherism*, London, Lawrence & Wishart.

HAMNETT, C. et al. (1989) (Eds) *The Changing Social Structure*, London, Sage.

References

HARRIS, C. and THE REDUNDANCY AND UNEMPLOYMENT RESEARCH GROUP (1987) *Redundancy and Recession in South Wales*, Oxford, Basil Blackwell.
HARVEY, D. (1989) *The Condition of Postmodernity*, Oxford, Blackwell.
HEBERT, R. and LINK A. (1989) 'In search of the meaning of entrepreneurship', *Small Business Economics*, 1(1).
HIBBERT, V. (1988) 'Childcare provision I: Employers head for the nursery', *Industrial Relations Review and Report*, 425, October 4, pp. 2–7.
HIBBERT, V. (1988), 'Childcare provision II: Allowances and other benefits', *Industrial Relations Review and Report*, 428, November 15, pp. 7–9.
HIBBERT, V. (1989) 'Bridging the career break', *Industrial Relations Services Employment Trends*, 431, January 10, pp. 6–9.
HMSO (1985) *Lifting the Burden*, Cmnd. 9571, HMSO, London.
HMSO (1986) *Building Business . . . Not Barriers*, Cmnd. 9794, HMSO, London.
HMSO (1988) *Releasing Enterprise*, Cmnd. 512, HMSO, London.
HOBBS, D. (1988) *'Doing the Business: Entrepreneurship, the Working Class and Detectives in the East End of London*, Oxford, Oxford University Press.
HOBBS, D. (1990) 'Business as a master metaphor: Working class entrepreneurship and business-like policing' in BURROWS, R. (Ed.) *Deciphering the Enterprise Culture: Entrepreneurship, Petty Capitalism and the Restructuring of Britain*, London, Routledge.
HOBSBAWN, E. (1988) *The Age of Empire*, London, Weidenfeld and Nicolson.
HOGGART, R. (1977) *The Uses of Literacy*, Harmondsworth, Penguin/Pelican.
HOLLINSHEAD, B. (1986) *Early Careers of Graduates*, Manchester, Centre for Educational Development and Training.
HOPE, K. and GOLDTHORPE, J.H. (1974) *The Social Grading of Occupations: A New Approach and Scale*, Oxford, Oxford University Press.
HURSTFIELD, J. (1977) *The Part-time Trap*, Low Pay Unit, Pamphlet No. 9.
HYWEL, F. and SMITH, D. (1980) *'The Fed:" A History of the South Wales Miners in the 20th Century'* London, Lawrence & Wishart.
IPM (1987) *Contract Compliance: The UK Experience*, London, Institute of Personnel Management.
INDUSTRIAL RELATIONS REVIEW and REPORT (1988) 'Paternity leave — A small step forward for mankind', *Industrial Relations Review and Report*, 410, February 14, pp. 6–11.
JENKINS, R. (1986) *Racism and Recruitment*, Cambridge, Cambridge University Press.

JENKINS, R. (1988) 'Discrimination and equal opportunity in employment: Ethnicity and "race" in the United Kingdom', in GALLIE, D. (Ed.) *Employment in Britain*, Oxford, Basil Blackwell.

JENKINS, R., BRYMAN, A., FORD, J., KEIL, T. and BEARDSWORTH, A. (1983) 'Information in the labour market: The impact of the recession', *Sociology*, 17(2), pp. 260–7.

JEWSON, N. and MASON, D. (1986a) 'Modes of discrimination in the recruitment process: Formalization, fairness and efficiency', *Sociology*, 20(1) pp. 43–63.

JEWSON, N. and MASON, D. (1986b) 'The theory and practice of equal opportunities policies; Liberal and radical approaches', *Sociological Review* 34(2) May, pp. 307–34.

JEWSON, N., MASON, D., WATERS, S. and HARVEY, J. (1990) *Ethnic Minorities and Employment Practice: The Experience Of Six Organizations*, Employment Department Research Paper No. 76, London, HMSO.

JOYCE, P. (1980) *Work, Society and Politics: the culure of the factory in late Victorian England*, Brighton, Harvester.

KANTER, R.M. (1977) 'The impact of hierarchical structures on the work behaviour of women and men', in KAHN-HUT, R. (Ed.) *Women and Work: Problems and Perspectives*, New York, Oxford University Press.

KEAT, R. and ABERCROMBIE, N. (1990) *Enterprise Culture*, London, Routledge.

KELLY, A. (1985) 'The construction of masculine science', *British Journal of Sociology of Education*, 8(3) pp. 305–26.

KELLY, A. (1988) 'Gender differences in teacher-pupil interactions: A meta-analytic review', *Research in Education*, 39, May, pp. 1–23.

KELLY, A. (1991) 'The enterprise culture and the welfare state: Restructuring the management of the health and personal social services', in BURROWS, R. (Ed.) *Deciphering the Enterprise Culture: Entrepreneurship, Petty Capitalism and the Restructuring of Britain*, London, Routledge.

KENDALL, W. (1984) 'Why Japanese workers work', *Management Today*, January.

KERR, C. and SIEGEL, A. (1954) 'The inter-industry propensity to strike: An international comparision', in KORNHAUSER, A. and DUBIN, R. (Eds), *Industrial Conflict*, New York, McGraw Hill.

LABOUR PARTY (1987) 'Labour's strategy for enterprise and small business', statement issued by Barry Sheerman, MP, House of Commons, 14 May.

LANE, T. and ROBERTS, K. (1971) *Strike at Pilkington*, London, Fontana.

LASH, S. and URRY, J. (1987) *The Ends of Organised Capitalism*, Cambridge, Polity.

LEE, G. and WRENCH, J. (1987) 'Race and gender dimensions of the youth labour market: From apprenticeships to YTS', in LEE, G. and LOVERIDGE, R. (Eds) *The Manufacture of Disadvantage*, Milton Keynes, Open University Press.

LEE, G. and WRENCH, J. (1983) *Skill Seekers: Black Youth, Apprenticeship and Disadvantage*, Leicester, National Youth Bureau.

LEWIS, J. (1985) 'Technical change in retailing: Its impact on employment and access', *Environment and Planning B: Planning and Design*, 12.

LGTB/CRE (1988) *Equal Opportunities and the Careers Service*, Luton, Local Government Training Board/Commission for Racial Equality.

LIPIETZ, A. (1987) *Mirages and Miracles: the Crises of Global Fordism*, London, Verso.

LLOYD, T. (1986) (Orig. pub. 1984) *Dinosaur & Co. Studies in Corporate Evolution*, Harmondsworth, Penguin Books.

LMNI (1987) *Report of the Labour Movement National Inquiry Into Youth Unemployment and Training*, Birmingham, TURC Publishing.

LOCKWOOD, D. (1966) 'Sources of variation in working class images of society, *Sociological Review*, 14(3) pp. 249–67.

LONDON BUSINESS SCHOOL (1989) *Economic Outlook*, 14(1) October.

LUSTGARTEN, L. (1987) 'Racial inequality and the limits of law', in JENKINS, R. and SOLOMOS, J. (Eds) *Racism and Equal Opportunity Policies in the 1980s*, Cambridge, Cambridge University Press.

MAGUIRE, M. (1986) 'Recruitment as a means of control', in PURCELL, K. et al. (Eds) *The Changing Experience of Employment*, London, Macmillan.

MAGUIRE, M. (1989) 'A study of women's employment', *Retail Trade Report to the Equal Opportunities Commission for Northern Ireland*, February.

MAGUIRE, M.J. and ASHTON, D.N. (1983) 'Changing face of the careers service', *Employment Gazette*, March.

MALLIER, A. and ROSSER, M. (1980) 'Part-time workers and the firm', *International Journal of Manpower*, 1(3).

MANDEL, E. (1990) *Long Waves of Capitalist Development: The Marxist Interpretation*, Cambridge, Cambridge University Press.

MARSHALL, M. (1987) *Long Waves of Regional Development*, London, Macmillan.

MARSLAND, D. (1988) *Seeds of Bankruptcy: Sociological Bias Against Business and Freedom*, London, Claridge Press.

MARTIN, J. and ROBERTS, C. (1984) *Women and Employment: A Lifetime Perspective*, London, Department of Employment/ESRC.

MARTIN, J. and WALLACE, J. (1984) *Women and Employment: A Lifetime Perspective*, Department of Employment/OPCS.

MARTIN, R. (1988) 'Industrial capitalism in transition: The contemporary reorganisation of the British space–economy', in MASSEY, D. and ALLEN, J. (Eds) *Uneven Re-Development: Cities and Regions in Transition*, London, Hodder and Stoughton.

MARTIN, R. and FRYER, R.H. (1973) *Redundancy and Paternalist Capitalism*, London, Allen and Unwin.

MARTIN, R. and WALLACE, J. (1984) *Working Women in the Recession*, Oxford, Oxford University Press.

MASON, C. (1990) 'Spatial variations in enterprise: The geography of new firm formation', in BURROWS, R. (Ed.) *Deciphering the Enterprise Culture: Entrepreneurship, Petty Capitalism and the Restructuring of Britain*, London, Routledge.

MASSEY, D. (1983) 'Industrial restructing as class restructuring', *Regional Studies*, 17(2) pp. 73–89.

MASSEY, D. (1984) *Spatial Divisions of Labour*, London, Macmillan.

MASSEY, D. and ALLEN, J. (1988) (Eds) *Uneven Re-Development: Cities and Regions in Transition*, London, Hodder and Stoughton.

MAYES, D. and MOIR, C. (1990) 'Small firms in the UK economy', *The Royal Bank of Scotland Review*.

McDOWELL, L. *et al.* (1989) (Eds) *Divided Nation*, London, Hodder and Stoughton.

McRAE, E.S. (1989) *Flexibility, Working Time and Family Life: a Review of Changes*, London, Policy Studies Institute.

MEADOWS, P. and COX, R. (1987) 'Employment of graduates: 1975–1990', *Employment Gazette*, April, pp. 191–200.

MEAGER, N. (1989) *Who Are the Self-Employed?* Anglo-German Foundation Self-Employment Project Working Paper No. 1, Institute of Manpower Studies, University of Sussex.

MILLS, C.W. (1940) 'Situated actions and vocabularies of motive', *American Sociological Review*, 5.

MIRA-SMITH, C. and LADBURY, S. (1989) 'Skills do not equal jobs: Current misconceptions in tackling unemployment', paper delivered to the Annual Conference of the Institute of British Geographers, Coventry Polytechnic, January.

MONOPOLIES AND MERGERS COMMISSION (1989) *British Coal Corporation. A Report on the Investment Programme of the British Coal Corporation*, Cmnd, 550, London, HMSO.

MOORE, K. (1987) 'Women's access and opportunity in high education: Toward the twenty-first century', *Comparative Education* 23(1) pp. 5–20.

MORGAN, K. and SAYER, A. (1988) *Microcircuits of Capital*, Cambridge, Polity.

MOSER, C. (1988) 'The Robbins Report twenty-five years after: And the future of the universities', *Oxford Review of Education*, 14(1) pp. 5–20.

MOSS, P. (1988) *Childcare and Equality of Opportunity: Consolidated Report to the European Commission*, Brussels, Commission of the European Communities.

MURRAY, R. (1988) 'Life after Henry Ford', *Marxism Today*, October.

MURRAY, R. (1989) 'Benetton Britain', in HALL, S. and JACQUES, M. (Eds) *New Times: the Changing Face of Politics in the 1980s*, London, Lawrence and Wishart/Marxism Today.

NATIONAL ECONOMIC DEVELOPMENT OFFICE (1986) *Changing Working Patterns, Report Prepared for NEDO in Association with the Department of Employment*, London, NEDO.

NATIONAL ECONOMIC DEVELOPMENT OFFICE (1988) *Young People and the Labour Market: A Challenge of the 1990s*, London, NEDO.

NEWBY, H. (1977) 'Paternalism and capitalism', in SCASE, R. (Ed.) *Industrial Society: Class, Cleavage and Control*, London, Macmillan.

NEWNHAM, A. (1986) *Employment, Unemployment and Black People*, London, Runnymede Research Report, Runnymede Trust.

NIESR (1986) *Young People's Employment in Retailing*, London, NEDO, July.

NIESR (1989) *National Institute for Economic and Social Research Review*, London, NEDO.

NOLLEN, S.D. (1989) 'The work-family dilemma: How HR managers can help', *Personnel*, May, pp. 25–30.

NORMAN, D. (1983) 'How a new plant made Pilkington reflect on its IR structure', *Personnel Management*, August.

NORTHERN IRELAND ECONOMIC COUNCIL (NIEC) (1985) *Economic Strategy: Distribution*, NIEC Report No. 49, March.

OAKLEY, A. (1974) *Housewife*, Harmondsworth, Penguin.

OAKLEY, A. (1981) *Subject Women*, London, Fontana.

OECD (1989) *Employment Outlook*, OECD, Paris, July.

O'HIGGINS (1985) 'Inequality, redistribution and recession: The British experience, 1976–1982', *Journal of Social Policy*, 14, pp. 279–307.

ORR, P. (1985) 'Sex bias in schools: National perspectives', in WHYTE, J., DEEM, R., KANT, L. and CRUIKSHANK, M. (Eds) *Girl Friendly Schooling*, London, Methuen.

PAHL, R.E. (1988) 'Some remarks on informal work, social polarization and the social structure', *International Journal of Urban and Regional Research*, 12, pp. 247–267.

PAYNE, G. (1987) *Employment and Opportunity*, London, Macmillan.

PAYNE, G. and ABBOTT, P. (1991) (Eds) *The Social Mobility of Women*, London, Falmer Press.

PEARSON, R. et al. (1974) 'Changes in the distribution workforce', *Retail and Distribution Management*, September/October.

PEARSON, R., PIKE, G., GORDON, A. and WEYMAN, C. (1989) *How Many Graduates in the 21st Century? The Choice is Yours*, Brighton, Institute of Manpower Studies Report No. 177.

PIORE, M. and SABEL, C. (1984) *The Second Industrial Divide: Prospects for Prosperity*, New York, Basic Books.

POLLERT, A. (1988) 'Dismantling flexibility', *Capital and Class*, No. 34.

POND, C. (1977) *Trouble in Store*, Low Pay Unit, London.

PRATT, A. (1990) 'Enterprise culture: Rhetoric and reality — The case of "small firms" and "rural" localities' in LOWE, P. *et al.* (Eds) *Petit Capitalism in Rural Areas: East-West perspectives*, London, David Fulton.

RAFFE, D. (1989) 'The transition from YTS to work; Content, context and the external labour market', paper presented to British Sociological Association Annual Conference, Plymouth Polytechnic.

RAFFE, D. and COURTENARY, G. (1988) '16–18 on both sides of the border', in RAFFE, D. (Ed.) *Education and the Youth Labour Market*, London, Falmer Press.

RAFFE, D. and WILLMS, J.D. (1989) *Schooling and the Discouraged Worker: Local Labour Market Effects on Educational Participation*, Centre for Educational Sociology, University of Edinburgh.

RAINNIE, A. (1989) *Industrial Relations in Small Firms: Small isn't Beautiful*, London, Routledge.

RAINNIE, A. (1990) 'Small firms: Between the enterprise culture and "new times"' in BURROWS, R. (Ed.) *Deciphering the Enterprise Culture: Entrepreneurship, Petty Capitalism and the Restructuring of Britain*, London, Routledge.

RAINNIE, A. and KRAITHMAN, D. (1990) 'Labour market change and the organisation of work', in GILBERT, G.N. and BURROWS, R. (Eds) *Fordism and Flexibility: Divisions and Change*, Basingstoke: Macmillan.

RAISTRICK, A. (1968) *Quakers in Science*, Newton Abbot, David & Charles.

RAJAN, A. and VAN EUPEN, P. (1990) *Good Practice in the Employment of Women Returners*, Brighton, Institute of Manpower Studies Report No. 183.

REES, G. (1985) 'Regional restructuring, class change and political action: Preliminary comments on the 1984–85 miners' strike', *Society and Space*, 2(4) pp. 389–406.

REES, G. (1986) 'Memorandum of evidence on the coal industry', House of Commons Select Committee on Energy, HC (1985–86) 196–1, pp. 326–333.

REES, G. and REES, T. (1989) 'The "enterprise culture" and local economic development: A review and evaluation', Report to the Scottish Development Agency, Cardiff, Social Research Unit, University of Wales College, Cardiff.

REES, G., WILLIAMSON, H. and WINCKLER, V. (1989) 'The "new vocationalism": Further education and local labour markets', *Journal of Education Policy*, 4(3) pp. 227–44.

RIDYARD, D. *et al.* (1989) 'Economic Evaluation of the Loan Guarantee Scheme', *Employment Gazette*, 97, (8) August, pp. 417–421.

RITCHIE, J. (1990) 'Enterprise culture as an educational phenomenon', paper presented at the *British Sociological Annual Conference*, University of Surrey, Guildford, April.

References

RITCHIE, J. (1991) 'Enterprise cultures: A frame analysis', in BURROWS, R. (Ed.) *Deciphering the Enterprise Culture; Entrepreneurship, Petty Capitalism and the Restructuring of Britain*, London, Routledge.

ROBERTS, K. (1987) 'ESRC — Young people in society', *Youth and Policy*, 22, pp. 15–24.

ROBERTS, K. and PARSELL, G. (1989a) 'Recent changes in the pathways from school to work in Great Britain', in HURRELMAN, K. and ENGEL, U. (Eds) *The Social World of the Adolescent. Intenational Perspectives*, De Gruyter, New York.

ROBERTS, K. and PARSELL, G. (1989b) 'The stratification of youth training', *Occasional Paper 8, ESRC 16–19 Initiative*, London, City University.

ROBERTS, K., DENCH, S. and RICHARDSON, D. (1987) *The Changing Structure of Youth Labour Markets*, Department of Employment Research Paper 59, London.

ROBINSON, O. (1988) 'The changing labour market: Growth of part-time employment and labour market segmentation in Britain', in WALBY, S. (Ed.) *Gender Segregation at Work*, Milton Keynes, Open University Press.

ROBINSON, O. and WALLACE, J. (1973) 'Measurement and problems of low pay in retail distribution', *Retail and Distribution Management*, September/October.

ROBINSON, O. and WALLACE, J. (1974) 'Part-time employment and low pay in retail distribution', *Industrial Relations Journal*, 5(1).

RODERICK, M. and FRYER, R.H. (1973) *Redundancy and Paternalism*, London, Allen & Unwin.

ROTHWELL, R. (1986) 'The role of small firms in technological innovation', in CURRAN, J. *et al.* (Eds) *The Survival of the Small Firm: Employment, Growth, Technology and Politics*, Aldershot, Gower.

ROWBOTHAM, S. (1973) *Hidden From History*, London, Pluto Press.

ROWLINSON, M. (1988) 'The early application of scientific management by Cadbury', *Business History*, October.

RUBENSTEIN, M. (1987) 'Modern myths and misconceptions: Equal opportunities make good business sense', *Equal Opportunities Review*, 16 December.

RUSSELL, A. (1987) 'Local élites and the working class response in the North West 1870–1895: Paternalism and deference reconsidered', *Northern History*, 23.

RUSTIN, M. (1989) 'The politics of Post-Fordism, or the trouble with "new times"', *New Left Review*, 175.

SABEL, C. (1989) 'Flexible specialisation and the re-emergence of regional economies' in HIRST, P. and ZEITLIN, J. (Eds) *Reversing Industrial Decline? Industrial Structure and Policy in Britain and Her Competitors*, Oxford, Berg.

SAUNDERS, P. (1986) *Social Theory and the Urban Question* (2nd Ed.), London, Hutchinson.

SCASE, R. and GOFFEE, G. (1982) *The Entrepreneurial Middle Class*, Beckenham, Croom Helm.

SCOTT, A. (1988) 'Flexible accumulation and regional development: The rise of new industrial spaces in North America and Western Europe', *International Journal of Urban and Regional Research*, 12, pp. 171–186.

SCOTT, P. (1988) 'Bluepoint or blue remembered hills? The relevance of the Robbins Report to the present reforms of higher education', *Oxford Review of Education*, 14(1) pp. 33–48.

SHARPE, S. (1976) *Just Like a Girl: How Girls Learn to be Women*, Harmondsworth, Penguin.

SHUTT, J. and WHITTINGTON, R. (1987) 'Fragmentation strategies and the rise of small units: Cases from the North West', *Regional Studies*, 21(1).

SILLITOE, K. and MELTZER, H. (1985) *The West Indian School Leaver*, 1, London, OPCS/HMSO.

SILVERSTONE, R. and WARD, A. (1980) *Careers of Professional Women*, Beckenham, Croom Helm.

SMITH, E. (1989) 'Women's vital role at work', *Employment Gazette*, March, pp. 118–21.

SMITH, L.D. (1986) *Carpet Weavers and Carpet Masters: The Handloom Carpet Weavers of Kiddrminster, 1780–1850*, Kidderminster, Tomkinson.

SOCIAL EUROPE (1988) *The Social Dimension of the Internal Market*, Commission of the European Communities, Office for Official Publications of the European Communities.

SOLO, R. (1985) 'Across the industrial divide: A review article', *Journal of Economic Issues*, 19(3) pp. 829–36.

SPARKS, L. (1981) 'A note upon retail employment and superstore development', *Service Industries Journal*, 1(3).

SPARKS, L. (1982) 'Female and part-time employment within superstore retailing', *European Journal of Marketing*, 6(7).

SPARKS, L. (1983) 'Employment characteristics of superstore eetailing', *Service Industries Journal*, 3(1).

SPARKS, L (1984) 'Recent trends and retail employment', *Retail and Distribution Management*, March/April.

SPENCER, A. and PODMORE, D. (1983) 'Life on the periphery of a profession: The experience of women lawyers', London, British Sociological Association (mimeo).

SPENCER, A. and PODMORE, D. (1987) *In a Man's World: Essays on Women in Male-Dominated Professions*, London, Tavistock.

STEDMAN JONES, G. (1971) *Outcast London*, Oxford, Oxford University Press.

STEINMETZ, G. and WRIGHT, E.O. (1989) 'The fall and rise of the petty bourgeoisie: Changing patterns of self-employment in the postwar United States', *American Journal of Sociology*, 94(5).

References

STOREY, D. (1982) *Entrepreneurship and the New Firm*, Beckenham, Croom Helm.

STOREY, D. (1983) 'Small firms policies: A critique', *Journal of General Management*, 8(4), pp. 5–19.

STOREY, D. and JOHNSON, S. (1987) *Are Small Firms the Answer to Unemployment?*, London, Employment Institute.

STOREY, D. and JOHNSON, S. (1987) *Job Generation and Labour Market Change*, London, Macmillan.

STOREY, D., KEASEY, K., WATSON, R. and WYNARCZYK, P. (1987) *The Performance of Small Firms, Profits, Jobs and Failures*, Beckenham, Croom Helm.

SWYNGEDOUW, E. (1986) *The Socio-Spatial Implications of Innovations in Industrial Organisation*, Working Paper No. 20, Johns Hopkins European Centre for Regional Planning and Research, Lille.

TARSH, J. (1988) 'New graduate destinations and degree class', *Employment Gazette*, July, pp. 394–413.

THRIFT, N. (1989) 'Images of social change', in HAMNETT, C. *et al.* (Eds) *The Changing Social Structure*, London, Sage.

TOWN, S. (1975) *After the Mines: Changing Employment Opportunities in a South Wales Valley*, Cardiff, University of Wales Press.

TOWNSEND, P., CORRIGAN, P., and KOWARICK, V. (1987) *Poverty and Labour in London*, London, Low Pay Unit.

TREWSDALE, J. (1988) *Womenpower No. 4*, London, Equal Opportunities Commission.

TRIST, E. and BAMFORTH, K. (1951) 'Some sociological and psychological consequences of the long-wall method of cutting coal', *Human Relations*, 4(1), pp. 3–38.

TROYNA, B. and WILLIAMS, J. (1986) *Racism, Education and the State: The Racialisation of Education Policy*, Beckenham, Croom Helm.

TROYNA, B. (1987) 'Beyond multi-culturalism: Towards the enactment of anti-racist education in policy, provision and pedagogy', *Oxford Review of Education*, 13(3).

URRY, H. (1989) 'The end of organised capitalism', in HALL, S. and JACQUES, M. (Eds) *New Times: The Changing Face of Politics in the 1990s*, London, Lawrence and Wishart.

VERMA G.K. and DARBY, D.S. (1987) *Race, Training and Employment*, London, Falmer Press.

WADDINGTON, D., WYKES, M., and CRITCHER, C. (1990). *Split at the Seams*, Milton Keynes, Open University Press.

WAGNER, G. (1987) *The Chocolate Conscience*, London, Chatto and Windus.

WALBY, S. (1986) *Patriarchy at Work: Patriarchal and Capitalist Relations in Employment*, Cambridge, Polity Press.

WALKER, A. and WALKER, C. (1987) *The Growing Divide: A Social Audit 1979–1987*, London, Child Poverty Action Group.

WALKER, A.G. and OWEN, J. (1984) 'Preliminary Report 11 to EDU on the lock industry', West Midlands County Council.

WALLACE, C. and CROSS, M. (1990) (Eds) *Youth in Transition: The Sociology of Youth and Youth Policy*, London, Falmer Press.

WASS, V. and MAINWARING, L. (1989) 'Economic and social consequences of rationalization in the South Wales coal industry', in DAY, D. and REES, G. (Eds) *Contemporary Wales 3*, Cardiff, University of Wales Press.

WEBER, M. (1971) *The Protestant Ethic and the Spirit of Capitalism*, London, Unwin University Books.

WEINER, M. (1981) *English Culture and the Decline of the Industrial Spirit 1850–1980*, Cambridge, Cambridge University Press.

WEISS, L. (1988) *Creating Capitalism: The State and Small Business Since 1945*, Oxford, Blackwell.

WENTZ, C.A., (1987) 'Preserving a union free workplace', *Personnel*, 64(10).

WHITTINGTON, R. (1984) 'Regional bias in new firm formation', *Regional Studies*, 18(3) pp. 253–6.

WHYTE, J. (1986) 'Reducing the waste of womanpower', *The Quarterly Journal of Social Affairs*, 1(3).

WILLIAMS, K. *et al.* (1987) 'The end of mass production?', *Economy and Society*, 16(3).

WINCKLER, V. (1987) 'Women and work in contemporary Wales', in DAY, D and REES, G. (Eds) *Contemporary Wales 1*, Cardiff, University of Wales Press.

WINTOUR, P. (1988) 'Fowler urges employers to give women better deal', *The Guardian*, 19 November.

WITHAM, J. (1986) *Hearts and Minds*, London, Canary Press.

WOOD, S. (1985) 'Recruitment systems and the recession', *British Journal of Industrial Relations*, 23(2) pp. 103–20.

WRENCH, J. (1987) 'The unfinished bridge: YTS and black youth', in TROYNA, B. (Ed) *Racial Inequality in Education*, London, Tavistock.

YETRU (1986) *They Must Think We're Stupid: The Experiences of Young People on the Youth Training Scheme*, Birmingham, Youth Employment and Training Resource Unit/Trade Union Resource Centre.

YOUNG, LORD (1986) 'Enterprise — the road to jobs', *London Business School Journal*, 11(1).

YOUNG, M. and WILMOTT, P. (1979) *Family and Kinship in East London*, London, Pelican.

ZAHAVI, G. (1988) *Workers, Managers and Welfare Capitalism: The Shoemakers and Tanners of Endicott Johnson 1890–1950*, Chicago, ILL., University of Illinois Press.

Notes on Contributors

Peter Ackers is a Research Associate at the University of Manchester Institute of Science and Technology. He was formerly a Research Fellow in the Human Resources Management Division of Wolverhampton Polytechnic Business School. He has written (mostly with John Black) on industrial relations in manufacturing industry in the West Midlands.

John Black is Principal Lecturer in the Human Resources Management Division of the Business School at Wolverhampton Polytechnic. He has written extensively on the history and current organisation of firms in the West Midlands.

Nick Buck was formerly a Research Fellow at the Urban and Regional Studies Unit at the University of Kent (1980–1989). He is now Chief Research Officer at the ESRC Micro-Social Change Inter-disciplinary Research Unit at the University of Essex. He is co-author of *Processes and Structures of Urban Life* (1982) and of *The London Employment Problem* (1986).

Roger Burrows is a Principal Lecturer in the Department of Administrative and Social Studies at Teeside Polytechnic. He previosuly taught at the University of Surrey and at the Polytechnic of East London. He has published papers in *Sociology*, *Sociological Review* and in other journals and edited collections. His edited book *Enterprise Culture: Critical Analyses* (Routledge) was published in 1990.

Tony Chapman has been a Lecturer in Sociology at Staffordshire Polytechnic since 1984. Prior to this he carried out doctoral research at Plymouth Polytechnic on patterns of occupational mobility of women and men based on data from the Scottish Mobility Study. He is currently working on a new comparative research project on equal opportunity programmes in Europe.

Michelle Connolly has been a research assistant in the Department of Sociology at Liverpool University since 1988. She has worked on a number of projects connected with the ESRC 16–19 Initiative, including a study of Liverpool's ethnic minority youth.

Malcolm Cross is Principal Research Fellow at the Centre for Research in Ethnic Relations, University of Warwick. He was formerly Deputy Director of the ESRC Research Unit on Ethnic Relations at the University of Aston and Lecturer in Sociology at the University of Surrey. He has authored or edited ten other books and more than 100 articles, chapters or reports, mostly on ethnic minorities, equal opportunities and labour markets.

James Curran is Midland Bank Professor of Small Business Studies and Director of the Small Business Research Unit at Kingston Polytechnic. He has published widely in academic journals and is the joint author of *Management Motivation in the Small Business* (Gower, 1973), and joint editor of *The Survival of the Small Firm* (Gower, 1986).

Sandra Hebron was previously a researcher on the 'Coal and Community' Project in the Department of Communication Studies at Sheffield City Polytechnic

Nick Jewson is a Lecturer in the Department of Sociology, University of Leicester. He has recently been conducting research, in collaboration with David Mason, into 'racial' and gender inequalities in the labour market.

Michael Maguire was until recently Research Officer in the Policy Research Institute at the Queen's University of Belfast and the University of Ulster. He was previously a Research Officer in the Social and Technology Policy Division at Aston University. He is the author of *Work, Employment and New Technology in Northern Ireland* and editor of *Unequal Labour: Women at Work in Northern Ireland*

David Mason is a Lecturer in Sociology at the University of Leicester. He has a long-standing interest in the sociology of 'race' and equal opportunities and has published widely in this field.

Glennys Parsell has been a Research Associate on the ESRC 16–19 Initiative since 1986. She has a background in the creative arts and has taught in schools, in further education and in a closed prison.

Geoff Payne is Dean of Human Sciences at Polytechnic South West, Plymouth. Formerly Director of the Scottish Mobility Study at Aberdeen University, he has written extensively on mobility and related topics, including *Mobility and Change in Modern Society* (Macmillan, 1987) and *Employment and Opportunity* (Macmillan, 1987).

Gareth Rees is a Lecturer in Sociology in the School of Social and Administrative Studies at the University of Wales College of Cardiff. He has written extensively on urban and industrial change and is currently carrying out research on the restructuring of industrial South Wales.

Ken Roberts is Professor of Sociology and Head of Department at the University of Liverpool. His books include *Youth and Leisure* (Allen and Unwin, 1983) and *The Changing Structure of Youth Labour Markets* (Department of Employment, 1987). He is currently working on the ESCR's 16–19 Initiative, on a study of indoor sports provision and on the quality of life in six UK cities.

Marilyn Thomas is a research student in the School of Social and Administrative Studies at the University of Wales College of Cardiff. She has an ESRC Collaborative Award in the Social Sciences, held jointly with Mid-Glamorgan County Council. Her research focuses on contemporary patterns of occupational and class change in the South Wales Coalfield.

John Wrench is Senior Research Fellow at the Centre for Research in Ethnic Relations at the University of Warwick. From 1976 until 1983 he was a Lecturer at Aston University, first in the Sociology Group and then in the Management Centre. His publications are in the areas of industrial safety, ethnic minorities and the labour market, trade unions and equal opportunities, and the Careers Service.

Maggie Wykes worked as a researcher on the 'Coal and Community' project. She currently teaches part-time in the Division of Communication Studies and English at Sheffield City Polytechnic. She is also carrying out doctoral research on 'Violence: Discourse, Gender and Difference' at the Centre for Socio-Legal and Criminological Research at Sheffield University.

Index